Curating Spaces of Hope

Curating Spaces of Hope

*Transformational Leadership
for Uncertain Times*

Matthew Barber-Rowell

scm press

© Matthew Barber-Rowell 2025

Published in 2025 by SCM Press

Editorial office
3rd Floor, Invicta House,
110 Golden Lane,
London EC1Y 0TG, UK

www.scmpress.co.uk

SCM Press is an imprint of Hymns Ancient & Modern Ltd
(a registered charity)

Hymns Ancient & Modern® is a registered trademark of
Hymns Ancient & Modern Ltd
13A Hellesdon Park Road, Norwich,
Norfolk NR6 5DR, UK

All rights reserved. No part of this publication may be reproduced,
stored in a retrieval system, or transmitted,
in any form or by any means, electronic, mechanical,
photocopying or otherwise, without the prior permission of
the publisher, SCM Press.

The Author has asserted his right under the Copyright, Designs and Patents Act
1988 to be identified as the Author of this Work

Scripture quotations taken from The Holy Bible, New International Version
(Anglicised edition) copyright © 1979, 1984, 2011 by Biblica (formerly
International Bible Society). Used by permission of Hodder & Stoughton
Publishers, an Hachette UK company. All rights reserved.

British Library Cataloguing in Publication data

A catalogue record for this book is available
from the British Library

ISBN: 978-0-334-06510-4

EU GPSR Authorised Representative
LOGOS EUROPE, 9 rue Nicolas Poussin, 17000, LA ROCHELLE, France
E-mail: Contact@logoseurope.eu

Typeset by Regent Typesetting
Printed and bound by
CPI Group (UK) Ltd

Contents

1	Introduction	1
2	Prologue: an Epilogue for the Temple Tradition	13
3	Living with Liminality	35
4	Spaces of Hope	69
5	A Movement of Hope	104
6	Gramsci's Intellectuals	148
7	Principles for Transformational Leadership	170
8	Shared Values	189
9	Conclusions	205

References   214
Index of Names and Subjects   229

1

Introduction

This book is a witness statement, a passion project that I have endlessly been trying to give away, and it is now my first book on a subject that has preoccupied me for at least the last 15 years. It is also a statement of intent for the academic and practical work that is most important to me. This may or may not be of interest to you, but I hope what is and what draws you in, and encourages you to engage with this volume seriously, is an invitation to sojourn as part of a movement of hope. This invitation has been consistent at the heart of the journey I have been on, as you will see in the pages to come. It is also in evidence through the roughly 80 gatherings and 1,500 participants, primarily in the northwest of England but from across civil society in the UK and around the world, who have contributed in some way, shape or form during that journey. In that sense, this book is for anyone who is seeking hope. It has a public theological persuasion, but as someone who is new to the field (this is my first book in public theology) my hope is that it doesn't just preach to the converted or appeal to those already in the club. If this book serves faithfully the tradition it is part of, the Temple Tradition, then it will not be confined to faith communities and will speak to interdisciplinary concerns as well. That is for you to judge.

At the heart of the book are transitions: already and always moving on through life, while trying to simultaneously understand what is reliable and constant. The first transition I talk about explicitly from my own experience is in Chapter 3, where I transition into unemployment during a global recession, at the age of 21. This is the beginning of my search for hope. At the heart of this book is a paradox: recognition that there is much that on the face of it doesn't make sense, but that if we each bring openly from what we have we can produce something that is more than the sum of our parts. As you will see in Chapter 3, I did not set out 15 years ago with this book or anything of the kind in mind. I could barely get up in the morning. In order for this book to exist I have been reliant on those who have contributed to it and supported me during my journey. In this sense, being independent is a myth, although paradoxically we have to find independence and establish our story and our skills and experiences to get on in the world. But the case I make is that we are also, critically, interdependent. If we bring our story and skills and experiences to bear together, we can and will see things transformed through the leadership we offer in service to one another. This is the social paradox. It is inferred throughout the book and addressed in Chapter 7. At the heart of this book is an argument that there is a pivotal place in public life for the things that we believe and the world views in which we root our lives. Yes, beliefs and world views speak to something personal and private, but they are also a rich resource for shaping our shared public spaces. And we need all the resources we can get our hands on. The things we believe in can change our lives and they can drive and motivate us to change the world. So you will also find here a call to action; a deep desire to see the world around us – the spaces, places and planet – transformed, for the suffering and oppression which affects more of us each day to be overcome not by force but by a deep commitment to one another and the content of our shared lives, which is rooted in the world views we hold and expressed as hope. Hope will be talked about in a number of ways in this book as we progress.

1. I will talk about personal hope, or my own experience of it. This will be from an evolving Christian perspective as that is my world view. I have been a Christian my entire life, marked by an upbringing in a Christian home, baptism, a personal commitment to my faith when I was a teenager, and confirmation. This kind of narrative, where hope is sourced from the world view that I hold, and understood in terms of the things that I do and things that have happened to me, will be explored in Chapter 3. This, I imagine, will give you a further sense of why the book has been written, but it will also set out for you an invitation to bring yourself to the conversation about hope, from your own positionality, belief base and world view.
2. I will explore shared hope, drawn from different perspectives, from people who have different world views and who operate in different spheres of life. Gathering a sense of hope in this way moves the conversation on from my own views on hope, and locates us in shared Spaces of Hope. These spaces were the basis for a movement of hope which started in 2016 and point a possible way of gathering together the different perspectives of those who live and journey alongside one another, in a way that can conceivably make life better. One could refer to this as 'curating' Spaces of Hope. I will turn to an etymology

of the term 'Spaces of Hope' later in this introduction and to terminology of curation in Chapters 3 and 7.
3 I will also map a much deeper, rigorous and resilient sense of hope. This is cocreated through a dialogue between our lived experiences and our world views and can be understood as the values we use to guide however we live. I deal with this throughout the book and address it through a fourfold typology of hope in Chapter 8.

These three different senses of hope move us from individual to shared to societal conceptions and manifestations of hope, and, as I will argue, offer us an interface for speaking our truths to one another in a way that is understood not only by people who are like you, or who have experienced what you've experienced, but by those who are fundamentally different from you. At the heart of this book, and the hopeful journey we are on, is the premise that differences should not be used to divide, to separate and to alienate, but to gather, to unite, to curate, to cocreate and to celebrate within public spaces and the public square, which are increasingly diverse and beset by crisis. In this book, the search for hope will be developed by reflecting on three main ideas. The first is the essential nature of lived experience; the second is about the crises that we face during the course of our day-to-day lives, experienced both in the communities that make up society and in the structures that shape it, locally and globally. The third idea draws on the first and second, and is to establish a basis for hopeful and resilient future. The phrase that I am using to characterize how to do this is *transformational leadership*.

In January 2024, Justin Welby, Archbishop of Canterbury, spoke at the Royal Society of Arts on the theme of courage. Welby's words conjured elements I would hope to see in a transformational leadership. Welby spoke of his predecessor, William Temple, and his volume *Christianity and Social Order* (first published in 1942) and the influence he had on the establishment of the welfare state in Britain. There was also reference to Carl Schmitt, the German lawyer who wrote *Political Theology* (1922) and *Political Theology 2* (1970), and whose work had close association with the Nazi party in the 1930s. These diverse points of reference can sit side by side within a conversation about courage, because Welby conceived of it as a 'contingent virtue', the point being that even leaders who have the darkest of intentions can go about realizing them by having the courage of their convictions. To make this point I will be working with Temple during this book, rather than Schmitt and the Nazis. The notion of contingent virtues means that we need to understand courage in a context, challenge the dark intentions of leaders who may otherwise appear courageous, and have an open dialogue about the sources of motivation we draw on and what they offer us in our shared public spaces. We can consider this a question of authenticity, which I pick up in Chapter 7. St Augustine, a much earlier political theologian, is attributed with the great saying that hope has two daughters: anger, as a response to the things we experience, and courage, to respond in the right way. One would expect to see a reference here, but to the best of my knowledge this attribution to Augustine is part of folklore; we glean the wisdom from it but it does not have the source we think it does, nor, I would argue, does that particularly matter. Notwithstanding, courage to act is in a contingent relationship with hope; the basis of hope is the means by which we bring about and express courage to respond to the crisis and injustice that we are angry about. With this in mind I will turn to the phrase that is at the centre of this work, Spaces of Hope, to offer an etymology of the term, which will evidence a heritage of salience for different world views and set out the ways in which I will define and develop the term.

An etymology of 'Spaces of Hope'

The first meaningful use of the phrase Spaces of Hope that I have been able to find is in the work of David Harvey (2000). Harvey is an eminent and celebrated Marxist theorist. His use of the term Spaces of Hope is as the title of a volume mapping intellectual contours of a post-McCarthy, postmodern public space using a Marxist or materialist framework and responding to significant social movements, including the anti-globalization movement in 1998. Harvey theorizes different geographies from a socialist perspective, and develops a conversation around utopia and utopianism, which, based on the title of the book, is taken as synonymous with the concept of hope.

The second substantial reference I found is in the edited volume by Professor Richard Phillips, *Muslim Spaces of Hope: Geographies of Possibility in Britain and the West*. This edited volume considers the work of Muslims, and the contexts in which they are doing it, as a marginally hopeful endeavour (Phillips, 2009, p. 1). The term Spaces of Hope is credited to Harvey, and is then used as a utopian lens through which to see and conceive of responses to the challenges facing Muslims in the public sphere. The volume itself came from a public dialogue in Liverpool Museum in 2008, which asked speakers to speak to the theme of 'Muslim Spaces of Hope'. It is a volume that is of interest but does not appear to have received any follow-up developing the term Spaces of Hope.

Next, there is Paul Cloke, Professor of Geography at the University of Exeter. Once again there is acknowledgement of Harvey as the originator of the term. Cloke brings Spaces of Hope into a Christian context and refers to it within the context of emergent postsecularity. I pick up on language of postsecularity in Chapter 4. Cloke appears to make only two references to the phrase, one in 2010 and subsequently in 2013. The first is in a European-wide study into the role of faith-based organizations, known as the FACIT project. As you will see in Chapter 4, this study is referenced in this work and it is the jump-off point for my use of the term Spaces of Hope. Interestingly, the FACIT project put 'Spaces of Hope' in quotes as if it is Cloke's phrase, but while his deployment of the term is in a faith-based context where Harvey's was not, his earlier use does not appear to make an attempt to define the term beyond the way that Harvey used it. The second use by Cloke is in a chapter with Sam Thomas and Andrew Williams where they frame the prophetic interventions of faith-based organizations as opening up Spaces of Hope in response to oppression or domination (Cloke et al., 2013, p. 7). The phrase then appears to drop from Cloke's later work relating faith-based organizations and urban geography; for example, it does not appear in the volume *Geographies of Postsecularity*, apart from an indirect reference to some early work of mine (Cloke et al., 2019, p. 122). I am grateful to Cloke for his work, because it comprises foundational elements of the literature review within my doctoral thesis (Barber-Rowell, 2021), which I have developed further here.

Finally, there is my own use of the term Spaces of Hope. I began deploying it in 2016 in the notional way, as a utopian lens such as used by Harvey, in specific faith-based contexts, such as in Phillips' work, and in a postsecular context such as that of Cloke. Over time the use of the phrase became synonymous with liminal spaces within communities and organizations, as evidenced in Chapter 3 of this book. The term also became a conceptual tool within dialogues that I facilitated and now comprises an element of my facilitation toolkit. But, as will be made clear in Chapter 4, I have both maintained and deepened this usage. I have taken the definition of Spaces of Hope beyond the notional or ethereal conceptual lens, and clarified and characterized it through ethnographic research and assemblage theory, to become a rich, relational and rigorous organizational paradigm, relating to faith-based and non-faith-based organizations alike within what I would refer to as postsecular contexts. I say more on this point in Chapters 3 and 4.

Now, though, I will turn to the crises that I believe are shaping the public sphere today.

Crises

Archbishop Justin Welby, in the 2019 William Temple Foundation annual lecture at Lambeth Palace, reflected on this theme. In a previous life, Archbishop Welby worked in the oil industry. He drew on the metaphor of the oil rig and the ways in which a rig is anchored in the ocean and prepared to do its job while being buffeted by storms. The Archbishop reflected on how to understand the weather itself. He noted:

> What are the storms that we are facing? Are the waves coming our way just weather, or are they a more existential threat such as climate change? Are they a storm that will pass or are they indicative of a new global pattern? We will need to identify and name these storms that we face. (William Temple Foundation, 2019)

Welby continued to note that while it is possible for us, metaphorically speaking, to create our own weather or shape the climate, while there are opportunities there are also challenges: 'Like nothing we have experienced since the Second World War, or in peace time since before that ... they are a challenge to liberty, to relationships both in our communities and globally' (William Temple Foundation, 2019).

But what are the storms we face? Indeed, what language should be used? Some refer to risk. For example, within sociology, Ulrich Beck refers to *Risk Society* (1992), *World Risk Society* (1998), and *World at Risk* (2009). The UK government's National Risk Register includes information about 89 risks, within nine risk themes – although several risks could and maybe should be categorized under more than one theme. The themes are: terrorism, cyber, state threats, geographic and diplomatic, accidents and systems failures, natural and environmental hazards, human, animal and plant health, societal and conflict and instability (HM Government, 2023). Hans Rosling, Professor of International Health and author of *Factfulness* (2018), written with his son and daughter-in-law, Ola and Anna, refers to five risks. These risks are global pandemic, financial collapse, world war, climate change and extreme poverty.[1] Chair of the William Temple Foundation Professor Simon Lee, speaking at Balliol College Oxford,[2] identifies eight crises: environmental, the cost of living, health (including the effects of the pandemic and the condition of the NHS), wars (including those in Russia and Ukraine, and Israel and Palestine), breakdown in trust in governments, culture wars, the breakdown of civic institutions (including faith groups), and educational institutions losing their way (2023a, pp. 48–9). Each of these crises would be enough on their own. We can ordinarily cope with one or two crises simultaneously. However, we are experiencing many storms, as Welby puts it, or risks, or a multiplicity of crises. Other sources, including the Bateson Institute and the World Economic Forum, refer to the experience of multiple crises as a poly-crisis, 'a cluster of related global risks with compounding effects, such that the overall impact exceeds the sum of each part' (Torkington, 2023). Chess Grandmaster and Director of Perspectiva, Jonathan Rowson (2021) is a helpful access point to discussion of 'meta-crisis'. Rowson's starting point is discernible as follows: 'the underlying processes causing us to gradually lose bearings in the world … the socio-emotional … the epistemic … the educational … the spiritual'.

Through this sense of the meta-crisis Rowson seeks to explore who 'we' are, how we 'know' things, how we 'learn' things and our capacity to 'imagine' and 'believe' things. My purposes are not to engage directly with Welby, Beck, Rosling, Lee, Bateson or Rowson as the central focus of my argument, but briefly to draw on their support to set out something of the breadth and scope of what is to come. My purposes are to articulate a lived response to crises, as expressed by the many people who have journeyed together to date, which we can view through the lens of curating Spaces of Hope and refer to as transformational leadership. As I conclude the book, I will circle back around to questions of how we might apply this approach to the pursuit of justice in the face of these poly-crises and meta-crises. It could be that this book later prompts an exchange about the nature of crisis and crisis response. Indeed there are others already speaking about this. For example, see *When the Dust Settles: Searching for Hope after Disaster* by Lucy Easthope, who is reputed to be 'Britain's top emergency planner'. So I will keep my attention on this book, where I refer to various crises: the mental health crisis in the UK, the Covid-19 pandemic, the climate crisis, wars and international conflicts, culture wars, poverty (including cost of living and energy crises) and institutional decline (including in higher education, faith-based organizations and government). The onset of these crises enable us to turn to what Thomas Kuhn refers to as a paradigm shift. This is a helpful term for positioning *Curating Spaces of Hope* and so I will turn to it now.

Paradigm shift

Thomas Kuhn (2012) characterizes the effect of multiple crises as begetting the revolutionary emergence of new paradigms. Kuhn refers to this as 'the tradition-shattering complement to the tradition-bound activity' (Kuhn, 2012, p. 6). As such, we reach a point where the old ways don't offer us what we need, so we need to conceive of new ways to tackle enduring challenges. Kuhn characterizes this in terms of a new paradigm or paradigm shift: 'an achievement, sufficiently unprecedented to attract an enduring group of adherents away from competing models of scientific activity. Simultaneously, it was sufficiently open-ended to leave all sorts of problems for the redefined group of practitioners' (p. 10).

The example that Kuhn uses is from physics, comparing and contrasting the paradigm put forward by Isaac Newton and a later paradigm put forward by Albert Einstein. Both Newton's and Einstein's work has some relationship with mass (m). For example, Newton's work is characterized by the formula $F = ma$ whereas Einstein's work is characterized by the formula $E = mc^2$. But Einstein's equation makes no sense in Newtonian mechanics. The terms of reference are different. It was not simply that Einstein's work extended from Newton's. It didn't. It is often the case that a new paradigm is formed where no preconceived or consciously acknowledged structure for it exists. Kuhn puts it like this: 'Instead, the new paradigm, or a sufficient hint to permit later articulation, emerges all at once, sometimes in the middle of the night, in the mind of [someone] deeply immersed in crisis' (Kuhn, 2012, p. 89).

New paradigms are considered to be 'incommensurable' from what has gone before (Kuhn 2012, p. 103): two different paradigms operating in the same field can view the same thing from the same direction and see entirely different things, such that what seems intuitive to one is invisible to another. And so new paradigms are often adopted as a wholesale shift, rather than step-by-step that take place over time; it is not instantaneous, it is often from generation to generation (Kuhn, 2012, p. 150).

The rest of the book will set out this paradigm shift. In Chapter 2, I offer a prologue for the book to come. I set out the Temple Tradition in public theology, which comprises the life, work and legacy of Archbishop William Temple, from his role leading the Life and Liberty movement, to his contributions to ecumenical movements or 'unity movements', through to the work for which he is most famous, *Christianity and Social Order*, which contributed to the ideation and formation of the post-Second World War welfare state in the UK. The purpose of this prologue is to offer an epilogue for the Temple Tradition. Eighty years after Temple's death, his work, while celebrated, has run its course. His contribution was to establish a basis for servant leadership that was interdisciplinary in nature, and sought to promote and develop the role of responsible citizens in public life. There are questions and inspirations that I take forward, which I use to guide the rest of the book. These range from the characteristics of a centrist reform movement, to the kind of philosophical framework that might be helpful, to the forms of leadership we need and where they might come from.

In Chapter 3 I offer a personal account and rationale for developing Spaces of Hope, as well as beginning the conceptual work that underpins the rest of the book. Through four stories, which span 15 years from 2010 to 2024 inclusive, I set out experiences of 'living with liminality', which is marked by a sense of being constantly in transition. The stories I tell in this chapter are titled 'There for you' (2010–2013), 'Hope and despair' (2014–2015), 'By their fruits, you will know them' (2016–2019), and 'Finding a way in the wilderness' (2020–2024). This tracks my journey from graduating into a recession created by the global financial crisis in 2008, through experiences of unemployment, poor mental health, loneliness and isolation, abuse and discrimination, into a social movement that became known as Spaces of Hope and offered the basis for a process of collective sense-making and community action out of 'living with liminality', which has informed the paradigm shift offered in this book.

In Chapter 4, I turn to Spaces of Hope itself, which I refer to in terms of a paradigm and methodology. This chapter speaks to the progression of Spaces of Hope beyond sense-making in liminal spaces characterized in Chapter 3 and begins to explore the conceptual questions emerging from the epilogue for the Temple Tradition in Chapter 2. I take on both of these challenges by redefining the vehicle used for responding to them in civil society. Temple referred to that vehicle as 'intermediate groupings'. You might also refer to them as charities or civil society organizations. A term I have already used above for this vehicle is faith-based organizations. I begin the chapter by setting out some further concepts that can help map transitions in different disciplines. I start with transition in understanding and framing of the role of world views in the public space, that is, the postsecular, based on the work of Jürgen Habermas. I bring Habermas' work into conversation with urban geography through the work of Cloke et al. (2019) to offer grounding for these transitions. I then contextualize this through a conversation about the diversity of the belief landscape in the UK which has transitioned away from a majority Christian one. I highlight the prevailing pre-pandemic context of 'liminality as the new norm' in social policy to show that there is a clear rationale for a paradigm defined by transitions. By mapping this conceptual landscape, I develop the basis for the emergence of Spaces of Hope as a new paradigm of faith-based organizations. I theorize this emergence using assemblage theory that uses differences to cocreate new forms of shared identity, locally understood. I bring this into a more practical conversation using ethnographic research within community spaces in a post-industrial town in the north-west of England. These include a high street characterized by unemployment and decline, an outer estate that is statistically one of the most depressed places in the country, and a town centre with anchor institutions in transition. From this basis, stories of hope provide a foundation for transformational leadership which I set out in the rest of the book.

In Chapter 5, I turn to the transition we all experienced in 2020, the Covid-19 pandemic, as a means of opening up a movement of hope. In this chapter, I consider what this transition meant for everyone as cocreators of a pandemic response across civil society. I do this initially using research from the pandemic, before turning to post-pandemic Spaces of Hope gatherings, which renewed its function as a vehicle for a social movement after lockdowns were over. These gatherings were curated from 2022 onwards. The account I offer maps the emergence of applications of the new paradigm and methodology, and what these mean for transformational leadership practice not just in local contexts but regionally, nationally and globally. These gatherings are formed: across a diversity of world views including Christianity, non-religious perspectives and Islam; a diversity of participants representing different institutions across civil society, including in education, the third sector and grass-roots politics; and a diversity of positionalities with traditional or formal leadership being set in dialogue with organic or informal leadership. These differences offer a basis for transformational leadership, rooted in contributions from across the public square.

In Chapter 6, I take up the question of diverse positionalities as a critical aspect of transformational leadership. To do this, I turn to the political theory of Antonio Gramsci. Gramsci's prison notebooks were formed during his life in Italy in the 1920s, and 1930s, shaped by national institutions, including the fascist government of the time, and also the Catholic Church. Gramsci's notebooks were also shaped by his time in prison. He spent eight of the last ten years of his life in prison as a political prisoner, during which time he produced his canon. While admittedly sporadic and incomplete, his work does help with the understanding of transformational leadership I am developing. The area on which I focus my attention relates to Gramsci's theory of the intellectuals. He uses 'intellectual' in a way similar to the way I am using 'leader' or 'curator'. Gramsci's theory of the intellectuals speaks to the positionality of leaders and the means by which a centrist and democratic movement, which operates with respect to existing institutions, might emerge. Gramsci offers two different positionalities and characterizes them as traditional and organic.

In Chapter 7 I turn to principles for guiding transformational leadership. These have emerged over the last ten years from the Spaces of Hope movement. I set out five principles: freedom, relationship, service, affect and authenticity. These principles are a guide through periods of transition. They can guide us from personal sense-making to collaborative working that is attuned to the limits imposed upon us by the crises of today, to stories of authentic hope and transformation that we can all share in, each from our own positionality or world view. These principles for 'curating' Spaces of Hope guide transformational leadership practice that transcends the hierarchies and organizational structures that we experience in society and are a means of guiding a movement of hope for the future.

In Chapter 8, I turn to the values that have both emerged from and underpin the Spaces of Hope movement: hope, unity and justice. I offer these as a means for taking the movement forward, and for drawing upon all the different sources of ancient and contemporary wisdom that shape us, our experiences and the stories that we use to shape and authenticate a hopeful, united and just future for all. I do this using examples from the movement over the last 15 years and point to policy recommendations that have emerged during the movement.

I conclude with a sense of the opportunities that lie ahead. While this book is 15 years in the making, it speaks to an experience that is just reaching midlife. New paradigms are for new generations. There are leaders now who see that, and are positioned to curate Spaces of Hope for the transformational leadership of generations of the future to flourish. So with that in mind this concluding chapter speaks both to the generation of leaders we have now and to a new generation of leaders to come. I will reflect on the opportunities that I see and will invite you to join in a movement that can transform our society into a more hopeful, united and just place for all.

Notes

1 The first version of this book was published in 2018, along with the paperback in 2019. So don't let anybody anywhere tell you that we could not have predicted a pandemic – they are either ignorant or have less than honourable intentions.

2 Both his and Temple's Alma Mater, albeit at different times.

2

Prologue: An Epilogue for the Temple Tradition

Pragmatically, things must end for others to begin. Theologically, there is death and following it comes life. Ecologically there are seasons where spring brings life, and autumn and winter see things fall fallow before the next season begins. Anthropologically, there are transitions. Paradigms shift. So while on the one hand, it might seem paradoxical to start with a finish, as it were, it is entirely natural. Beginning with this epilogue will set out the limits of the Temple Tradition and open up questions that I will take forward into the rest of the book. The Temple Tradition has contributed to the centre ground in Anglican social thought for the past century, but anyone who knows that also knows that it has declined in relevance and over the last 40 years has become a marginal influence, albeit a respected one. Nonetheless, the Temple Tradition marks the public theological context from which this book emerges and I will turn to it now.

The Temple Tradition

The 'Temple Tradition' represents the contributions of Archbishop William Temple (1881–1944) to the public theological landscape of twentieth-century Britain as Bishop of Manchester (1921–29), Archbishop of York (1929–42) and Archbishop of Canterbury (1942–44). *The Dictionary of National Biography* heralded Temple as the ecclesiastical figure with the most impact on the twentieth century in England and possibly the world. He was listed alongside other public figures including Winston Churchill, Bertrand Russell and George Bernard Shaw (Hastings, 1995, p. 68). There are multiple accounts that specifically address Temple's life and work. Iremonger (1948) offered the official biography following Temple's untimely death from gout in 1944. Stephen Spencer, Advisor for Theological Education to the Anglican

Communion, has offered multiple accounts of Temple's life. Initially there was *William Temple: A Calling to Prophecy* (Spencer, 2001). Chapters on the Temple Tradition followed in *Anglican Social Theology* (Suggate, 2014) and *Theology Reforming Society* (Spencer, 2017). Most recently there has been *Archbishop William Temple: A Study in Servant Leadership* (Spencer, 2022). My purposes here are to establish the Temple Tradition in terms of Temple's positionality, theological and philosophical outlook, and his legacy. This requires a sense of the man and his contributions during his life, as well as the publications we have to refer to today. *Christianity and Social Order* (first published in 1942) was Temple's foremost publication. It offers the most succinct expression of Temple's approach to leadership through his life, so I will use that publication primarily to gauge Temple's relevance today for a twenty-first-century context. I will also consider Temple's legacy viewed through the lens of the William Temple Foundation with whom I have had an association for over a decade, initially as doctoral candidate (2014), as a Temple Scholar (2019), as an Honorary Research Fellow (2021), as a recipient of a Temple Postdoctoral Research Fellowship (2022), as Communications Officer (2023) and Secretariat to the Board of Trustees (Present).

Temple's leadership

Temple can be characterized as an organizer, clergyman, social reformer, thinker, writer and ultimately a servant leader (Spencer, 2022). He developed this multifaceted positionality throughout his life and ministry. University in Oxford, at Balliol College, was a key period for Temple, where he established relationships with William Beveridge and R. H. Tawney. These later became significant for the formation of the post-Second World War welfare state in Great Britain. During his time at university, Temple discerned a calling to ordained ministry. This is not entirely surprising given that Temple's father, Frederick Temple, was Archbishop of Canterbury (1896–1902). However, it is worth noting that Temple's own journey to ordination was not straight forward. He was initially refused for ordination by the Bishop of Oxford, Francis Paget, because of theological differences. Temple appeared not to hold suitable views on the virgin birth. However, in the time that followed, Temple's position was reformed sufficiently for his path to be cleared to become ordained. Shaw (2023) dispassionately attributes this clearing of the way to Temple's 'cultural capital' exhibited by the Temple family relationship with then Archbishop of Canterbury Randall Davidson, who ultimately said that Temple should be ordained.

During his time at university, Temple joined the Oxford Medical Mission in Bermondsey and also spent time at the Toynbee Hall settlement. By attending thesse different missions, Temple saw hardship and poverty, and this in turn helped him to develop his own views. In 1905, Temple became cosecretary of the Workers Educational Association with founder Albert Mansbridge. The WEA advocated for new forms of partnership within universities, which empowered workers to have more of a say in, even coproducing, their education. This approach to education by the WEA was radically different from others in its day (Spencer, 2022, p. 19). Temple continued as president of the WEA, winning multiple re-elections, until 1924 (Spencer, 2015, p. xiv). Temple was also involved in the Student Christian Movement (1908–09)[1] and was inspired by the Anglo-Catholic and integrative theological approach espoused by church leaders such as Henry Scott Holland and Charles Gore. In 1910 Temple also attended the Edinburgh Missionary Conference as an usher. This gathering is noted by Spencer as 'the first big ecumenical activity of the new century' (2022, p. 131). This is the first step of what later became Temple's journey into ecumenical leadership. These commitments point to Temple's own theological position 'standing in the centre' (Spencer, 2022, p. 21). Temple's different commitments confronted him with the need for change in both the church and society. At times this put him at odds with senior church leaders, including Holland and Archbishop of Canterbury Randall Davidson. In response Temple led the Life and Liberty movement, which was designed to open up access to the gospel for all in society. Spencer summarizes this challenge:

> If the gospel was to be heard the body proclaiming it would need to be reformed and many ancient abuses removed ... a campaign was needed, to free the church from its identification with the anachronistic establishment of the past ... it needed self government. (2022, p. 34)

The Life and Liberty movement succeeded. By 1920, self-government in the Church of England was enshrined in an Act of Parliament. Directly following this movement, in 1921, Temple was named Bishop of Manchester. In a letter to his brother, Temple noted an affinity with Manchester. He wrote saying, 'Somehow I have always felt that I should go to Manchester one day ... I should have a better chance of doing some good there than anywhere else' (Iremonger, 1948, p. 282). Likewise, Temple was welcomed by Manchester. A quote from the *Manchester Guardian* reflected: 'Nothing is needed here than that the Church should be brought into close touch with every progressive movement in moral, economic, social, and educational matters, and no one is better fitted to effect this than the brilliant son of the late Archbishop of Canterbury' (*Manchester Guardian*, 1920).

As Bishop of Manchester, Temple was a national figure and sought to address the mandate highlighted in the *Guardian*. He established the Diocese of Blackburn to reduce the size of the bureaucracy within the Diocese of Manchester and to devolve powers to local contexts. Temple sought to work with others to broker greater rights for workers through the Conference on Politics, Economics and Citizenship (COPEC) gathering and as part of the 1926 miners' dispute, but both failed to gain traction with political leaders of the time, Ramsay McDonald (Labour) and Stanley Baldwin (Conservative). Broadly speaking these interventions were a failure at the time (Spencer, 2022, pp. 123–4). And Temple attracted detractors. Conservative theologian Ronald Knox questioned whether Temple's approach was about keeping up with the Joneses and seeing what they would swallow. Temple responded, 'I'm not a spiritual doctor, trying to see how much Jones can swallow and keep down. I'm more respectable than that. I am Jones himself, asking what there is to eat?' (Iremonger, 1948, p. 162). However, Hastings makes the case that Temple's efforts were not wasted:

> Immediate consequences were small. Its importance lay within a longer process of adult education whereby the leadership, clerical and lay, of the church was being weaned from high Tory attitudes to an acceptance of the Christian case for massive social reform and the development of a welfare state. In this it and its like were almost over successful. (1995, p. 179)

Further evidence of this kind of commitment by Temple is seen in the establishment of the Board of Women's Work in 1922, which among many activities provided training for deaconesses in the church (Spencer, 2001). When Temple left Manchester for York, 80 women wrote to Temple, telling him that they 'Desire to thank you for your sympathetic and fair treatment of your own workers. From your first coming into the diocese, you have shewn equal respect and consideration for women's work as for men's ... [you have] given dignity and authority to our work' (Iremonger, 1948, pp. 307–8).

PROLOGUE: AN EPILOGUE FOR THE TEMPLE TRADITION

Further evidence is also available through Temple's development of the term 'welfare state'. As Bishop of Manchester, Temple used the term 'welfare state' for the first time in 1928, at the Henry Scott Holland Lectures in Liverpool. Temple set up the 'power state' on the one hand and the welfare state on the other. The power state model drew influence from Austrian and Prussian states before the First World War, which sought to coerce their citizens for the state's own ends and would work to preserve the sovereignty of the state at the expense of individual freedoms. This was contrasted with Temple's welfare state, which existed to serve the people and communities that made up the nation. While welfare state is a term that has become synonymous with Temple, Simon Lee (2023a) notes that it is a term that he did not have a great personal affinity with, hence its diminishing use by Temple in the years before the establishment of the post-Second World War welfare state itself. Nonetheless, the original orientation and outlook of the welfare state is synonymous with the devolved, inclusive and person-centred vision Temple sets out in his work, which holds open space for preserving individual liberties alongside the need for the order of things by the state. This is captured in an address Temple gave, 'The Pilgrims of the United States', in New York in 1936:

> In all nations there is to be detected the swing of a pendulum from one side to the other between [freedom and order]. Sometimes central authority is being more developed, sometimes local liberties are or individual rights; always the pendulum is swinging, but in some countries the swing is very violent and it seems that they must either have liberty or order but are hardly capable of both.

It was during Temple's time in Manchester that he established his commitment to ecumenical ministry, which he continued during his time in York and Canterbury and for which he was given the informal title of 'Bishop of Unity'. Temple supported unity movements across all the main expressions of it in his time. These included the Faith and Order movement, which held its first conference in 1927 in Lausanne and its second in Edinburgh in 1937. Temple was elected chair of the movement in 1929 and was at every annual meeting thereafter. He was also involved in the founding of the World Council of Churches, and the British Council of Churches, which became Churches Together in Britain and Ireland, both of which are still in operation today. Temple is the only leader to operate across these different movements. As such he has a unique role in ecumenical and unity movements within the

Christian church. Had he not died in 1944 he would have been the first chairman of the World Council of Churches too (Spencer, 2022). During the Second World War, Temple's commitment to pursuing unity across difference was powerfully expressed. In 1943 he offered a broadcast, on behalf of the Provision Committee of the World Council of Churches, to Germany entitled *Is Christ Divided?*

> I think of many very dear German friends, whom I yearn to meet again, knowing that when we meet it will be to find our fellowship in allegiance to Christ unbroken and undiminished. For this unity of the Christian people in every land is not a construction of human beings. It is not, in the ordinary sense, an international fellowship. That phrase suggests that we start from our various human groupings and seek ways of drawing these nearer to one another. But Christians do not begin in that way at all. They do not construct the unity, nor develop it out of their aspirations. They find that they are united across all barriers or gulfs of division; and this unity is in their one Lord, Jesus Christ. (Temple, 1943, cited in Spencer, 2015, p. 161)

He embodied his desire for unity beyond embracing different Christian traditions as well. Temple established the Council of Christian and Jews to gather in solidarity with the Jewish community and to seek support from across the Christian church. While Temple adopted a position of seeking unity and reconciliation with the German church, at the beginning of the war Temple also clearly objected strongly to the treatment of the Jews and to the wrongdoing of the Nazis themselves, and saw younger generations from Great Britain as responding clearly and decisively to the challenge:

> The prevailing conviction is that Nazi tyranny and aggression are destroying the traditional excellences of European civilisation and must be eliminated for the good of mankind ... Our people are confident, not in their own righteousness as individuals or as a nation, but in the justice of the cause to which they have now dedicated themselves. (Temple, 1939, cited in Spencer, 2015, p. 194)

In unpublished papers from 1941, collated and published in *Christ in All Things* (Spencer, 2015), Temple returns to his distinction between welfare state and power state. He is more explicit here in his distinction and his application of both. He notes:

PROLOGUE: AN EPILOGUE FOR THE TEMPLE TRADITION

> We get the conception of the welfare state, according to which the state exists for the sake of its citizens, both collectively and individually. But if the other doctrine of man is true, then each individual exists for the state, which is itself the object of his final allegiance and the prosperity of which is the measure of right and wrong – the conception of the power state. The Nazi philosophy takes this position and the conduct of the Nazi Government follows from it with perfect consistency. (Temple, 1941, cited in Spencer, 2015, p. 199)

What stands out from Temple's leadership is both the breadth of his commitment to different constituent groups and the depth of his commitment to his faith in Christ, and indeed the power God has to be a unifying force in the face of utter evil. While it is entirely reasonable to see the shortcomings in the early years of Temple's time as Bishop of Manchester, it is those same failures that prepared him for seeking justice in the face of existential crises that were shaping the nation and the global context in which he was leading. From his time in Manchester, through his time as Archbishop of York and Archbishop of Canterbury there was a continuity to what Temple did. Spencer summarizes: '[Temple] offered insight into the way things are, with a compelling and hopeful vision of the way they could be, with the principles, values, and specific goals needed to get there' (2022, p. 191). The strength of Temple's approach was highlighted in a domestic context in 1941 through the Malvern Conference, which sought to contribute to a vision for recovery and for the future of the nation, after the Second World War (Spencer, 2022, p. 124). Malvern served to catalyse a movement which for Temple at least culminated in his work *Christianity and Social Order* being taken up by a much wider audience outside the bounds of the church. This movement beyond the church will have come in no small part from Temple's prominence in the war years. For others who lived longer than Temple, this movement contributed to a wider social reform agenda and the realization of what Temple termed the welfare state. A point of note at this stage: along with Temple's emphasis on personal emancipation, collective unity and limits to the role of the state, that is, to seek the welfare of people in communities throughout the nation, Malvern also highlighted Temple's views on the environment, repeated later in *Christianity and Social Order*:

> The fundamental source of all wealth is Land. All wealth is a product of human labour expended on God's gifts; and those gifts are bestowed in the land, what it contains and what it nourishes. Most truly the

Malvern Conference declared that 'we must recover reverence for the earth and its resources, treating it no longer as a reservoir of potential wealth to be exploited, but as a storehouse of divine bounty on which we utterly depend.' (Temple, 1976, p. 113)

In order to make full sense of the high-water mark in the Temple Tradition, *Christianity and Social Order*, we will return to the roots of Temple's formation as a leader – university. I have set out different developments that followed Temple's time in Oxford. This period was influenced by the philosophy and social reform of T. H. Green, who taught at Oxford in the 1870s. Skinner (2023) offers a succinct summary of the 'Greenian Moment'; the influence of Green at Balliol over those who followed him, and on the liberal tradition in the early twentieth century. Skinner notes how Green's influence was beyond his philosophy and pursuit of social reform in that he realized a legacy through his followers, including Temple, Tawney, Beveridge, Toynbee and Clement Atlee. The Greenian Moment was characterized by an idealist liberal philosophical tradition. He was heavily influenced by G. W. F. Hegel who thought that society was shaped by its historical development. In addition to his philosophy, Green also engaged with the poorest communities around Oxford and sought to develop social reform agendas. Green's influence in this area led to the establishment of Toynbee Hall, which was a laboratory for the shaping of Balliol alumni who sought not only to develop their minds but to develop their experience in impoverished communities. As I note above, Temple and his contemporaries spent time at Toynbee Hall when they were at Balliol, which contributed to their views on social reforms. These views were nurtured by Edward Caird who was Temple's Master at Balliol College. Caird's view was that they were not training professional philosophers but were preparing public servants for government, the church and the law (Spencer, 2001, p. 3). In terms of Temple's philosophical outlook, this Greenian influence showed up most clearly in his early title, *Mens Creatrix* (Temple, 1919). There Temple set out a philosophy of mind. It was premised on the fact that early forms of life did not have sentience, or the capacity to think for themselves. As humanity emerged, capacity to think for ourselves folowed, which allowed an understanding of the incarnation of Christ to emerge too. Temple's perspective drew on a breadth of different resources. He felt that the achievements of human culture – the Greek and Roman empires, for example, the natural sciences and the arts and morality itself – were all facets that contributed to the emergence of and revelation of Christ. They all provided markers of the evolution of humanity and a move towards conceiving of and apprehending the manifestation and revelation of the incarnate Christ. Temple notes:

> The whole process of that revelation which has been going on through nature, through history and through prophets, comes to complete fulfilment in the Incarnation ... Only in the life of Christ is this manifestation given. What we see in Him is what we should see in the history of the universe if we could apprehend that history in its completeness. (Temple, 1919, pp. 317–18)

Temple's view was that Christ incarnate was articulated most clearly in the Gospel of John; 'The word was made flesh and we behold his glory.' For Temple, the Gospel of John did not stand opposed to or aside from other sources of culture and philosophy that shape society. Rather, they are part and parcel of it (Spencer, 2022, p. 51). The influence of Green, his philosophy and his social reform agenda was seen in Temple's politics too. Green argued for the positive role of the community in shaping people and vice versa. This view entailed a conception of freedom not as an absence of restraint, which aligned with the negative freedom articulated by John Stuart Mill's liberalism (see Mill, *On Liberty*, 1859), but as a presence of opportunity for all, which transformed both inner and outer dimensions of our lives. Temple embodied this sense of freedom during his different episcopal roles. He received high praise from his contemporary Reinhold Niebuhr:

> The primary significance of his life lay in his ability to carry the radical social implications of their Christian faith into higher ecclesiastical office than any other churchman. The real fact is that Dr Temple was able to relate the ultimate insights of religion about the human situation to the immediate necessities of political justice and the proximate possibilities of a just social order more vitally and creatively than any other modern Christian leader. (Niebuhr, 1944, pp. 584–5)

It is in *Christianity and Social Order* that Temple sets out his approach to leadership most clearly and where he expresses freedom in a positive sense as a tenet for the incarnational leadership of the church in society. Temple's leadership was embodied by Life and Liberty, the formation of the Diocese of Blackburn, his work across ecumenical movements, the Council of Christians and Jews, during the war years, at Malvern, and many other examples. Temple builds on this by offering guiding social principles for citizens to take up and use to guide their own leadership.

He also ventures a suggested programme of policy agendas, noted as 'middle axioms', to be taken forward. This combination of three approaches – embodied leadership, guiding principles and a suggested agenda – characterize Temple's approach, which received endorsement from early twentieth-century economist John Maynard Keynes, as well as Balliol contemporaries R. H. Tawney and William Beveridge (Spencer, 2017, p. 1856).

Principles for leadership

In the latter half of *Christianity and Social Order*, Temple set out three guiding principles that were a generally accessible frame of reference for anyone to take up. The first principle was based on the liberty and autonomy of the individual. The relationship between personal autonomy and the structure of society is a key one for Temple. Indeed he acknowledges the art of governing within this relationship: 'the art of government, in fact, is the art of so ordering life that self-interest prompts what justice demands' (Temple, 1976, p. 65). Liberty or freedom is also something about which Temple offers a caution. He warns against freedom being frittered away through superficial or selfish undertaking. The simple fact of the matter for Temple is that he sees humankind as implicated in original sin:

> When we open our eyes as babies, we see the world, stretching out around us, we are in the middle of it; all proportions, and perspectives, in what we see, are determined by the relation – distance, height, and so forth – of the various visible objects to ourselves. This will remain true of a bodily vision as long as we live. I am the centre of the world I see; where the horizon is depends on where I stand ... So each of us takes his place in the centre of his own world. But I'm not the centre of the world, or the standard of reference between good and bad: I am not and God is. In other words I put myself in God's place. That is my original sin. (Temple, 1976, p. 60)

Temple does not associate that original sin with guilt that we must carry with us throughout our lives, but does caution that it is a condition and an environment that we are in and that we would be wise to find our way out of. He notes that this can be done through education, which can mitigate the impact of conditions on us and can subject us to trust and beauty. This can move us beyond our self-centredness but ultimately,

Temple argues, it is Divine Love that is needed to save us (Temple, 1976, p. 60). However, Temple was not naive or indeed idealistic. Elsewhere, in *Christus Veritas* (1924) Temple reflects, 'Of any emancipation from selfishness itself, or any attainment of perfect fellowship in self-surrender to the absolute good, our historic progress hitherto gives no promise whatsoever.'

So within Temple's (1976) first principle, freedom, while offering no guarantees, he located a sense of freedom with respect to God, using the doctrine of Imago Dei, being created in the image of God. So at the foundation of things, Temple wants to promote the right that everyone has to express their humanity fully in all that it entails, through their own deliberate choices, created in the image of God. And, in order to facilitate this freedom as deliberate choice, Temple argues that society should be structured for the 'widest possible extension of personal responsibility' or the '[full expression of our] personalities' (1976, p. 67). In terms of how this then implicates our freedom, Temple argues that freedom should be defined as freedom 'for' as opposed to freedom 'from' others. So this is not negatively defined in terms of freedom being a simple absence of coercion, as per J. S. Mill (1859), or as per Isaiah Berlin's 'negative freedom' to be free from interference. As has been made clear earlier, Temple sets individuals in relationship with the rest of creation and, through education, that relationship can be nurtured. The purpose of this is not to be bound to the state or endless collectivism per se, but to be resourced by the state to act as responsible citizens in society. Temple is candid in his derivation of freedom, as he notes that while the subject of the book (*Christianity and Social Order*) is not personal conversion, he cannot define freedom perfectly, as that perfect freedom can only be achieved through perfect faith:

> That is, a complete personal response to the love of God – only the love of God working upon his conscience, heart and will can set him free from the self-centredness, which, otherwise will vitiate both his own life, and his contribution to the life of society. (1976, p. 69)

Nonetheless, Temple is still hopeful that seeking that sort of freedom can facilitate self-control, self-determination and self-direction for all (1976, p. 68). In fact, Temple regards our spiritual lives as dependent on freedom to choose a course of action. The example he gives is that even Jesus did not intervene when Judas moved to betray him (pp. 68–9). For Temple, freedom is a political act ultimately shaped through relationship with God, people and laws that shape society.

Temple's second principle was fellowship, or a right to social relationships (1976, pp. 69–73). This second principle suggests that our full humanity lies within a deep sense of interdependence:

> No man is fitted for an isolated life; everyone has needs that he cannot supply for himself, but he needs not only what his neighbours contribute to the equipment of his life but their actual selves as a compliment to himself. Man is naturally and incurably social. (Temple, 1976, p. 69)

Temple (1976) emphasizes this point by highlighting our influence on one another throughout our lives and across our different social units: families, home life, education, work life, in urban and rural contexts, including civic associations, or the intermediate groupings that make up society. Temple notes that it is these groupings where freedom is realized most fully. He also notes that in politics there are often spaces that are disregarded and forgotten, instead focusing on the individual or the state, and nothing in between (1976, p. 70). Temple argues strongly, 'it is impossible to lay excessive emphasis on this point' (p. 71); our personalities are formed (contrasted with individuality) through our relationships with the people and groupings that make up society, and the more we associate and express ourselves across 'networks of communities and associations and fellowships ... [the richer our personality is] ... it is in these that the real wealth of human life consists' (p. 71). And it is these in turn that should be attended to by the state, as a means of promoting human well-being and nurturing citizens. This is the welfare state as Temple saw it.

Temple's third principle was service, or the outworking of freedom in relation with others. Service is the point at which thought turns to word and deed expressed as responsible citizenship. Temple suggests that we should always check our personal decisions with reference to external considerations, that is, with respect to those we are in relationship with; in our families and within the communities and networks we are part of, as well as wider society (1976, pp. 73–7). Temple's principles showed how individuals might engage with wider society and might contribute to a shared life, mediated through two things. The first is the work of what he referred to as intermediate groups within civil society; educational institutions, faith institutions, political and civic associations, and others, and their role in serving society. The second type of service Temple refers to is a call to make our individual occupations, our means of making a living, forms of service. Temple notes:

PROLOGUE: AN EPILOGUE FOR THE TEMPLE TRADITION

> To make that choice on selfish grounds is probably the greatest single sin that any young person can commit, for it is the deliberate withdrawal from allegiance to God, and of the greatest part of time and strength. This does not mean no attention is to be paid to inclinations. Inclination is often a true guide to vocation; for we like doing what we can do well, and we should give our best service by giving scope to our own attitudes and talents. But a young man who is led by his inclination to take up teaching or business or whatever it may be, must nonetheless make his choice because in that field he can give his own best service. This will enormously affect the spirit in which he does his work and his dealings with the other people engaged in it all with whom it brings him into contact. (Temple, 1976, pp. 73–4)

Temple does not simply lay the responsibility at the feet of young people, however. He is clear that all groups of people in society should seek to serve in the same way, that is, for good reasons, and based on the skills and experiences they have. Temple also cautions that the way in which we serve should not be to the detriment of other groups, so we should always be expressing our liberty or freedom for others, and, tellingly, a person should not force their own standard on someone else who is not yet ready to receive it,

> ... for it is the essence of spiritual faith that it is freely accepted ... let him live by that as far as he can, and let him invite others to join him in that enterprise, but let him not force that standard on his fellows, and least of all on those dependent on him. (Temple, 1976, pp. 75–6)

Temple offers these three – freedom, fellowship and service – as a general guide to be taken forward by responsible citizens who can enact them through the intermediate groupings that make up society. In the concluding part of *Christianity and Social Order*, Temple turns to ways of regulating the applications of these three principles, such as using concepts of love and justice (Temple, 1976, pp. 78–82), the purpose of which was ultimately to support the agenda of rebuilding the nation after the war. I have given an example of the vehement way in which Temple attributes both love and justice, through his breadth of associations and arenas in which he offered leadership: from student movements and reforms agendas, including education for all and prioritizing women's ministries a *long* time before it made the list of priorities for the national church, to the formation of associations across difference within the ecumenical movement, nationally and globally, and across religious divides as the Nazis persecuted the Jews in the Second World War. It is there that Temple also showed the depth of his love and the extent of his justice, making clear his support for the war effort in defence of those who cannot defend themselves.

Regarding the question of whether it is loving to bomb German cities, Temple said, 'By "love", we must be guided … It must of course be "love" for all concerned – Poles, Czechs, Norwegians, Dutch, Belgians, French, and so forth – not only for Germans' (Temple, March 1944, in Spencer, 2015, p. 166).

Regarding the commandment, 'Thou shalt not kill', Temple said:

> The mosaic sixth commandment is more accurately represented by the Prayer Book than by the Bible version, for the word in the Hebrew does not refer to killing of any kind but to murder, that is to say to killing for personal advantage or the satisfaction of personal passion. There is a great deal in the Gospels that is very terrible, as well as all that is said there about love and peace, and we have no right to take one part without the other.
>
> I am quite sure that at present it is a duty to fight the war through and win it … (Temple, July 1944, in Spencer, 2015, p. 209)

Looking to the future, beyond the war, Temple returns to the people for whom he is writing, present and future generations. He sets out on the final two pages of the main text of *Christianity and Social Order* what he believes to be six core ideas that he believed might be endorsed in the future. These include:

1 the rights of children to grow up in a family and community that is decent and offers dignity and a means of being in happy fellowship in a safe environment;
2 access by children to education, until they reach maturity, to make clear their aptitudes and to allow them to develop, inspired by a faith in God;
3 each citizen should have enough income to live in a home and bring up children in conditions described;
4 each citizen should have a voice in the industry they are working in and the knowledge that their labour is being directed for the well-being of the community;
5 each citizen should have time off each week (two days in seven) and annual leave from their employed work to enable a full personal life to enjoy their interests;

PROLOGUE: AN EPILOGUE FOR THE TEMPLE TRADITION

6 each citizen should have liberty to worship, to express themselves and to assemble and to associate. (Temple, 1976, p. 97)

Temple then elaborated on these six at the end of the book in an appendix running to 16 pages. The most significant part to my eye is not the presentation of these ideas, but the manner of them. Temple sets out ideas that he hoped many would agree with. He was also careful to qualify his programme, noting:

> I think it's most improbable that every Christian should endorse what I'm now going to say. But it seems right to indicate how I personally think we should do well to begin. Very likely better ways than these can be found for the realisation of our sixfold aim; very likely one or another of my proposals is definitely ill-founded and would, in fact, frustrate its own object. I offer them as suggestions for criticism rather than for adoption, and beg that readers will consider them in that spirit. (Temple, 1976, p. 99)

Temple also offered three further qualifications:

1 He offered his appendix in response to the question, 'What would you *do*?' But he denies that there is a distinction between talking and doing. He notes: 'By talking we gradually form public opinion, and public opinion, if it is strong enough, gets things done' (Temple, 1976, p. 114). Nonetheless Temple notes he is willing to give an answer to the question being put to him without claiming any special skill with which to answer it.
2 Let no one quote this as Temple's conception of a political programme Christians ought to support. Temple does not believe there can be such a programme. It is presented as one option among many.
3 Temple asks that the political proposals that have been made are not substituted for the truths of the gospel as the mark of a real Christian.

In all things, Temple offered leadership that was contextual and critical, which both recognized his own limitations and sought to open opportunities for others to offer their view, or to form one of their own. This pragmatism pointed to the ability of Temple to conceive of a new vision for faith in public life, emanating from the incarnate Christ expressed through humankind, and realized in society through the mediation of the welfare state. While Temple was clear about this as a possible pathway, he presented it in such a way as to leave space for the views of those who saw the world differently to him, including notably the views of those that the welfare state was for. When *Christianity and Social Order* was published in 1942 it sold 131,000 copies, which made in its time a significant and popular volume well beyond the limits of the Christian church. Temple died from gout in 1944 at the age of 63. His death meant that he did not get to see his work come to fruition through the establishment of the post-Second World War welfare state and an enduring legacy for himself.

Temple's legacy

As a centrist, consultative and prophetic leader, Temple held wide appeal in the years following his death. However, he was not universally admired. This is apparent in the contrasting views of different Bishops of Blackburn. In a volume celebrating the fiftieth anniversary of the establishment of the Diocese of Blackburn, Bishop of Blackburn Alan Chesters praised Temple and his legacy:

> William Temple was a prophet, albeit a rather reasonable, jovial and consensus seeking one. One might be tempted to say that he was the kind of prophet the Church of England at its best should produce ... he helped to bring hope and new opportunities to the lives of millions. (Chesters, 2001, p. vi)

More recently, another Bishop of Blackburn, Philip North, claimed the negative impact of the welfare state on people and communities in the north of England as a rationale for calling Temple and his legacy into question. Offering a review of Stephen Spencer's writing on Temple, North said, 'Spencer's account of the life of William Temple adds to the rich body of hagiography, but fails to address the charge that the Temple legacy [the welfare state] has added to the sense of dependency that afflicts so many northern working-class communities' (North, 2016).

I would suggest that North might hold a different view if he consulted some of Temple's writings on the subject.[2] Beyond the Diocese of Blackburn, theologian and philosopher John Milbank, whose influence was notable as part of the Red Tory and 'Big Society' agenda forged by the Conservative/Liberal Democrat coalition government in 2010, also criticized Temple. Milbank suggested that Temple had handed over the incarnational mission of the church to the state and saw the state as a more complete expression of the church's social mission than the church itself (Milbank, 2011).

Beyond the welfare state, the Diocese of Blackburn, the incarnational mission of the church, Temple's legacy was also marked by the formation of an institution in his memory. This was done initially by the formation of William Temple College (1947–71), which supported theological development and training for male and female lay leaders, based at St Deiniol's Library (now known as Gladstone's Library), in Hawarden, North Wales.[3] The college was run initially by David Jenkins before leadership was passed to Mollie Batton. It followed the tradition that Temple had set up in his time in Manchester. The college was then moved to Rugby School where Temple had been headmaster. The college later became the William Temple Foundation (1971–present). The Foundation has variously styled itself as a 'college without walls' and a 'public theology think tank', under the leadership of successive directors, Ronald Preston, John Atherton (PhD supervised by Preston), Malcolm Brown (PhD supervised by Atherton), and Chris Baker (PhD supervised by Atherton). A milestone for the Foundation was its consultative role leading the *Faith in the City* report (1985), which analysed the role of the church in urban contexts in the UK and made recommendations to guide the church's response. However, *Faith in the City* was characterized as the 'high-water mark' for the Temple-Preston-Atherton axis and influence and marked a point from which the Temple Tradition began to decline in influence (Sedgwick, 2018).

Temple tradition in transition

The publication of *Faith in the City* catalysed a turn away from Temple's work, 40 years after Temple's death, and towards Liberation Theology within Anglican social thought, represented in part by the establishment of the Church Urban Fund. However, this shift left some, including former Foundation Secretary Malcolm Brown, feeling '[theologically speaking] almost naked' (Brown, 2014a, p 11). Brown reflected during an obituary for Bishop David Jenkins, who founded William Temple College in Hawarden, that by the 1990s interest by the Church of England in the Foundation had dissipated:

> In the 1990s, the House of Bishops often met for its annual gatherings at Manchester Business School. We tried to interest them in the work of the Foundation, but with little effect. We were even refused permission to put leaflets around the tables in the bishops' meeting room. But David accosted me one evening in the bar. 'Don't bother with this lot,'

he said loudly. 'All they want to do is put their arms around each other and say, "It's alright to cry even though you are a bishop!"' (Brown, 2016)

Brown moved on in 2000, and the William Temple Foundation moved from the Business School at Manchester University, where it had been established by Ronald Preston, to Luther King House where Chris Baker assumed the role of Development Officer under the continuing guidance of Atherton. Baker completed his PhD in 2002 and followed the prominent influence of Atherton at the Foundation until his death in 2016. During this period, another professor, Samuel Fergusson Professor Elaine Graham, emerged as a prominent influence on the Foundation. This relationship and the one with Atherton is noted in 2002 at the opening of the Manchester Centre for Public Theology, relationships that ran throughout their careers (William Temple Foundation, 2002). In 2008, Baker moved to the University of Chester and established the Centre for Faiths and Public Policy at the Theology and Religious Studies Department there, of which the William Temple Foundation became part. Graham joined the department at Chester in 2009 as Grosvenor Professor of Research, and Atherton also joined as a Visiting Professor. This was part of a continuing transition for the Foundation, including a move away from its long-term home in Manchester where the roots for Temple's work in the north of England can be found. This transition saw the emergence of a new network of associate research fellows who worked together to produce a progressive agenda for the new-look Foundation. In 2014 the William Temple Foundation officially relaunched itself, 70 years after Temple's death. Assistant Director: Communication and Development, Charlotte Dando, wrote:

> Our makeover, however, is not simply a matter of aesthetics. We continue to promote the economic, social and political wellbeing of society, but we've taken some time to carefully evaluate who we are, how we should work, and how we can best act on our values of social justice. (Dando, 2014)

The new-look foundation maintained an interdisciplinary approach under the influence of Atherton until his death in 2016. Following this, Baker and Graham offered a 'festschrift' for Atherton, through the co-edited volume *Theology for Changing Times: John Atherton and the Future of Public Theology*. They opened it with their tribute to Atherton:

PROLOGUE: AN EPILOGUE FOR THE TEMPLE TRADITION

To read the eight major volumes of public theology that spanned John Atherton's extraordinarily rich and consistent output from the early 1980s up to his death in 2016 is to swim in an immense tide of human experience, social history, global upheaval and religious and secular change. John's public theology captures a period in history that is still shaping our collective experience. The last 40 years have been an era of turmoil and often traumatic disorientation: from the rise of Thatcherism and the big bang of financial deregulation, the collapse of the post-war global consensus and the break-up of the Soviet Union, growing social inequality and the decline of Christianity in the West, through to 9/11, the rise of grass-roots protest such as the Occupy movement, global religious revival and the current moment of dangerous and febrile nationalist populism across Europe and the USA. John's work accurately and presciently captures these historical and social movements in a way that no one else in public or political theology has done. (Baker and Graham, 2018, p. 1)

Under this umbrella of Atherton's influence others were also making their own contributions. Dando developed contributions around inter-faith engagement and as Assistant Director was the first signifier of a diversification in the leadership of the Foundation. John Reader was a parish priest and the leading voice within the William Temple Foundation on Continental philosophy. Reader's PhD was on the work of Jürgen Habermas, which gave him a grounding in European social thought. Reader wrote prolifically on themes of Continental philosophy, the environment and the post-digital age, and established the Ethical Future Network at the University of Oxford which produced a variety of outputs up until his death in 2023. This network comprised a distinct group of scholars globally respected in their own right, which in the end was largely independent of the Foundation and its Fellowship. Reader was also influential in recruiting staff to the Foundation, with consecutive Communications Officers after Dando being recruited from Reader's networks. Baker's work was developed through numerous collaborations. These included entrepreneurial ventures. The Spiritual Capital Development Company was piloted by Baker in 2015 with the support of a Dr Shanon Shah, who is now Director of Faith for Climate and holds posts at both the University of London and King's College London. Power and Baker Consultants was piloted in 2017 in partnership with Dr Maria Power, a former senior research fellow of the Foundation and a Senior Research Fellow at the Las Casas Institute for Social Justice at the University of Oxford. There was also a move to work with me to consolidate Spaces of Hope as a leadership consultancy during the course of completing my PhD, but I did not take this up. In terms of academic collaborations, these were interdisciplinary. In public theology this was primarily with Elaine Graham. In urban geography, Baker worked with pioneers in that field, Justin Beaumont and, in particular, with University of Exeter geographer Paul Cloke, who died in 2023. Both Beaumont and Cloke led the development of concepts of postsecularity. As an independent scholar, Beaumont produced a substantial edited volume in 2018 exploring postsecular theory. Cloke's leadership in the area of thinking included being lead author on the 2019 volume *Geographies of Postsecularity*. Baker partnered with Reader on a theological and philosophical exploration of the urban, *A Philosophy of Christian Materialism: Entangled Fidelities and the Public Good*. Baker's policy work initially explored ideas of religious and spiritual capital, rooted in a Marxist critique of faith-based social action, which contributed to capital theory pioneered by Robert Putnam. This began following Baker's PhD in 2002. More recently, policy work switched to mapping the faith and belief landscape in social policy with Professor of Faith and Public Policy Adam Dinham at Goldsmiths College, University of London. In 2017 links with Goldsmiths College meant a Temple Scholarship Programme could be established. Scholars included community organizer Val Barron, environmental activist Matt Stemp, journalist Yasmin Duwan and chaplain Gill Reeve. I started my PhD supervised by both Baker and Graham at Chester and later became a scholar at Goldsmiths, supervised by Baker and Dinham. Scholarship projects began to conclude from 2020 with my submission. Barron and Reeve submitted in 2023, post-pandemic.

The transition continued with the story of the Foundation and the Temple Tradition coming full circle. Under the direction of the new Chair of the Board, Simon Lee, the Foundation hosted three symposia that marked the eightieth anniversary of *Christianity and Social Order*, at sites across the UK resonant with the life and legacy of Temple: Canterbury Cathedral, Balliol College and Blackburn Cathedral. At Balliol College, *Christianity and Social Order* was studied with regards to historical and contemporary contexts to assess any enduring relevance 80 years on. Matthew Grimley noted that while premature, Temple's death meant that he departed while his work was at its height. He quoted former Bishop of Durham Henley Henson, 'I think [Temple] is "*felix opportunitate mortis*", for he has passed away, while the streams of opinion, in church, and state, of which he had become the outstanding symbol and exponent, were at flood, and escaped the experience of their inevitable ebb' (Grimley, 2023, p. 16).

PROLOGUE: AN EPILOGUE FOR THE TEMPLE TRADITION

Lawrence Goldman (2023, pp. 20–8) found the scope of *Christianity and Social Order* to be limited to its time, and Stephen Spencer (2022, p. 15) was uncertain of the extent to which *Christianity and Social Order* was transferable into a twenty-first-century context. Anthony Reddie[4] offered contemporary nuance, querying who gets to exert power and influence as Temple and others did? Reddie's challenge followed:

> Imagine three Black working-class women sat on a park bench in Handsworth, inner-city Birmingham ... discussing their hopes and visions for Britain in the future. Can one imagine in what universe these working-class Black women would be able to envision a world where their views, hopes and intentions would eventually be realised as social policy? (2023)

Simon Lee (2023a, p. 48) noted that society today faces different challenges to Temple, which must be considered appropriately – the climate crisis and Covid-19 pandemic – alongside enduring issues that Temple would recognize: the cost of living crisis, wars (namely Ukraine and the Israel–Palestine conflict), breakdown of trust in and structure of institutions. The final word was from Baker who had stewarded the transition of the Tradition since 2001 via the work of the Foundation with Atherton, Graham, Reader and others. Baker conceded the demise of the Temple Tradition, while also acknowledging that Temple's work might offer some inspiration and a call to action for new generations (Baker, 2023, pp. 52–6). In 2024 the William Temple Foundation began a return to its roots. This strategy has been led by Simon Lee and has sought to open up space for questions of where hope might be found in uncertain times in the public square. This agenda was characterized in terms of *Radical Hope*, with the etymology of 'radical' being a return to the roots of things. I will say more about *Radical Hope* in Chapters 5 and 8. In terms of a return to the roots of Temple's life and legacy, the Foundation is exploring a return to its identity as a college offering education for all. In summer 2024, the Foundation began this process with a virtual Festival of Public Theology.

In this prologue, I have explored the work of William Temple, his legacy and the transition the Temple Tradition has gone through both in terms of the influence of Temple's thought and in terms of the institution that bears his name. In the end, what I can see from Temple is a philosophical, theological and public tradition, which works from the centre, as opposed to left or right, and seeks to walk with and be in conversation with, and ultimately be curated by, those who are outside institutional structures, in a way that seeks the common good. The critique of *Christianity and Social Order* at Balliol in 2022 shows clearly the limits of Temple's own work for today. However, it does also raise questions to take forward. These include:

- What might an interdisciplinary reform movement from the centre look like today?
- What might the philosophical framework for it be?
- What forms might leadership take?
- Where might leadership come from?
- What kind of principles might guide leadership?
- How might intermediate organizations be conceived?
- How might the different conditions within the twenty-first century be accounted for?
- How might the public square be framed?
- How might different world views be engaged within the public square?

In what follows I will consider these questions. In the next chapter I offer a conceptual basis of 'liminality', which is taken from the anthropological work of Arnold Van Gennep and, later, Victor Turner.

Notes

1 Which later became the press that has published this book, SCM Press.

2 To my view, he has not taken into account that (a) Temple died before the welfare state was brought to fruition, so (b) a wise assessment of Temple's views would be found with respect to what Temple actually said, which was (c) to draw a sharp distinction between the power state (being more indicative of the Thatcher-run government of the 1980s) and his vision for the welfare state.

3 The library was used as the private study of archbishops and other such dignitaries. The brief residency of Temple College, with its service of lay leaders, hinted at the potential offered by the library for wider public use. This came to fruition in the 1980s under the Chairmanship of the Revd T. P. Davies who was Rector of Hawarden from 1977 to 1992. During this period the library went through a substantial conversion, which opened it up to use by the public and encouraged access to education for all.

4 Anthony Reddie is the first Professor of Black Theology in the history of the University of Oxford. His role in the symposium alongside Dr Saiyyidah Zaidi, the first Muslim scholar to complete a PhD in public theology in Britain, was symbolic of a shift in the orientation and identity of the Foundation, to a make-up more reflective of contemporary society.

3

Living with Liminality

> Religious faith, wherever it is encountered, invariably enables the faithful to maintain their poise and position; and also in moments of challenge, cope with crisis and change ... it highlights how adherents might be guided through periods of liminality, maintaining the core of their faith whilst at the same time being appropriately adaptive. Sometimes faith can be disruptive and revolutionary. Sometimes it can be glacial . . . [it nonetheless] enables adherents to negotiate those external forces it cannot control. (Percy, 2021)

In this chapter, I will set out the lived experience that has characterized and developed the basis for Spaces of Hope. I will set this out in four sections, offering a narrative that runs from 2009 to 2024. This 15-year period is used to introduce myself as the author and to articulate my positionality as an account and rationale for what you will read in subsequent chapters. This chapter is also used to provide a conceptual basis for the book to come, in terms of liminality. I do this by beginning with some simple parameters for the concept of liminality, derived from the work of Arnold Van Gennep and then Victor Turner who coined and developed the term. Liminality has roots in anthropology – that is, the study of people – and is related to ethnography as an immersive research method, which I turn to in Chapter 4.

Liminality

We can trace the concept of liminality back to the work of Arnold Van Gennep (1873–1957), *Les Rites du Passage*. Van Gennep's work considers how people transition through a passage or process of change, usually associated with coming of age or growing up.

> The life of an individual in any society is a series of passages [for example] from one age to another and from one occupation to another

> ... every change in a person's life involves actions and reactions ... Transitions from group to group and from one social situation to the next are looked on as implicit in the very fact of existence. (Van Gennep, 1960, p. 2)

Van Gennep's work was with tribes in Africa, and maps the rites of passage that young men went through, guided by the elders of the tribe. The rite of passage was the process where younger members of the tribe are prepared to become full members, adult members, who in time would bring the next generation through into full membership of the tribe as well. The rite of passage is characterized as a liminal process, from the Latin *limen*, meaning threshold. So a liminal process is the crossing of an initial threshold, transitioning into a liminal experience, the experience itself, and then crossing a second threshold to transition beyond the liminal experience. In this way, the process or rite of passage can be characterized as pre-liminal, liminal and post-liminal. Within this process, the liminal experience is ultimately one of submission, submission to the conditions in which one finds oneself and to the creators of those conditions.

> Whoever passes from one to the other finds himself physically and magico-religiously in a special situation for a certain length of time: he wavers between two worlds. It is this situation which I have designated a transition, and one of the purposes of this book is to demonstrate that this symbolic and spatial area of transition maybe found in more or less pronounced form in all the ceremonies which accompany the passage from one social and magico-religious position to another. (Van Gennep, 1960, p. 18)

The rite of passage and the three phases of the liminal experience set out by Van Gennep are based within a tribal context, within a given community. Victor Turner (1967 and 1969) developed understanding of liminality beyond this and defined it in terms of the threshold between structures and communitas. Turner argues structure and communitas are two major models of human relatedness, which are juxtaposed and alternating (1969, pp. 360–1). The first, structure, is an ordered, hierarchical system, which separates people in terms of more or less. The second, communitas, is different. Communitas is relatively unstructured and characterized by equal individuals who are not under the authority of others in that environment. In this sense, liminality is the experience of communitas relative to structure. It is noteworthy that Turner uses the term communitas, as opposed to community. Communitas denotes the experience of social relationships, as opposed to a community, which Turner sees as a bounded 'area of common living' (Turner, 1969, p. 360). Turner presents rites of passage and communitas as essential parts of social life. Liminality, understood relative to structure and communitas, highlights that there cannot be high (position, status, etc.) without there being a concomitant low, and as such being high requires also the experience of being low. Turner (1967) describes transitioning within the liminal period as 'a process, a becoming, and in the case of rites [of] passage, even a transformation' and offers analogies with water boiling to produce steam and a grub forming into a moth (p. 4). A liminal period or communitas has different cultural properties from those of a structure. Liminality is a disorienting, non-binary and seemingly contradictory process where the subject of the liminal process is both invisible, not present within structures, and also symbolized in potentially bizarre ways (1967, p. 6). Turner notes:

> liminality may perhaps be regarded as the [antithesis] to all positive structural assertions, but as in some sense the source of them all, and, more than that, as a realm of pure possibility whence novel configurations of ideas and relations may arise. (1967, p. 7)

Liminality can be both a period of waiting and the removal of status between recognized and accredited encounters, and it can also be a novel, foundational and formational process of challenge and change. In submitting to the liminal period, there is a relinquishing of preliminary status and opening up of the potential for the absorption of power within a new status (Turner, 1967, p. 11).

A pertinent example of this is found where Turner notes that the then Prince Charles was sent by his father, Prince Philip, to bush school in the outback in Australia so that he could learn 'to rough it', as part of his process of becoming a man (1969, p. 360). Another example is the King's coronation in 2023, where Prince Charles became King Charles III, a process during which he was stripped to his undergarments before millions of people in the UK and billions of people around the world (albeit obscured by screens), before being re-dressed in the garments that symbolized his power and authority as monarch of Great Britain.

From here, I will take forward that liminality is something experienced as a rite of passage which takes place in different aspects of social life, characterized by transitions in and out of liminal periods, which are marked out by thresholds demarcating the pre-liminal, liminal and post-liminal periods between structure and communitas. Living with liminality is something that I believe we all have to do in different ways at different times and, as I will argue, it is pre-requisite for the development of transformational leadership. To illustrate that point, I will share from my experience, through four periods of my life entitled 'There for you', 'Hope and despair', 'By their fruits you will know them' and 'Finding a way in the wilderness'. These titles are taken from emics that characterized the different periods of time.[1] I use them as a means of mapping my changing perspectives as I lived with liminality. These stories provide an account of different liminal experiences: from stepping out of education and into the world of work after completing my graduate degree, under the influence of global factors such as the global financial crash; to the personal struggles and sense-making that took place through education, in the work place and through personal and professional relationships; the process of becoming political in outlook while making sense of how to seek God in environments where that is seen as a suspicious thing to do; moving from hope as a refuge amid day-to-day struggles, to a means of building resilience in the face of existential uncertainty. The quote from Percy (2021) used to open this chapter speaks to the temporality of faith while within liminal spaces; sometimes things can move at a pace, other times they are glacially slow. These accounts speak both to short periods of deep intensity and also take place over periods of years. During this time my own conception of God and my relationship with him has deepened and transformed. As I develop these accounts, I invite you to consider whether anything resonates for you and also to ask what your own stories of living with liminality might be.

There for you (2010–13)

In 2009 I graduated from my undergraduate degree, a BSc in Environmental Science. I studied topics such as exploration geology, environmental policy and sustainable development. My plan had been to go into the oil industry, but the careers advice before graduating was to 'get a temp job'. The global financial crash in 2008 had restricted opportunities in the job market. For graduates this meant that they were competing with Masters and PhD students for entry-level jobs in their industry. I found work at the sports retailer I had worked at during my A-level years. However, by the end of October 2009, I had been made redundant. This is not what was supposed to happen. In the months following, I experienced poor mental health as the realities of being unemployed set in. In January 2010, my dad shared an advert for a role as a sales assistant at the local petrol station. I applied for and secured this job. I worked ten hours a week over two shifts serving people for their groceries and fuel. At that time, ten hours a week was all I could manage. I had secured work in the oil industry, but this is not what I had anticipated. I worked at the petrol station for a further three and a half years.

Those who worked there wore a uniform emblazoned with the slogan 'There for You'. This spoke to the functional role of a shop assistant and offered an invitation for customers to ask us for help. For me, this slogan pointed to the deeper calling I felt I had on my life, to express my faith through the things that I did, but there and then I did not know how to. The conservative evangelical gospel message that I had grown up with was something that had shaped me personally. I had and still have a deep faith in God, but in these moments it did not offer me much in terms of dealing with the challenge I was facing. Sharing the good news of Christ crucified with colleagues in the back office was more likely to receive ridicule than encourage anyone to relate to me or my world view. I knew this because, while I was on the till, my supervisor would periodically change the shop television to the God channel. For those who haven't worked in a petrol station, there is a button behind a till that is used to authorize the use of the fuel pumps. In 2010 it was a legal requirement that somebody was behind the till while the pumps were in use, so that they could be turned off if there was a problem. So, when I was serving behind the till, I could not move. Having the God channel projected into the whole shop, with nobody else around, was my supervisor's way of mocking me without saying a word. As people entered through the door of the shop, the television was mounted on the wall to the left and the tills were on the right. As people walked in, they heard what was happening on one side of them, they saw me on the other and drew their own conclusions. If anyone asked, the awkwardness was justified by the fact that I was a Christian and this is what I was into. For clarity I *do* like God. I *don't* like environments where people are coercively controlled, publicly ridiculed and shamed because of something that is important to them. I needed to find my way out of oppressive environments like this.

In September 2010, I started a Masters degree at the University of Keele. I studied for a Masters in Environmental Politics, which included political theory, studies on human motivations, environmental theories, namely sustainable development characterized in the Brundtland Report

(1987) in terms of 'common but differentiated responsibility', which meant that we all have a part to play to a greater or lesser extent in responding to global environmental concerns based on the resources we have and the impact we have had on the world. Other areas of study included Limits to Growth and Garrett Hardin's *Tragedy of the Commons*, which in turn led me to the work of Nobel prize-winning economist Elinor Ostrom, which offered the foundations for theories of coproduction today. Questions about human motivation within economics and the environmental movement stood out to me, including the *Transition Movement* led by Rob Hopkins. This movement emerged from Totnes in Devon and uses theories of permaculture. It responds to the crisis of peak oil, where the available resources have peaked and the following decline, matched by increased demand, will create a resource crisis. I even ventured as far as theorizing a model for responding to common problems, drawing on a contextual reading of different and contrasting motivations, which might be deployed as a movement for change. My essay was identified as original in its thinking by our tutor for green political theory, and I later applied for a PhD at Keele, but nothing came of this. During my study at Keele, I also developed a project that helped me to see afresh the way that a personal faith in Christ could help me contribute within different environments. I went with the Church Mission Society to the Democratic Republic of Congo (DRC), to the second city, Lubumbashi, with a mission partner called the Congo Children's Trust, which offered person-centred care for street children at Centre Kimbilio and Maison Kimbilio.[2] Street children were prevalent in the DRC with numbers of 250,000 reported including substantial numbers in the main cities. Time in the DRC provided a visceral example of the impacts of a failed state on the communities within it, including the most vulnerable (see Acemoglu and Robinson's (2012) *Why Nations Fail: The Origins of Power, Prosperity, and Poverty*). In previous centuries the DRC was a series of smaller nations, before they were amalgamated under the colonial rule of Belgium, who brutally ravaged the nation for its natural resources. When the Belgians left, civil war ensued, before President Mobutu was installed and changed the name of the country to Zaire. Mobutu was at the heart of a geopolitical struggle between the USA and the USSR during the Cold War. The abundance of natural resources available in the DRC meant that Mobutu was in a powerful position.[3] However, the wealth was not shared with the Zairian people. This is summarized by the folkloric Article 15 of the DRC constitution, summarized as 'debrouillez-vous' in French and translated as 'fend for yourself', because there will be no help from the state.[4] With only nominal institutions and non-existent public infrastructure, it is true to say that it was faith-based organizations who offered the only sustained support to people in the DRC. In response to what I had seen I combined my Masters studies with this trip to the DRC to generate a sustainable energy project, called *Sustainable Kimbilio* or sustainable refuge. I sourced funds and solar panels for Maison Kimbilio and wrote the project up for my dissertation.

This period opened my eyes to what it meant to be there for others beyond serving them fuel. I had continued to work all the hours available at the garage, while also studying, confined to my cell behind the till.

At the beginning of 2013, after I had completed my Masters study, I had arranged a six-month placement with a church in an urban priority area to explore faith-based sustainable development further. This was in Winsford, an overspill town from Stoke, Liverpool and Manchester.[5] While known as a priority area, the town felt as if it wasn't a priority for anyone. I was brought in to support the development of social action projects and a community festival, which were responding to the policy of austerity implemented by the Coalition government. We opened a foodbank, one town over from where I also still worked at the petrol station. On the second week of opening the foodbank, I found myself serving somebody who I recognized from the petrol station.[6] My hope is that I served them well.

During my time there, the parish church celebrated 150 years since it opened its doors. My brief was to deliver a community festival, celebrating that church in that town. We called it the Delamere Street Festival. I worked with councillors and a lot of different people and groups: to gain permission to host the event, the council; to close one of the main arterial routes into the town, the local nightclub owner; to help us host music across three stages on the site we established, five of the local primary schools; to conduct a history parade, and to share music with us, the owner of the local funfair; to bring rides down to the local car park for children to use; and 30-plus local charities, whom we convened in a 'not-for-profit market' that was positioned at the centre of the festival. This gave residents the opportunity to access services and support as if they were shopping in the town centre. This approach gave local people agency rather than the indignity of being funnelled into services and treated as burdens on the state. Through this project, we engaged thousands of people and raised thousands of pounds for charity, too. The festival delivered something deeply significant in the town and a festival has taken place there each year since.[7]

In 2010, I had no job, depression and a limited outlook on life. Nearly four years on, I had acquired voluntary commitments, life experience, work. I had secured further education, delivered a project overseas and served in an urban priority area offering a framework for replicating success in the future. This period had shown me, in a visceral way, both the impacts of punitive economic ideology and the fend-for-yourself style policies that can emerge, and the potentially life-limiting effects of controlled environments and unjust structures they can create. From being unemployed and depressed and not knowing how to communicate what was important to me and the faith that I held dearly, I had learned something of what it meant to live and work in different environments, and something of how to communicate my faith in a way that allowed me to embody the slogan that I had worn for so long, 'there for you'.

Hope and despair (2014–15)

While working in the urban priority area, I had established connections with a faith-based organization called Link Up. Link Up convened prayer breakfasts and worship gatherings for faith leaders in the area. These gatherings were ecumenical and placed emphasis on unity between churches of different denominations. Link Up also ran the 'Standing In The Gap' project,[8] commissioned by Cheshire West and Chester Local Authority to research the different ways faith groups were contributing to the delivery of public sector services.[9] Link Up took inspiration from sources of guidance such as the Nicene Creed and the Bible. For example, Jeremiah 29.7 is prominent on their website and in their work: 'Seek the welfare of the city ... and pray to the Lord on its behalf ... for in its welfare, you will find welfare.'

This was embodied by members of the Link Up leadership group, including Free Church pastor and chaplain of Chester City Football Club Guy Lister, pastor and entrepreneur Gary Atkins, and the Revd Andy Glover who had moved from Stoke to become leader of Hoole Baptist Church in Chester and committed 30-plus years of his ministry to building and sustaining Link Up and associated unity movement work, in a manner that has had a huge impact (Link Up, 2015). In 2024, Glover was named Canon Ecumenical at Chester Cathedral in recognition of his leadership and commitment to the welfare of the city. I conducted mapping work and produced case studies of the different faith groups and their social action work, and the way in which they contributed to the communities that they worked in.[10]

Case studies I researched included:

- *Project Andrew*, a narrowboat supporting people living on the waterways near Ellesmere Port and sharing time, support and the Christian gospel with them.
- A *pana football project*, used by the local faith-based youth provision in Blacon in Chester, in partnership with the police, to reduce anti-social behaviour.
- A *Methodist connectivity hub* in Neston, with computers and free internet, and a cafe for refreshments alongside a foodbank.
- *Wellbeing High Street*, which appeared similar to the 'not for profit market' I had convened years earlier.
- *Night Church*, run by the Revd Gaz Thomas, which provided assistance within the night-time economy, including a base for the street pastor team, the police, provision of worship space and a cafe space run by volunteers.
- *Elsie Ever After*, offering a Christian bereavement service that developed support for bereaved parents to combat the postcode lottery of bereavement provision in the area.

During my association with Link Up, I was looking for ways to progress my interests and the different ideas that I had been considering, and if possible a grounded approach to seeing these ideas play out. At this time, Gary Atkins pointed me in the direction of Chris Baker from the William Temple Foundation. Chris was based at the University of Chester, and while I knew nothing of him or the Foundation at the time, I was told we would have things in common. I began my PhD part-time at the University of Chester in 2014, exploring hopeful expressions of care and social action in response to austerity, with Link Up as a case study.

I had moved on from the petrol station in the autumn of 2013, and took up a full-time role as a lettings agent in a new town. I had not considered this career path previously, but it was something that I was advised to consider by a Christian friend of mine, and so I did. While I had learned a lot about myself in the previous four years and was keen to progress through work with Link Up and my PhD, I felt I had lacked independence. I was 25, but did not feel I had achieved independence. I moved to a new town, had my new full-time job, and a set of side-projects as an outlet for my real passions. I had also become aware of a café church in the centre of town called Restore, which was pioneering something new.[11] The pioneer leader the Revd Tim Watson was a poet, spoken word performer, artist and liturgist. Watson produced liturgies, including *Restore: A Service of Compline and Examen* (2014b), *Old Lost and Broken Dreams: Poems Litanies Prayers and Blessings* (2014a) and *Lighting Beacons: A Liturgy for Life* (2015). He was inspired by the work of Dietrich Bonhoeffer, a link found in his own postgraduate study (2012). The following quote from Bonhoeffer was his starting point:

> The restoration of the church must surely depend on a new kind of monasticism, which has nothing in common with the old but a life of uncompromising discipleship, following Christ according to the Sermon on the Mount. I believe the time has come to gather people together and do this. (Bonhoeffer, 1935)

Restore gathered weekly and studied the Bible. We read the book of Jonah in some detail. The message related to the question of how to respond to the call that God has put on your life. Jonah 1.1–3 reads:

> The word of the LORD came to Jonah son of Amittai: 'Go to the great city of Nineveh, and preach against it, because its wickedness has come up before me.'
>
> But Jonah ran away from the LORD and headed for Tarshish. He went down to Joppa, where he found a ship bound for that port. After paying the fare, he went aboard and sailed for Tarshish to flee from the LORD.

With hindsight this study of Jonah offered a chastening reminder of how dangerous and costly it can be to seek independence without seeking God. This was made crystal clear during 2014 and 2015. As a young single man, I was working in the private rented sector. It was not well regulated. The workplace culture was a huge challenge. I received personal attention from colleagues that I had not received the likes of before. There appeared to be nothing in place to guide what was acceptable at work. I didn't know what to do. This was symptomatic of my naivety, and also indicative of working as a junior male colleague to predominantly older female senior colleagues in that professional environment. What I experienced was a dynamic characterized by different values that divided the powerful and the powerless, where the colleague who shouted loudest won, and the landlord who paid their management fee was favoured over tenants who were only paying their rent. My perception of what it meant to be independent was severely challenged in this environment. In that place, independence meant having power and money. If you didn't have money you were powerless.[12] In this new environment, there was no oversight, everyone was complicit, and I submitted to the control of others. I found myself in a personal relationship that lasted about 18 months. What transpired was devastating. The power dynamics in the office transferred to my personal life, so that I became pretty well powerless to control anything that was going on in my life. I was instructed to stop going to church, because I couldn't be trusted to go alone. I didn't know what the consequences would be but I was fearful enough to comply. My ability to practise my faith and to find an outlet was limited. From time to time I would get access to fragments of the Bible from TV shows, which offered words of comfort. These words stayed with me from 1 Peter 1.7: 'These have come so that the proven genuineness of your faith – of greater worth than gold, which perishes even though refined by fire – may result in praise, glory and honour when Jesus Christ is revealed.'

By 'these', Peter meant trials. I saw my independence consumed by others. The only safe place for me to be was in my car or out on appointments for work where I conducted property inspections. Otherwise, I was trapped. In this way, my work and the office administration processes were genuine spaces of refuge and sources of hope for me. They gave ways out from the pain and intensity of my life as it was. While cocooned behind the wheel of my car, I would listen to titles such as *Searching for Sunday* by Rachel Held Evans, and *Accidental Saints* by Nadia Bolz-Weber, which examined how to live faithfully in a situation that Nadia (I imagine with some confidence) would characterize as 'fucked up'.

By January 2016, I had fled the relationship and the behaviours and conditions that are characterized within the Serious Crime Act (2015) as part of domestic abuse and coercive and controlling behaviour. During that time I was also subject to what the Theft Act (1965) sets out as blackmail. The case law refers to blackmail as 'like murder of the soul'. In the fallout from this period of my life I had lost my home, my job, my car, my financial stability, my social networks, my health and my dignity. To compound matters, when I sought help from the police, I simply wasn't believed even though I provided the requisite evidence to prove my case.[13] The refusal of the police to listen to me led to further offences being committed against me, which they then refused to act on because to do so meant acknowledging their own individual prejudices and systematic failings during the first investigation.

During 2014–15 I saw first-hand what both hope and despair looked like. During this period, the following verse from Romans 5.2–5, became prominent for me:

We boast in the hope of the glory of God. Not only so, but we also glory in our sufferings, because we know that suffering produces perseverance; perseverance, character; and character, hope. And hope does not put us to shame, because God's love has been poured out into our hearts through the Holy Spirit, who has been given to us.

Across 2014–15, everything in my life had changed again. I had been disabused of the notion of independence without dependence on God. However, while there was acute suffering, there was also hope. I moved to a new town and found new work and began to rebuild my life.

By their fruits you will know them (2016–20)

In April 2016, I took up new part-time role as a community development worker for a church in the centre of Stockport in South Manchester. In the first week of this role, further offences were committed against me, in full view of my new employers, which was mortifying. As I was seeking to move on with my life in an entirely different town, now in Greater Manchester, I was attacked again. I received support this time from health professionals and made a conscious choice to set down what had gone before so that I could move forward with my life. One thing that helped me with this was my commute to work with my Dad. He has 38 years in public service, with 30 years in the police. After retirement from the police, he worked for Greater Manchester Fire and Rescue as a Community Partnerships Manager. We would drive to work 'before the traffic', as Dad would put it, and he would drop me at the church office before carrying on round the M60 to his offices. It transpired later that he was working with people in the public sector that I was also, serendipitously, talking to about partnerships through the Spaces of Hope movement. Sharing different parts of the journey helped me to move forward.

In the sermon on the mount Jesus encourages relationships to be given priority over the law (Matthew 5.25) and gives clear instructions about how to respond to people who persecute you:

'You have heard that it was said, "Eye for eye and tooth for tooth." But I tell you, do not resist an evil person. If anyone slaps you on the right cheek, turn to them the other cheek also. And if anyone wants to sue you and take your shirt, hand over your coat as well. If anyone forces you to go one mile, go with them two miles.' (Matthew 5.38–41)

This was a radical and transformational argument and spoke literal truth into what I had experienced. If differences can be reconciled relationally there is more opportunity to move forward well. If the law is relied upon, justice may not be served.

After the devastation, I was also briefly able to reconnect with Watson and members of the Restore community who embodied the fellowship one might find in the writings of Bonhoeffer. We attended Greenbelt Festival in the summer of 2016 as a collective called Dreamers Who Do. We were a group of lay and ordained Anglicans, Methodists and Baptists who held space for worship, prayer and dialogue for 'misfits in a field', as the Greenbelt story puts it (Greenbelt, 2024). My journey has been punctuated by a breadth of practices from charismatic sung worship to monastic prayer gatherings with different groups, which gave me a rootedness in my relationship with God, although not in one parish for an extended period of time. This rootedness in my relationship with God gave me a support while I journeyed from place to place.

My role as a community development worker was initially for two years. The work was framed using an asset-based community development approach, deployed widely by the Church Urban Fund in the Church of England. This included the deployment of social action projects in a manner akin to my work in the urban priority area in 2013. However, after six months, it became clear that this parish context was not conducive to this kind of initiative and something else was emerging. Fr Lythall, the rector of the parish I was working in, wrote to the bishop:

> Matthew's role has organically developed to be something rather different – and more effective – than originally envisaged [and] has highlighted that the potential for [Community Development] work in St Thomas' parish is actually rather smaller than anticipated ... Further, from a strategic viewpoint, I feel that Matthew's potential is not being utilised as best it might in the context as it stands. The work Matthew has done to date has been exemplary – even pioneering – and has highlighted, for me at least, that he would better serve the church in a wider capacity, taking a broader approach.

This was an encouragement after the mortifying experience of my first week on the job. In terms of the strategic viewpoint referred to, my work found resonance with both the 'Missioner' department within the Diocese of Chester, which focused on worship, mission and evangelism, and the 'Social Responsibility' department, which was separate and focused on social action initiatives. There is an affinity with social responsibility work in the Temple Tradition through the linkage with John Atherton. Both departments – Missioner and Social Responsibility – addressed the Anglican five marks of mission: (1) to proclaim the good news of the kingdom; (2) to teach, baptize and nurture new believers; (3) to respond to human need by loving service; (4) to seek to transform unjust structures of society, to challenge violence of every kind and to pursue peace and reconciliation; and (5) to strive to safeguard the integrity of creation and sustain and renew the life of the world (Richards, 2017). My practice, while only loosely defined at this stage, appeared to be emerging between the two departments. In terms of a broader approach, what Fr Lythall was referring to in practice was an experimental series of community dialogues, which joined different agendas together by highlighting potential points of connection and shared interest. We were gathering in cafes and community centres, listening as different narratives formed and stories were told. People were talking about different things that gave them hope. Formal and informal gatherings emerged, which we began to call 'Spaces of Hope'. Our narrative was about rooting relationships in things that last. We sought to serve people and communities by seeking health, hope and relationships with God. Our mantra was, 'By their fruits you will know them' (Matthew 7.16 and 20). Verse 16 speaks to the way in which false prophets might seek to do damage to us, and likewise verse 20 is about the way in which faithful and prophetic contributions can be seen and understood. One person had heard about what we were doing and joined us from South Shields. They asked, 'How could we provoke the church or churches of today to learn from history, and to move forward into new and emerging Spaces of Hope that are relevant for today and today's context?' (Barber-Rowell, 2021, p. 45).

Another delegate, who was programme lead for the Health as a Social Movement initiative led by the Royal Society of Arts and supported by Stockport Council, wondered if Spaces of Hope represented something that could 'stand side by side with people and communities, but also having the ability to step into and have a foot on both sides and to do most of the work in that space in between, in that liminal space?' They continued, 'I wonder if it represents an idea whose time has come?'

In the months that followed we commenced a pilot project to explore the extent to which a Spaces of Hope movement could emerge. Key to our gatherings was storytelling. In Stockport this included the stories of women such as Pam Robinson who led community work in Edgeley for many years, Marie Flint who worked with children and young mums in

Offerton and who is now ordained, and Sue Heap who was the administrator for the civic church in the town. It is out of the faithful presence and humble service of these women and many others that a movement would emerge if it was going to. The prophetic influence of impressive female leadership was emphasized at a 2017 gathering when the Bishop of Stockport, Libby Lane, characterized what she saw:

> Spaces of Hope brings together all our different parts and elements into a shared public space to be able to discuss openly and fully with one another, each from our own experience and belief base and world view and with our expertise, in order to discover how we best care for one another ... I think the opportunities for Spaces of Hope are almost endless because they will be necessary and valuable in every community, potentially. (Barber-Rowell, 2021)

Later in 2017 at a gathering at Chester Cathedral, numerically the largest of the movement, we reflected on public sources of hope and despair shaping what was becoming characterized as the postsecular city.[14] Professor Elaine Graham, Canon Theologian at the cathedral, noted:

> It's impossible to gather today without acknowledging that we stand in the shadow of the dreadful events of the attacks first on Westminster Bridge then at Manchester Arena and in Borough Market in London at the weekend ... undeniably religious identity and theological belief have been significant ingredients of our current political context, local, national and global. And it only goes to show I think how faith is a vital element of the complex issues of identity culture politics and radicalisation that face us today ... But we should also recognise that faith, whether that's religious, formally in a creedal or organisational way, or less so has inspired, and continues to do so, acts of kindness and humanitarian service. (Barber-Rowell, 2021)

This context set out the real tension presented by different world views and their influence on public life. Our gathering moved to dialogue about finding hope in the darkness of the recent events, and within the city and region we live in. The Bishop of Chester (1996–2019), the Rt Revd Dr Peter Forster, joined us later in the day. At the time of this gathering, the Bishop of Chester was the longest-serving diocesan bishop in the Church of England and the longest-serving bishop in the House of Lords. Bishop Peter offered this encouragement:

'I have come that they may have life, life in all its fullness.' If I were trying to name in a contemporary spirituality what people in our society strive for, it would be something like that: 'life in all its fullness'. I think dialogue between people of different faith communities, people of no faith and people with an interest in human flourishing to gather together and to explore what human flourishing might mean in today's world and our society must be a good thing. (Barber-Rowell, 2021, p. 44)

The movement developed in a number of ways from here. In late 2017 a contemporary worship collective called The Gathering formed at the cathedral. The worship band had been regulars at Restore and had attended the cathedral dialogue. The Gathering convened for 12 months across 2018, with people from across the city and the diocese worshiping together. Another legacy was support for inter-faith dialogues in the Cheshire East local authority area, after a collective of local authority staff, clergy and community workers had joined us for the dialogue. This culminated in a conference held by the local authority in 2018. Later in 2017 a further gathering was held with Salt of the Earth Network, one of the sponsors from Chester Cathedral. We developed dialogue that related Spaces of Hope to their key focus, which was industrial mission and faith in business.[15] This dialogue resulted in a further gathering in 2018 where we shared emerging ideas around Spaces of Hope and leadership at 'Salt Sunday', a regional gathering celebrating the industrial heritage of mid-Cheshire, which historically has been a global supplier of salt. The themes of worship and social action continued also with an invitation to take Spaces of Hope to the New Parish Conference in Birmingham in 2018. I led sung worship at the gathering over two days and held a dialogue with pioneers and practitioners from different denominations and different parts of the UK and USA. Influences from the USA were present in the North West too. Dr Lance Wallnau is a pastor and business leader who campaigned in support of Donald Trump for president of the USA in 2016. Wallnau characterized Trump as 'God's Chaos Candidate', who would 'be a wrecking ball to the spirit of political correctness', before Trump became the nominee for president (Wallnau, 2016). This narrative drew from the Old Testament and the role of a secular Persian King Cyrus set out in Isaiah 45. Wallnau did not believe that Trump was a Christian but he did believe that he was anointed to become president.[16] Wallnau's narrative made connections between this Christian promotion of Trump for president, the strategy behind it championed by Steve Bannon and the Brexit vote in the UK.

This offers some additional context for the breadth of religious movements and positionalities present in the North West at that time.

The Spaces of Hope gatherings I had been commissioned to deliver were based around sharing stories, which we opened up through dialogue using principles that had emerged from the movement. The experimental approach that we were using was to 'curate' Spaces of Hope.[17] We utilized a common definition of curation, which is in two parts: first, to draw together different objects as one would in a gallery or an exhibition, which can be gathered within a broader theme or idea;[18] and, second, to show care for one another as the priest would do in a parish in the role of cure of souls.[19] This broad process of curation was accompanied by guiding principles that had been discerned during the Health as a Social Movement pilot work. As part of the Spaces of Hope Hubs Network commissioned by Stockport Council in 2018, we trialled some guiding principles to develop things. These drew inspiration from the social principles offered by William Temple, set out in Chapter 2. We sought to develop these principles with new names that spoke of a more practical view rather than a philosophical one.[20] We also moved from three to seven principles. These comprise the following: taking responsibility, thinking relationally, serving publicly, facilitating agency, recognizing authenticity, honouring identity and cultivating connectivity (see Table 1 for notional definitions) (Barber-Rowell, 2021, pp. 50–2).

These principles were presented as notional or experimental terms of reference that could be interpreted subjectively by those using them. The process of working out meaning was a strength of the gatherings and enabled people to take ownership of them. The gatherings were as much about testing the principles as they were about guiding a conversation within the movement at the time. Collectively these seven principles marked a transition from personal sense-making (taking responsibility, thinking relationally and serving publicly), through to shared story (facilitating agency, recognizing authenticity and honouring identity), and on to broader connection (cultivating connectivity). We used a storied approach to navigate the principles with community members and policy-makers with gatherings hosted in diverse community settings (see Table 2).

Table 1

Principles for Curation (Stockport, 2017)	Definitions/Rationales
(1) Taking Responsibility	The first principle is based on Temple's first social principle of freedom. Temple said that freedom is the greatest possible expression of our personality. Based on this tenet, the first principle of Spaces of Hope is promoting a personal undertaking of taking responsibility.
(2) Thinking Relationally	The second principle Temple explores is fellowship. He describes a right to social relationships; supported by this, the second principle of Spaces of Hope is thinking relationally.
(3) Serving Publicly	Temple's third principle is service. This is rooted in the idea of freedom, not from people but for people. The third principle of Spaces of Hope, therefore, is serving publicly.
(4) Facilitating Agency	Temple offered three principles to be taken up by individuals, but in order to mobilize them within an organizational paradigm, we need to consider how we build on the actions of one and translate them into the actions of many. To this end, the fourth principle of Spaces of Hope was facilitating agency.
(5) Recognizing Authenticity	The fifth principle took a mutual undertaking reflected in the biblical passage, Matthew 7.15–20, which cautions against false prophets and offers a guideline for recognizing them, and provides us with the language of knowing them by their fruits. Here we take the sense of authenticity as being defined by an external check against what people produce.
(6) Honouring Identity	Once we have identified different outputs as being like good fruit, it is critical to make space for them, and maintain them within our conceptions of people and groups.
(7) Cultivating Connectivity	The final principle, of cultivating connectivity, builds from a personal decision-making approach into a relational movement that responds to the different and creative imaginations that emerge from the gatherings held. This final principle encouraged a cyclical or iterative approach to deploying the other principles across what we do.

Table 2

Names of community settings	Descriptions of the community settings
Friendly Fridays – Cheadle Heath	A well-being gathering convened at a local community centre based on the five ways to well-being.
The Space – town centre	A town-centre location offering hospitality in particular for those who are disabled (The Space was run by the charity Disability, Stockport).
Alvanley GP Surgery – Woodley	Hosted by the Patient Champion, and attended by the lead GP and Practice Manager.
Marple Methodist Church – Marple	A hub hosting multiple activities that serve the community but facing questions around sustainability.
Olive ROC Cafe – Edgeley	A faith-based social enterprise cafe operating on the High Street in a deprived community utilizing support from a national faith-based infrastructure organization, Redeeming Our Communities.
Stockport Baptist Church	A church that offered homelessness provision (contributing to the Bed Every Night campaign pioneered by Mayor Andy Burnham in Greater Manchester), a prominent food network, and regional support for Iranian refugees.

In addition to the physical gatherings, we gathered on social media as well. Twitter hashtags were used to curate content and share it with our network. Videos were produced at the gatherings and circulated as tweets and threads for others to view and comment on. Each Monday evening we also convened a Spaces of Hope Twitter hour that shared ideas and dialogue about things happening in different communities. These overlapped with other Twitter hours from the Heatons in South Manchester, in the Borough of Tameside and the Borough of Oldham, which were oriented towards a community health-based conversation.

As the movement grew, Spaces of Hope came to the attention of the Inquiry into the Future of Civil Society in England. This work sought to explore activities that were taking place below the radar and what might traditionally have been referred to as grass-roots settings. This included faith movements, including Islamic, Christian, Jewish and non-religious expressions. The inquiry covered the work of the Spaces of Hope movement in 2018 and summarized it as follows:

> bringing together innovative mixes of civil society actors – from professional community practitioners through to individual community activists – to 'meaning-make' as a response to experiences of pointlessness and emptiness in personal, community and professional life. (Civil Society Futures, 2018)

A local cafe manager who was interviewed by the Inquiry reflected:

> Spaces of Hope has these deep roots in terms of kind of engaging intellectually, engaging philosophically but also wanting to put in simple ways of practising the things that we care about. The majority of the [other] offers at the minute don't have this open and transparent process. (Barber-Rowell, 2021, pp. 53–4)

Another respondent, a senior local authority officer, spoke passionately about the importance of love and hope and of religion as one of the possible sources of that while also stressing her own atheism:

> I think that in the past I've worked for local authorities for a lot, a number of years and in the past, we've had a situation where the policy team has been the policy team … and [use] this kind of council speak … talking in the language of hope or hearts over the last relatively short amount of time there's been a shift. (Barber-Rowell, 2021)

Spaces of Hope gatherings raised interesting questions for the inquiry. The lead researcher reflected:

> In a public sphere which has struggled to talk about religion and belief, how might faith-based actors be held to account? Should public spaces attempt to preserve the idea of secular neutrality? Or does that stifle the fullest explanations of why certain actors act … In an increasingly religiously diverse landscape these questions have traction … Spaces of Hope appears to open [these] questions up and this in turn is opening up an innovative space in public policy making and practice … In the context of civil society futures this poses the question of how to talk and think about faith. Should the sector continue to behave

as though England is simply secular and therefore faith is a private matter to be discussed only in 'public reasons'? Or should it move beyond the binaries of secular–sacred and public–private to recognise a reality which is much messier, ordinary and lived? (Civil Society Futures, 2018)

The movement continued for over three years, beyond the scope of the initial community development work at the parish church as Fr Lythall had foreseen. There were a number of gatherings that explored Spaces of Hope, lived experiences and the theme of mental health; one in mid-Cheshire with community groups, which was convened by the Department of Social Responsibility, and another called Re:Mind at Methodist Central Hall in Manchester, convened by the Mosaic Social Justice Network who were working between ecumenical faith groups and the public sector to explore this theme. At these gatherings I shared my story, the emerging movement, and the place of hope in responding to questions of mental health. The gatherings and community research drew in close to 1,000 people across 70-plus organizations, through around 40 gatherings.[21] Respondents noted specific values that characterized the gatherings: 65% of respondents associated Spaces of Hope with values of personal vulnerability, personal freedom and social connection, and 40% understood people's suspicions and perceptions towards one another due to different cultures and world views to be barriers to Spaces of Hope. One-third of respondents said that the dialogues had catalysed something new within their own work and 90% of respondents said that they valued the dialogues and would participate in them in the future (Barber-Rowell, 2021, pp. 47–8).

The final gathering took place in late 2019, in Stockport. It comprised the Social Responsibility Network Annual Conference, jointly hosted by the Church of England and the Diocese of Chester. Curating Spaces of Hope was deployed as the learning methodology and it was applied to the theme of 'church on the high street'. We visited spaces around the town that had contributed to the movement, so that the stories of hope might be shared and taken back to different towns across the country.[22] This was the last gathering I ran in Stockport. Following this, I moved out of the area. I had been humbled and transformed by my time there. I had entered into the town in a state of trauma and into a new role where I knew no one. I left as a trusted broker of spaces and stories of hope across civil society.

Finding a way in the wilderness (2020–24)

On 26 March 2020, Boris Johnson told us all to 'stay at home'. At this stage I was engaged to Phoebe, who is now my wife. We had a choice either to move in together in Liverpool or to stay living separately and wait for the pandemic to pass. We moved in together. I began the pandemic in a new home in a new city. The first ten weeks of us living together were the final ten weeks of writing up my PhD. Our wedding, scheduled for June 2020, was cancelled. It was a chastening period but it was a deep blessing to be together.

As the first lockdown began, food and support networks mobilized across the country. These were coordinated by faith groups and third sector groups. I volunteered in Clubmoor where we now lived, packing bags and delivering food around the community on behalf of our local food network. The evangelical church we attended was well networked, due to the large-scale social action initiatives it led in the north of the city through the Community Network. As of 21 May 2020, 152 new volunteers had picked, packed and provided over 25 tonnes of food to 2,000 people (Barber, 2020).

While these new networks mobilized to respond to the crisis, other things ended. I personally lost work developing a future leaders summit for Cumberland Lodge, an education charity and social enterprise based in Windsor. They had asked me to map the faith and belief landscape for 2040 and use this to set out policy briefings for leaders now and in the future. The immanence of the pandemic experience made it clear to the project lead at Cumberland Lodge that their 20-year vision for the faith and belief landscape was fanciful at best and a new strategy was needed for their work. This 20-year time span had been developed in part around statistics that said the faith landscape in 2040 would be 60% non-religious of which 20% would be humanist. It may or may not be, but what was apparent in our exchanges as the pandemic set in was that the framing for a new vision for leadership by faith groups should not be dictated by a particular reading of the stats, or handed down by institutions, but rooted in the lived experience of the future leaders themselves. The pandemic meant we did not have the chance to gather people to discuss this, as per the project plan, so we agreed by mutual consent to part ways in March 2020.

Whereas I had been able to complete my PhD research by the end of 2019, others were not so lucky. Gill Reeve, Research Fellow from the William Temple Foundation, reflected on having her own doctoral work in Liverpool decimated by the pandemic:

> Gradual despondency caused me to consider my options. I could suspend my studies, give up; start again on a different topic ... Covid-19 has brought immense pressures to cities such as Liverpool ... which even in pre-Covid times had high levels of social deprivation. And whilst the government recently expressed a commitment to 'levelling up' it is difficult to be hopeful about this. (Reeve, 2020)

Just because work was scarce did not mean one could stop looking for it, as tough as it was. In the years before the pandemic, I had done a variety of additional jobs including assessing no-fault car insurance claims, recruitment and sales roles, and in 2018–19 I had even worked as a pizza delivery guy. In contrast, in June 2020 an opportunity came up to be one of a team of five commissioned by the All-Party Parliamentary Group on Faith in Society to research Covid-19 responses by faith groups in partnership with local authorities during the first lockdown. Later in 2020–21, I was also asked to deliver a feasibility study for the Diocese of Liverpool, scoping a ten-year strategy for realizing the General Synod commitment to delivering a net zero carbon footprint by 2030. The strategy I set out was rooted in the iterative development of local mission that both emancipated the laity and was developed under the authority of the bishop, through education, confidence building, technical mapping and prophetic vision for change catalysed by storytelling across new networks and alliances. This strategy also addressed existing governance and administration; for example it called for the Diocesan Advisory Committee (DAC) to recruit experts on sustainable technologies that could enable sound faculty decisions (the Church of England planning system) to be made, and support for parish-level funding to be offered in an informed and timely manner. In 2021–22, I found work with a team of parishes in St Helen's, also within the Diocese of Liverpool, scoping and securing resources for engaging in local mission while building ecological resilience through funding technological change. The Team Rector noted:

> [The] calm and measured approach encouraged [the] PCC to have confidence in their vision, and bring it into reality ... we now have a great heating system, a flourishing food pantry, several external rentals to help ensure the building pays for itself in future and isn't a drain on parish giving. We opened a pre-school nursery too ... The approach taken was to really listen to our context, of which nothing was known previously [by Matthew]... [His] approach was equally at home engaging children as it was meeting with council representatives

[and] experience of net zero strategies and ecological solutions has been vital ... particularly where parishes are anxious about the future or resistant to change. (Personal correspondence)

The projects that I found myself working on during the pandemic were complemented by time as a churchwarden, where I supported our parish to find their way through the turmoil of this period. For those without a working knowledge of the Church of England, which could easily be a great many reading this, churchwarden is a legally recognized role. They are licensed lay leaders who are trustees of the church and recognized within Canon Law (church law) as being part of and senior to the other trustees who are on the Parochial Church Council (PCC). Canon Law (section E1) says:

> The churchwardens when admitted are officers of the bishop. They shall discharge such duties as are by law and custom assigned to them; they shall be foremost in representing the laity and in co-operating with the incumbent; they shall use their best endeavours by example and precept to encourage the parishioners in the practice of true religion and to promote unity and peace among them. They shall also maintain order and decency in the church and churchyard, especially during the time of divine service. (Archbishops' Council, 2016)

As a researcher working nationally, it was possible to see the emancipatory role available to laity during the pandemic and in response to crises. In my role with the diocese regionally, it was possible to see ways of making this work from a governance and administration perspective. In my role as local consultant for a team of churches and in my role as churchwarden for one parish, it was possible to see how this might play out with some success, although at times there are also pronounced and intractable tensions and regrettable failures in leadership. This tension between governance and authentically emancipating lay leadership is a perennial one that I sought to highlight in a solution-oriented way in each role I had. Some were heeded and some were not. In October 2021, after 12 months in the role, I stepped down as warden. I was encouraged to knock the dust off my feet, which invoked a Bible passage from Matthew 10.14: 'If anyone will not welcome you or listen to your words, leave that home or town and shake the dust off your feet.' In the months that followed, two local leaders employed in that context (one ordained and one not) and a regional leader with oversight of this parish all stepped down as well. Who can ever know why these things happen?

I do not. However, I do not believe they would have done so had the questions I raised as warden not been entirely legitimate.

The year before, in September 2020, Phoebe and I had married in our local parish church. We had been given the use of the space and the church technology. Our friends who were ordained conducted the ceremony. It was a hybrid ceremony with the legal limit of 30 people in person. We had another hundred or so people present online. We temporarily occupied an otherwise vacant worship space. We rearranged the furniture to sit in the round. We laid greenery, lighting and decorations on the ground to form a pathway down which Phoebe walked. The ceremony was a rite of passage within a rite of passage within a rite of passage. It was shaped by the pandemic experience, while moving into a new city, while committing our lives to one another before our friends, and God. As part of the ceremony, one of our readings was from Isaiah 43.18–21:

> Forget the former things;
> do not dwell on the past.
> See, I am doing a new thing!
> Now it springs up; do you not perceive it?
> I am making a way in the wilderness
> and streams in the wasteland.
> The wild animals honour me,
> the jackals and the owls,
> because I provide water in the wilderness
> and streams in the wasteland,
> to give drink to my people, my chosen,
> the people I formed for myself
> that they may proclaim my praise.

We felt encouraged to enter into the covenant of marriage. However, we didn't comprehend the possibility of the imminent prophetic significance of this passage into the wilderness through what had taken place after I became churchwarden. Following a year of wandering, in late 2022, we began to attend Liverpool Parish Church. The historic parish of Liverpool dates back to 1215 and became a strategic centre of leadership and civic partnership in the city over many centuries. The parish church held space to encounter God in the mystery of the gospel and the eucharist. We found a welcome at the church. We contributed as members of the electoral roll, we served at communion and we shared fellowship. I was invited to hold a Lenten dialogue about lay leadership in uncertain times. The following year we formed a cycling collective that logged kilometres cycled, to count the cost of, raise awareness of and confidence to respond to the climate crisis, which we also linked to Lent. I noted in the *Liverpool Echo* at the time:

> Ash Wednesday is an act of humility, identifying people who are made from dust and to dust will return. After this, there is a sombre and transitional period during Lent and then a wonderful season which is captured by Easter. In our public life today, we have public leaders who don't show humility or self-reflection. They don't expose themselves to temptation or trials to authenticate their leadership and that's what Jesus did before he went into his ministry. It can feel out-of-step in the way our political life works today but I think it is a really powerful thing to do and be involved with. (McAuley, 2024)

However, what was abundantly clear at this stage was that things are only for a season. Transitions from one season to the next are inevitable. The Rector of Liverpool was the Revd Dr Crispin Pailing MBE who, in his ten-year tenure, oversaw the recovery of the parish and its renewal as a self-sustaining church. In May 2024 he resigned his orders in the Church of England as a protest against what he saw as insurmountable issues in the church and the way it was governed:

> I cannot, in good conscience, continue to have a representative role in an organisation which perpetuates bias and discrimination against sections of society ... In contrast to the institutional actions which show such disregard for so many human beings, it seems to me that the majority of individuals and communities across the Church of England speak with the voice of inclusion. (Ashworth, 2024)

The clear contradictions that Pailing identified within the church as an institution and the pressures that puts leadership under were different from those I saw as churchwarden, but speak to a broader requirement for reform. This critique must be balanced with an acknowledgement that leadership and authority are deeply challenging responsibilities to take on. We must see even those we disagree with as God sees us. These episodes brought into focus for me the need for reimagining how we relate to God and the rest of his creation, including the different virtual and physical spaces and structures that we occupy, inhabit, transition through, or make our home. A personal encouragement during this time comes from Psalm 37.3–9:

> Trust in the LORD and do good;
>   dwell in the land and enjoy safe pasture.
> Take delight in the LORD
>   and he will give you the desires of your heart.
> Commit your way to the LORD;
>   trust him and he will do this:
> He will make your righteous reward shine like the dawn,
>   your vindication like the noonday sun.
> Be still before the LORD
>   and wait patiently for him;
> do not fret when people succeed in their ways,
>   when they carry out their wicked schemes.
> Refrain from anger and turn from wrath;
>   do not fret – it leads only to evil.
> For those who are evil will be destroyed,
>   but those who hope in the LORD will inherit the land.

In May 2022, while wandering in the wilderness, two years after submitting my PhD and completing numerous freelance projects, I found stable work. I began working part-time with the Diocese of Manchester as part of their Transformation Programme. My role was to develop eco projects that are both part of national church strategy and derived from local leadership in its pursuit of church and community transformation. My brief responded to the General Synod's commitment in 2020 to deliver net zero carbon across all dioceses by 2030. The Diocese of Manchester is blessed with a faithful and pioneering cohort of lay and ordained leaders who have been exploring ecological mission since well before the formalizing of a commitment to the net zero policy. Within my role I was asked to develop a relational and networked approach to supporting both lay and ordained leaders in parishes across the diocese. Initially my work related to the technical mapping of carbon footprints. The Energy Footprint Tool (EFT),[23] as the process is known, can be perceived as a dry paper exercise and indicative of unwieldy diocesan bureaucracy. However, it also represented a simple and effective means of galvanizing team-based and relational working across parish and diocesan administration, honouring both the licensed lay roles of warden and treasurer, and the informal but no less valuable roles of lay activists who champion issues such as the environment. In 2021, diocesan submissions of EFT were at 29%. In 2022 it was 49% and in 2023 it was 59%, which was the highest return in the northern province. In 2024 we built on this with 60%. Over this period, around 89% of churches across the diocese had engaged in the process at least once. We designed a process for commissioning 'eco champions' (lay leaders) with a specific brief to resource and support missional engagement in their deanery. We also designed and delivered a new lay leadership training resource called Eco Stepping Stones, on which our champions are trained. Of the resource, the Bishop of Manchester said:

> We see our response to the ecological crisis as a non-negotiable. We recognise that our actions can affect people in our parishes, diocese, nation and around the world, whilst supporting our colleagues from across different faiths and none to deliver a just transition, through our mission. Join us by taking our Eco Stepping Stones course. (Diocese of Manchester, 2023)

The resource was coproduced by an interdisciplinary team from the diocese, including wisdom and insight from the Diocesan Environment Officer, the Revd Grace Thomas, Head of Serving Communities, Alison Peacock, Head of Church Growth, the Ven. Mike McGurk, Head of Lay Development, Kim Morgan-Jones, Director of Transformation, Dan Caffrey, and Communications Officer, James Newman, along with ordained and lay leaders committed to responding to the climate crisis. These modest early outcomes from this eco-transformation work speak to the potential that can be opened up when lay and ordained leaders work together across community spaces and administrative structures to develop leadership together.

My journey through the wilderness has been one of perpetual transition: the transition into the pandemic, the transition into a new city, the transition into marriage, the existential and professional transition out of doctoral studies, the transition into and out of parish life. There were multiple transitions into and out of different freelance roles, some of which have been cited in this section: research assistant, independent scholar, William Temple Foundation Research Fellow, Len Collinson Postdoctoral Fellow, Honorary Research Fellow at Liverpool Hope University, Dean's Scholar at Virginia Theological Seminary, fundraiser, project manager, strategic advice consultant, behaviour insights consultant, facilitator and curator, communications officer, Secretariat to the Board, and author. There have been others too. I note these titles only for the purposes of highlighting the necessity of reinventing ourselves and changing our personas as part of the constant pressures that change can bring, with new confines, parameters and professional responsibilities signified by new hats to wear. In some spaces I found myself meeting and working with senior strategic leaders with oversight of institutions in cities; in other spaces I was a volunteer supporting community-based social action; in others I held no status and was for all intents and purposes invisible to those who did hold positions of power and influence; in others I was being diminished as people sought to limit my opportunities for personal and professional growth and development. So be it.

As an honorary fellow at Liverpool Hope University, I attended a weekly Eucharist which is held for staff and students. It has been organized by a thoroughly decent lay leader while the post of chaplain has been in vacancy. Two sermons are worth highlighting here as they speak to the richness of transition. The first related to the account of the road to Emmaus (Luke 24.13–35) and the way in which Jesus, who was thought to be dead, joined in a journey with some others midway along their road, sojourned for a while and later left them, their lives transformed. The second related to the road to Damascus conversion of Saul of Tarsus to the Apostle Paul. Saul was not a Christian. He was a Jew who violently persecuted Christians. On the Damascus road he became incapacitated and was forced to stop his journey, but in spite of how personally profound the experience was, he was not alone. He was guided by those around him to a safe space, before he was met by Ananias, a stranger, who prayed for him and spoke into his life in a way that saw it transformed. Saul encountered God, and his view of the world changed completely. Paul became a foremost proponent of the good news (Acts 9). The existential change that these transitions brought about is characterized as metanoia, or spiritual conversion, or a fundamental change of heart. From my own perspective, I would recognize the transitions I have set out as ones of metanoia, a transformation or conversion and heart change. It might not happen overnight. It might take years. This was the case while I found out what it meant to be 'there for you' at the beginning of the chapter. It is highlighted by the deep dissonance experienced in my section 'Hope and despair', as well as the fruitfulness of different spaces in the story 'By their fruits you will know them'. It is also the case that these transitions and conversions offer us experience that can contribute to finding a way in the wilderness. What I found during each season is that my experiences related to transitions not only in my life, but to experiences of others found in the zeitgeist. These were transitions to a deeper search for personal authenticity, understandings of relationships with others, the things we do that define us; the fruit we produce, and our personal and collective agency to bring about change.

Evidence of this wider search intensified during the Covid-19 pandemic and as lockdown restrictions eased and numerous gatherings began to take place. From March 2020 we got together with fellow companions of the Northumbria Community in weekly online gatherings where we shared the liturgy of *Celtic Daily Prayer*. These gatherings, with German companions with whom we had connected pre-pandemic at the monastic house in Northumberland, were a source of continuity, connection and spiritual nourishment while sojourning with friends and God. These new spaces opened up just as physical spaces lay dormant and lifeless. During this period I also attended a retreat in Northumberland which explored the theme of social change. My attention was drawn to the book of Ecclesiastes:

> Whatever your hand finds to do, do it with all your might, for in the realm of the dead, where you are going, there is neither working nor planning nor knowledge nor wisdom ...
>
> > The race is not to the swift
> > or the battle to the strong,
> > nor does food come to the wise
> > or wealth to the brilliant
> > or favour to the learned;
> > but time and chance happen to them all ...
>
> The quiet words of the wise are more to be heeded than the shouts of a ruler of fools. (Ecclesiastes 9.10–12, 17)

We want change and it may or may not come. We might think we know enough but things are not working and we might not understand how, but I believe that God uses everything. I took that encouragement from these verses. In 2021, I gathered with others to consider the future of citizen engagement in the city of Liverpool. Guest speakers included Jon Alexander, author of *Citizens*, who advocated the shift to a new citizen story, and Dr Camila Vegara, author of *Systemic Corruption* which calls for an end to unaccountable leadership and exemplifies the need for new publics and a new democratic movement for change. In 2022, I attended the Liverpool Salon at the Atheneum to participate in a dialogue about 'Practical Utopias', drawing on influences from the Chartist movement, Port Sunlight and the 2012 Olympics, offering a long view of possible sources of hope for the future in the city. Similarly, the Royal Society of Arts Northern Coffee House gatherings online offered a chance to meet and share ideas and connect. And, then there were Spaces of Hope gatherings that emerged from 2022 onwards, which unearthed different sources of hope in the face of crises. These gatherings held space for people and organizations from across the north-west of England and internationally. They culminated with a question of where we might find radical hope in a year of election. In 2024, 82 nations around the world were voting for new national leaders. The point at the heart of these gatherings and this book is the extent to which our involvement as leaders in society goes far beyond the occasional formal means, that is, submitting our vote at the ballot box and pointing to someone else we want to see step up, as important as that is. The point is that leadership starts with the informal expressions and experiences of day-to-day life. It starts with each of us and it is ongoing.

In this chapter I have set out the process of living with liminality, characterized by rites of passage and processes of transition between structures and communitas. I did this initially with respect to a global financial crisis, transition into unemployment and depression, before finding my way into the world of work and discovering a sense of vocation. This rite of passage was characterized by further study and social action in the Democratic Republic of the Congo and an urban priority area in the north-west of England. Following this, my next transition was through a chastening period of hope and despair, which deepened my understanding of what it means to respond to God's call on one's life through the story of Jonah, and what Bonhoeffer refers to as 'uncompromising discipleship'. I also learned something of what it meant for God to care for our souls, when someone set out to harm mine. Following this, liminal spaces opened up to form a social movement known as Spaces of Hope, which are known by their fruits. Finally, living with liminality was something we all shared through the Covid-19 pandemic and institutional decline, which I have referred to as finding a way in the wilderness. These processes have been set out as a means of offering a personal witness statement for my role as curator in what is to come, and also as a means of offering a conceptual basis of liminality and transition, for the Curating Spaces of Hope paradigm and methodology that I will now turn to in Chapter 4.

Notes

1 'Emic' is an anthropological terms that refers to the study, description or articulation of something from the perspective of those who have experienced it and are from that particular culture. Emic can be contrasted with 'etic', which means to study, describe or otherwise articulate something from a perspective that is outside that culture.

2 Kimbilio means 'refuge'.

3 As a result of the position Mobutu found himself in, he was adorned with riches from the outside, for example the Muhammad Ali boxing match named the 'Rumble in the Jungle'. This was a gift from the USA which put Zaire and Mobutu on the global stage, but also sought to enhance the role of the USA in the DRC.

4 *Footsteps of Mr Kurtz* (Wrong, 2000) offers a powerful exposition of Mobutu's influence. His kleptocratic regime ended in 1997, followed by another civil war.

5 The town was divided in terms of these different identities, with estates named after prominent areas from the old cities; for example, Dingle in Winsford was named after Dingle in Liverpool.

6 I was aware of anecdotal evidence that it was common practice for people accessing foodbanks to travel to other towns, so as to avoid people they knew and the feeling of shame that could be associated with accessing the foodbank. I served them their food at the foodbank and the following month served them in the petrol station as well.

7 As the work unfolded, I was constantly told by the parish priest that we would secure funds for a longer-term post. After the festival had been delivered, I was tasked with completing funding applications to this effect. But a couple of months later the vicar told me to stop. He told me that he was going to hand me over to a retired priest in the parish and that there would be no more conversation about any of it because, as he put it, this was just something priests had to do sometimes. To put this deeply patronizing sentiment into context, I was a 25-year-old postgraduate at the time and the priest was in his mid-30s. I knew my position was without any guarantees. I knew the risk of pursuing an entrepreneurial initiative from my experience with Sustainable Kimbilio, but I felt cast aside, that it showed poor leadership and placed no value on the skills and abilities of a lay member of the church. Later, in 2013, the vicar apologised for the way he had treated me.

8 A title inspired by the prophet Ezekiel.

9 Link Up's work was also a pioneering contribution to what became Cinnamon Network, which for a season championed social action initiatives across the UK.

10 I was grateful to the leadership of Link Up, who recognized my commitment to the journey I was on, and for the opportunity and support they gave me. The work of Link Up was connected to the ancient Celtic traditions of spirituality, drawing inspiration from the work of Robert Mountford on St Chad (see *The Mantle of Chad*, 2013) and dialogue characterized by 'unblocking ancient wells', which explored the way our history can shape how we live today.

11 This community gathered for approximately 12 months before being disbanded. The diocese had withdrawn support for it. The reason I heard given was that it was never a sanctioned church, it did not limit itself to parish boundaries and there were no mission communities in the diocese. With hindsight, I wonder, was this pioneer community an illegal gathering? This is quite likely, and the Bishop of Chester as the ultimate authority did not approve, but Bonhoeffer, while weighing the risks and the cost of being found out, might well have done!

12 As I reflect on this period in the estate agent's office, I can look back on my experience behind the till at the garage, tethered to my tiny cell under constant surveillance, with some fondness.

13 This was borne out by two sources with training and expertise in the field. One was a duty solicitor who had never met me but, following a brief reading of my evidence, went into bat for me. The other was both a former police chief inspector and union leader who had retired and was working with a domestic abuse charity.

14 I pick up this language in Chapter 4 and define it there.

15 The emerging movement and the links with themes of leadership, business and values meant that there were numerous offers from business leaders whom I had met and academics, in addition to my PhD supervisor, to turn Spaces of Hope into a legal entity that had directors and could offer services. The people positioning to support me had much longer careers and larger professional networks than I did and they felt that they could bring Spaces of Hope to new markets and pioneer new thinking. While I had explored some modest entrepreneurial initiatives through Kimbilio Sustainability and the Delamere Street Festival, it did not feel like the right thing to take up the offer of turning Spaces of Hope into a business or social enterprise. I stepped away and focused instead on continuing the formation of what has emerged in these pages.

16 Wallnau connected his advocacy of Trump to the Seven Mountains Prophecy, which was drawn from the work of Jonny Enlow (*The Seven Mountain Prophecy: Unveiling the coming Elijah Revolution*, 2008). The mountains or spheres of society are media, government, education, economy, religion, celebration/arts and family. This school of thought was connected to a third idea: marketplace ministries rooted in the work of Ed Silvoso (*Ekklesia: Rediscovering God's Instrument for Global Transformation*, 2017).

17 While the movement was emerging, various methodologies were explored for framing and facilitating the spaces that were emerging. These included social accounting, pinpoint facilitation and different hosting techniques, including open space, world-cafe, appreciative inquiry, and Theory U. However, what was taking place was somehow different and needed further exploration beyond the scope of these tools.

18 Since 2020, one of my exposures to this kind of practice has been via my father-in-law. He is a guide at an art gallery in Milton Keynes. His role is to help people navigate their way through the different exhibitions, holding space, opening up stories, and drawing attention to the different details of the artist's work. My father-in-law enjoys telling a good story. From time to time my wife and I are recipients of artefacts related to the exhibitions, which you will find around our home, from a bespoke vase, to an album assembling prints of a photo exhibition, and also a book offering an unlikely comparison between the artist formally known as Prince and Charles Dickens. We are also blessed with the stories that give these different gifts their context.

19 I have had more than what I would assume is the normal amount of exposure to ordained leaders. My grandad was rector of numerous parishes in North Wales from the 1960s through to the turn of the millennium. My mother-in-law has also served numerous parishes faithfully since long before we met. My brother and sister-in-law are both ordained in the Church of England. This is to say nothing of three of my close friends who are ordained and a credit to their orders. This has given me different perspectives on what it means to have the cure of souls.

20 As you can see, these were not developed in a rigorous way at this stage.

21 The number 40 is a number that for some has significance in the Bible through its association with periods of testing and transition. The flood that destroyed the earth in Noah's time was caused by rain for 40 days and 40 nights, followed by a rainbow as a sign of hope. Moses was on Mount Sinai for 40 days and 40 nights. Before Samson's deliverance, the Israelites served the Philistines for 40 years. Once the Israelites escaped from Egypt they wandered in the wilderness for 40 years. Goliath taunted Saul's army for 40 days before David arrived to defeat Goliath. The number 40 appears in the prophecies of Ezekiel and Jonah. Jesus was in the wilderness for 40 days before his ministry commenced.

22 Stockport is not only noteworthy for the movement that emerged, but also as the source of the River Mersey, which is the boundary between the ancient kingdoms of Northumbria and Mercia. St Chad is thought to have carried the gospel south through Northumbria and then from Chester to Lichfield in Mercia, sojourning, worshipping and sharing fellowship before residing in Litchfield as the first Bishop of Lichfield. Our gathering was joined by the 99th Bishop of Lichfield, Michael Ipgrave, who chaired the Social Responsibility Network in 2019. This ancient reference was included in the conference, to acknowledge the history of the places in which we were gathering, and to explore contemporary synergies, inspiration and sources of hope for the future.

23 EFT is a simple tool for opening up data on carbon consumption in each parish. The deployment of this resource gains insights that can be used at parish and diocesan levels to guide day-to-day energy consumption, technical support and fundraising.

4

Spaces of Hope

In this chapter, I will continue to develop the conceptual foundations for transformational leadership. This work is found in my doctoral thesis, submitted in April 2020. In Chapter 2, I set out the Temple Tradition, the characteristics of Temple's leadership and the questions that arise, while also acknowledging the declining influence and relevance of his work today. In Chapter 3, I set out stories of transition and the concept of liminality as an anthropological basis from which Spaces of Hope also emerges. In this chapter I set out further terms of reference for Spaces of Hope, drawn from the social movement referred to in Chapter 3 and derived from diverse positionalities and different forms of leadership that engaged in a shared pursuit of hope. The Spaces of Hope movement was based on the commitments of citizen leaders in the first instance and became related to the contributions of what Temple would refer to as intermediate groupings or, as we might understand them, civil society or faith-based[1] organizations. In this chapter I will set out Spaces of Hope as a new paradigm and consultative methodology of faith-based organizations, with the means of framing and relating social movements to the cocreation of and leadership by citizens and these organizations alike.

I will build on the conceptual foundations offered in Chapter 3 by offering a means of mapping the differences that flow through liminal spaces, drawing on new materialist philosophy rooted in the work of Gilles Deleuze and Félix Guattari. This may require some slightly heavier conceptual lifting than the first three chapters, but it will ultimately serve the wider project by opening up spaces to further research and practice. A new materialist approach offers some conceptual grammar for mapping the differences and the creative potential that make up our lives, expressed through the stories of shared lived experience. It enables the mapping of transitions between the different liminal spaces we occupy, in a manner that is sensitive to both the human and non-human aspects of those spaces. The benefits of this will become clear in the chapters that follow. The benefits of the conceptual work in this chapter will also come into their own in Chapter 7 when the principles to 'curate' the affective flows of difference as transformational leadership are set out. To begin, however, I will turn to a number of literatures to map some key conceptual transitions in political philosophy: the postsecular turn in sociology of religion; the diversifying belief landscape; and, in social policy, liminality as the new norm. These interdisciplinary literatures set the stage for the emergence of Spaces of Hope as a new paradigm of faith-based organizations, which I will turn to now.

Faith-based organizations

First, what do we mean by faith-based organizations (FBOs)? I will explore this question with respect to wider welfare contexts, different typologies of FBO and the prevailing crisis of definition. An FBO is an 'organisation [embodying] some form of religious belief in the mission statements of staff and volunteers' (Beaumont and Cloke, 2012). FBOs are providers, protesters and policy influencers, and everything in-between, making a contribution to voluntary activity and public service across society. This is well documented in the USA (Beaumont, 2008a, 2008b) and in European contexts (Beaumont and Cloke, 2012). There are several useful typologies that can develop initial understandings of FBOs in health and welfare contexts.

The first is Esping-Andersen's (1990) typology for three different types of welfare regime: the Nordic, social democratic regime; the continental conservative (or corporatist or Christian democratic); and the liberal regime. Additional regimes were added later, including analysis of Mediterranean and Eastern Bloc countries and their welfare contexts. The third of these regimes characterizes liberal Anglo-Saxon approaches that advocate market-based solutions and means-tested social assistance, which includes but is not limited to the UK. While the term 'welfare state' originated from William Temple in the UK, the UK model is now one of many welfare regimes.[2]

With regards FBOs, further typologies that help to begin this discussion are Cnaan et al. (1999), who identify FBOs by scale, ranging from local congregations to religiously affiliated international organizations. This study does not really consider the faith dimension. Smith (2002) identifies faith-related groups by the role of belief, ranging from faith-saturated groups through to completely secular groups. Smith offers a clearer understanding of how the 'F' of FBOs is understood. Herman et al. (2012) provide some suggested styles of FBO without claiming an exhaustive list. These are characterized in terms of spaces of engagement: for example, spaces of community, sanctuary, faith, care, learning, market interaction and so on. Beaumont and Cloke (2012) welcome these parameters as part of the Europe-wide FACIT project,[3] but also point to FBOs as possessing multiple differences, with this variety of meaning leading to FBOs 'defy[ing] straight forward definition' (p. 10). This has led to as many typologies as there are studies, so we are cautioned against seeking out ideal-type classification.

This point is given clarity by Johnsen (2014), who highlights a central problem with current understandings of FBOs within the UK, namely that it is not clear what the 'F' in FBO really stands for. Without a clear understanding of the difference that the 'F' (faith) makes, it becomes increasingly difficult to examine FBOs. Johnsen finds that it is increasingly difficult to discern between FBOs and secular equivalents, which is encouraging an uncritical homogenization of FBOs and other civil society actors, while different discernible characteristics are there to be identified. 'Faith' played a role in establishing welfare provision in the UK, but it is barely visible in the twenty-first century. Nonetheless, Johnsen argues that, on the one hand, the 'F' should neither be used to seek nor oppose the inclusion of FBOs and, on the other, suggests that different sources of motivation for FBOs should not be ignored. This points to a distinct category of stakeholder in welfare provision, namely FBOs. But it also highlights the need for FBOs to be redefined to allow their distinctiveness to shine, which is acknowledged but otherwise hidden through homogenizing analysis. In this chapter I will set out a means of opening up these differences, offering a heterogeneous analysis of faith-based organizations and their contributions. To develop this case I will turn first to the work of Jürgen Habermas, who engages with the pre-political motivations of those who contribute to civil society, and conceives of a place for different world views in public life through his theory of the postsecular.

The postsecular

The term postsecular can be traced back to Andrew Greeley (1966) who discussed the role of neo-gemeinschaft communities flourishing within a secularizing Catholic Church. The use of the term postsecular I am concerned with is that adopted and popularised by Habermas, a Marxist social theorist from the Frankfurt School. Habermas's use of the term postsecular represented a substantial and surprising turn within his work in the early twenty-first century. This turn has been picked up within public theology by numerous thought leaders including Elaine Graham in her book *Between a Rock and a Hard Place* (2013) and discussion of the postsecular in the public square in her 2017 keynote address to the Spaces of Hope Movement at Chester Cathedral. Habermas's turn to the postsecular acknowledges a new visibility of religion in the public square. This turn took place at the beginning of the twenty-first century and through dialogues with Cardinal Ratzinger (later Pope Benedict XVI) in 2004 exploring the pre-political foundations of the democratic state, recorded in *The Dialectics of Secularisation: On Reason and Religion* (Habermas and Ratzinger, 2004). Habermas and Ratzinger found much common ground, which offered the foundation for Habermas to further develop his thinking around the postsecular.

For Habermas, there were a series of events that clarified the limits of secular understandings of the public sphere and required new ways of understanding what was going on between those of different world views. The first was the 9/11 terrorist attacks on the World Trade Center in the US, then a series of three events in one weekend in 2007: the autocratic intervention of President Sarkozy in religious riots in France; the intervention by Archbishop Rowan Williams regarding the role of Sharia law in UK law; and the death of nine Turkish Muslims in a fire in a tower block in Germany, the circumstances of which were considered to have been indicative of xenophobia. Habermas referred to this in terms of the western world being on a *sonderweg*, or special path, which was characterized by *kulturkampf*, or cultural struggles, in terms of how individuals and groups related to and contributed to society, while also speaking openly about their different world views. How differences are treated is central for Habermas's conception of the postsecular. Habermas argues against an either/or or us/them approach, characterized by a politics of identity, or as he put it, 'an anti-racist racism' (2008a, p. 29). Instead, Habermas advocates an approach that does not deny the continuation of the secular, but also does not conceptually prioritize one difference over another, or exclude one to the benefit of another. As such he presents the postsecular as a means of *embracing differences* where all are equally burdened with the task of articulating their world views as part of civil society. This being said, the postsecular cannot be taken uncritically. Parmaksiz (2018) offers a dispassionate assessment: 'the concept cannot be much more than an eloquent way to disguise a sophisticated religious revivalism'. Beckford (2012) argues that while the postsecular is talked about widely, it does not possess any meaningful definition or application, noting six separate definitions. Others argue that it simply describes swathes of history, which are recognized in other areas of the literature, or simply ignores existing literatures regarding the role of religion in the public sphere (Kong, 2010; Ley, 2011; Wilford, 2010: Calhoun et al., 2011). With these critiques in mind, I do not take the postsecular to be a universally applicable concept, nor a foregone conclusion, but rather a question of how different world views are treated and how they are set in dialogue with one another as a pre-political basis for informing the contributions of different people to civil society through intermediate groupings, as Temple would put it, faith-based organizations as Cloke and Beaumont would frame it, and Spaces of Hope as I will go on to argue. Olson et al. point to engagement with the postsecular in this way as an interplay or co-production informed by the religious and the secular in a specific location:

> Postsecular theory is concerned with understanding the coproduction of the religious and the secular in modern societies and the discourses, practices, and moral and political projects associated with this co-production. Whereas secularisation theory asserts clear divisions (spatial, social, and political) between religion and other social functions and structures, postsecular approaches reflect on the maintenance, contestations, and meanings attributed to these divisions (2013, pp. 1423–4).

The question then becomes, where might these coproductions take place? Cloke et al. consider specific geographies of postsecular engagement which might emerge. They note that:

> The being of postsecularity is conditioned by a co-productive relationship between faith and reason, involving a commitment to solidarity and an openness to difference. It is about doing something together based on an acceptance of the unknowns and unknowables in particular contexts and being open to what could emerge ... It can reflect to varying extents both a relaxation of secular suspicion towards spirituality and related re-enchantment, and a willingness to take religious values out into the secular world ... reflecting a blurring of sacred and secular spaces and subjectivities through the co-production of hopeful imaginaries, hopeful ethical sensibilities, and hopeful practices. (2019, p. 8)

Cloke et al. characterize the emergence of geographies of postsecularity in three ways. The first emergence is through the production of social movements (p. 9). The second is through the expressions of care and social action that take place in the city, typically within the community and voluntary sector (p. 12). The third emergence is through pedagogical engagement (p. 16). For my purposes, the first of these is in evidence in Chapter 3 in the section 'By their fruits you will know them', through the social movement that enabled the emergence of Spaces of Hope. The second and third of these are in evidence as this chapter and the book go on. I will now turn to the transitions taking place across the belief landscape in the UK.

Different beliefs, values and world views

Clarke and Woodhead have said that we are experiencing 'the single biggest change in the religious and cultural landscape of Britain for centuries, even millennia' (2018, p. 4). This is a substantial claim. So what is meant by it? Sociological research into religion has offered multiple theories in recent decades. The 'spiritual turn' (Houtman and Aupers, 2007) and the more recent 'rise of the nones' (Putnam and Campbell, 2010; Woodhead, 2016, 2017) highlight the diversifying landscape and the context in which a new means of coproducing values should respond. The spiritual turn in the UK emerged during the twentieth century as a response to the confluence of unwavering secularization and religious deinstitutionalization. This was coupled with spirituality as counterculture in the 1960s, developing into New Age thinking in the 1980s (Houtman and Aupers, 2007, pp. 305–6). More recent assessments of this culture include 'Do-it-Yourself Religion' (Baerveldt, 1996), 'Pick and Mix Religion' (Hamilton, 2000), or a 'Spiritual Supermarket' (Lyon, 2000) and even 'eclectic if not kleptomaniac process ... with no clear reference to an external or deeper reality' (Possamai, 2003, p. 32). The spiritual turn is a move to a more subjective view of the world, away from paternalism and reliance on and submission to institutions and hierarchies, and a move towards individual agency and capacity to decide for oneself. Aupers and Houtman (2003) argue that this movement is enabling choice and curtailing a monopoly on wisdom. Where once Christendom defined our western context, increasing deinstitutionalization, modernization and increasing spirituality brought this to a halt.

Sociologists have disagreed about the significance of this shift. Bruce has seen the reducing salience of religious perspectives as confirmation of a secularizing public sphere (2002, p. 105). Berger drew different conclusions, and stated that the secularization thesis, a body of work he made substantial contributions to, was 'essentially mistaken' (1999, p. 2) as he saw this deepening spiritual subjectivity as a consequence of modernity acting to undermine the close association between modernity and secularization (pp. 119–20). Houtman and Aupers suggested post-Christendom spirituality represents 'gnosis', or an epistemological third way, defined by 'the self [as] divine and by the immanent conception of the sacred that goes along with it' (2007, p. 308). This points to a subjective sense of self (Giddens, 1998), and the pursuit of personal authenticity (Giddens, 2008) within a more fluid and emergent landscape. Heelas and Woodhead (2005) proposed that this spiritual subjectivity was a driver for cultural change away from paternalistic and hierarchical forms of religious prescription. They conducted the Kendal Project, where spiritual practices aimed at improving psychological well-being have grown in contrast to institutionally religious adherence in the service of and to an external God. This latter perspective has halved relative to the population since the 1960s. Baker and Dinham (2017) note that experiences uncovered by this research are representative of new forms of spiritual fluidity analysed in sites such as Kendal and Glastonbury in the UK (see Partridge, 2006), at festivals and online.

More recently, the 'rise of the nones', that is, people of no religious affiliation, was identified in the United States by Putnam and Campbell in *American Grace: How Religion Divides and Unites Us* (2010). Linda Woodhead conducted research into the nones in the UK in 2016 and 2017. She found that nones do not fit neatly into one demographic. Of those identifying as nones, different genders, ethnicities and races are equally likely to be present. The 'rise of the nones' in the UK coincided with a reduction in numbers affiliating with Christian identity. Woodhead (2017) tracks this shift. In 2013, 41% of people identified as a 'none'. In 2015, this figure was 50%. In 2019 the British Social Attitudes Survey found that the nones were 53% of the population in the UK (Curtice et al., 2019).[4]

The relevance of the long view in this literature was highlighted by the 2021 Census for England and Wales (Office for National Statistics, 2022). The census surveyed religious affiliation and sets out a more nuanced transition in the landscape relative to the British Social Attitudes Survey data. This was done with a larger data set, with 94% (56 million people) of eligible residents answering the question, which was up from 92.9% or 52.1 million in 2011. The census found that the nones do not comprise more than 50% of the population; they are 37.2% of the population, which is up from 25.2% in 2011. There was a drop in those identifying as Christian (46.2% down from 59.3% in

2011). There was an increase in those identifying as Muslim (6.5% up from 4.9% in 2011). Hindu affiliation rose from 1.5% (2011) to 1.7% (2021). Sikh affiliation rose from 0.8% (2011) to 0.9% (2021). Buddhist affiliation also rose, from 0.4% (2011) to 0.5% (2021). Jewish affiliation saw a numerical rise of 6,000, from 265,000 to 271,000 people. These data show that a landscape that was once taken for granted as majority Christian is no longer so. The big indicator of this is the 'rise of the nones', which accounts for a 12% increase in those not affiliated to a religion.[5] From this analysis of the belief landscape in the UK, it is clear that there is a diversity of world views shaping the public square, and an increasingly nuanced assessment of them is needed.

Liminality as the new norm?

To take further account of the need for a nuanced and heterogeneous engagement with world views, Baker, Crisp and Dinham (2018) question whether there has been a turn to 'liminality as the new norm' in social policy, acknowledging the crises and transitions shaping day-to-day life and the policy landscape. Through research funded by the Arts and Humanities Research Council (AHRC) they engaged global experts in interdisciplinary dialogue and explored the postsecular belief policy landscape. Drawing on the conceptual work of Victor Turner, they set out experiences of liminality in terms of

> the increase in globalised, fluid and frictionless environments, punctuated by market efficiency and new technology, along with intense flows of migration, ideology, innovation, investment and knowledge that show little respect for existing forms of local identity and community. What is produced are increased expressions of social and economic inequality, fear and anxiety, populist politics and challenges to identity and democracy. (pp. 5–6)

The mapping of this shift connects the framing of public engagement with different world views. The public space had been subject to secular assumptions that were famously summed up by Alastair Campbell's characterization of the New Labour government, 'We don't do God' (Brown, 2003). Faith-based organizations were open to suspicion of proselytizing (Cloke et al., 2013, p. 32) and were seen essentially as either an asset to be harnessed or a problem to be solved (Baker and Dinham, 2018, pp. 27–8). As narratives of the postsecular emerged, the contested nature of the public sphere was brought to the fore, promoting the kind of research done by Baker and Dinham. These factors increase the importance of mapping the diversifying belief landscape, the analysis of faith-based organizations, and the conceptual framing of liminality offered in Chapter 3 and here. In turn, it heightens the need for a paradigm that is conceptually sensitive to differences as co-constituents of identity. To develop my case for this, I will consider literature from continental philosophy.

Difference and creative potential

In Chapter 2 I set out the work of William Temple, which drew its philosophical underpinning from T. H. Green. In order to answer the questions from the end of Chapter 2, a new philosophical root is needed. Here, I will turn to a new materialist framework characterized as assemblage theory drawn from the work of Gilles Deleuze and Félix Guattari. This philosophical outlook is oriented to differences, the relationships between them, the way they flow and transition, and how they can be mapped as they transcend scales, bringing local and global differences into dialogue with one another. Deleuze addresses differences by considering questions of everyday life.[6] This has been an enduring theme in continental philosophy, noted through post-structural and post-modernist thinkers, such as Jean-Paul Sartre, Michel Foucault and Jürgen Habermas.

To understand Deleuze's approach, it can first be contrasted with other continental philosophers, such as Jaques Derrida and Deleuze's contemporary Michel Foucault. All three worked to identify new ways to escape from the limits of structure and conformity that shape our day-to-day lives. Foucault's approach to the question, 'How might one live?' is 'historical', with the framing of now itself being framed by what has gone before. Derrida's approach was linguistic, with the words we use offering irreconcilable constraints upon our lives. Within the question, 'How might one live?', one could expect to find notions of being or ontology that help us to analyse and understand our lives. These were central to my own journey set out in Chapter 3 and a lucid engagement with different philosophical outlooks and world views as the Curating Spaces of Hope movement progressed. Both Foucault and Derrida reject ontology in this sense; Foucault with particular emphasis on human ontologies, and Derrida by virtue of the tools (language) one uses to define any ontology. Essential nature is doomed by their implicit reference or antithesis to things that 'are' being excluded as 'non-essential'. Both Foucault and Derrida reject ontology because it seeks to understand what 'is' through a pure form of being that acts to constrain behaviour through structure and narrow conformity, which is what is being escaped from in the first place. Deleuze on the other hand takes a different approach. While being interested in the same question, 'How might one live?', as well as being interested in finding ways out of the limitations of preconceived structure and conformity, Deleuze embraces ontologies. Todd May notes that 'to read Deleuze is to be introduced into a world of proliferating beings and new forms of life' (2005, p. 15). A contrast opened up by Deleuze is the contention that ontologies are a means of adequately inquiring about life and revealing fresh answers. Deleuze adopts new assumptions. Rather than 'discovery', that is, to identify what is already there, Deleuze's approach is one of 'creation'. In order to recognize creation rather than discovery, Deleuze acknowledges that instead of identity being a fixed and completed form for each thing that is discovered, differences exist, which can create new forms of what is, new identities. May summarizes:

> [Deleuze] abandons the search for conceptual stability and [begins] to see what there is in terms of difference ... [reaching] beneath the identities our world presents to us in order to touch upon the world of difference that both constitutes and disrupts those identities. (2005, p. 19)[7]

Key to this discussion is that Deleuze is not seeking out a means of articulating truth; he is seeking to create perspectives about what there is to draw upon in day-to-day life. For my purposes, this orientation to difference is helpful as it opens up access to the sources of truth that people rely on, found in the different world views that Habermas holds space for and that are present within the UK belief landscape today, as opposed to debating the validity of those truth claims themselves.

For Deleuze, difference is conceptualized as understanding what is going on 'between' things, such that we can understand both what makes up one thing and how it relates to another (2014, p. 37). In this sense, relationships form and ontologies emerge out of the multiplicities of concrete differences and the creative potential differences have, and the way in which both contribute to day-to-day life (p. 360). To be clear, Deleuze's understanding of difference is that the substance of things, the multiplicity as he puts it, possesses both potential and concrete content and expression. It is the combination of the concrete and the potential that is yet to be realized that, taken together, can help us to understand changing relationships through time and space (p. 241).

In order to map these changing relationships, Deleuze and Guattari offer us *A Thousand Plateaus*, where they introduce the rhizome as means of modelling emergence and flow of difference. Rhizomes are subterranean forms or root systems that are expressed in a wide range of diverse ways (Deleuze and Guattari, 2016, p. 5). Rhizomes are fluid and connected spreads that elude hierarchical structures and controls which within Deleuzian grammar are described as arborescent. This is the kind of distinction Turner (1967) makes between communitas and structure. Rhizomatic characteristics help us to understand space that is uncertain, thoroughly context specific, and governed by processes other than traditional structures. In this way rhizomes enable liminal spaces, where normal rules and structures have been suspended, and the multiplicity of differences within them to be mapped. This mapping enables the creative potential and concrete production of liminal spaces to be grounded and understood. This is helpful in terms of making sense of how one might live and, in turn, lead. However, in order to map differences in this way, further parameters are needed.

For this, Deleuze and Guattari (2016) offer us assemblage theory to map rhizomatic flows of difference that transition across different spaces. An early definition of assemblage from Deleuze and Parnet (2007) is 'a multiplicity constituted by heterogeneous terms and which establishes liaisons, relations between them' (p. 52). Deleuze and Guattari develop their first understanding of assemblages as a territory: 'The territory is the first assemblage, the first thing to constitute an assemblage; the assemblage is fundamentally territorial' (2016, pp. 375–6).[8]

A territory is both a passage and is in the process of passing into other territories, as assemblages are in the process of passing into other assemblages. Assemblages adhere to the principles of rhizomes[9] and express different social and material flows simultaneously (Deleuze and Guattari, 2016, p. 24). It is not a case of identifying one single assemblage, territory or space, but more that there are multiple assemblages, territories or spaces, which offer meaning from what is going on between them. In terms of the terminology used for this work, it is plural, that is, Spaces of Hope, not space of hope, for this reason.[10] Assemblages are expressed across two axes. The first is the content/expression axis, that is, what they are made of and how that substance is shared (Deleuze and Guattari, 2016, pp. 82–4). The second is the deterritorialization/ reterritorialization axis, that is, the transition into and out of territories, assemblages or spaces (Deleuze and Guattari, 2016, pp. 376–80).[11,12]

To aid understandings of spaces or territories, consideration should be given to the relationships between the differences flowing through them and the affect each relationship has on one another. These three terms, territories, relationship and affect, make up three key underpinning theses upon which assemblages are premised. The content of assemblages has no ontological status in and of itself. Its ontological status is only produced when the relationship with the other content within the assemblage is examined (Deleuze and Guattari, 2016, pp. 142–4, 304). So, assemblages are always productive, either in a progressive or regressive way (p. 4).

To make more sense of the productive nature of assemblages, I will turn to Bruno Latour's Actor Network Theory (ANT) which looks at the 'trail of association between heterogeneous elements' (Latour, 2007, p. 5). By considering these associations we can look at relationships differently. So I am not seeking simply to identify a thing among other things – a black sheep among a herd of white ones for example[13] – but noting the nature of connections between different things that would not otherwise be considered. What would we find, for example, if we looked beyond (not discount or ignore, but look beyond) the sheep's wool as determinant of its association and belonging? I would consider this question in the same way as looking beyond the uniform with the 'there for you' slogan that I wore in the petrol station. Latour notes that the nature of what is social, or associates with one another, is thrown into doubt by the uncertainty we are surrounded by. His examples prophetically include 'a new vaccine ... new job ... new political movement ... new laws ... new catastrophe ...' (Latour, p. 6).

Because of the influence of new and different things, Latour is interested in the possibilities of potential associations and the connections that we experience, while also being clear that we must redefine who and what we refer to when we say 'we' (2007, p. 6). In terms of understanding the social, Latour notes that it 'must be much wider than what is usually called by that name, yet strictly limited to the tracing of new associations and to the designing of their assemblages' (p. 7).

A sometimes controversial element of ANT, but an element that informs and enriches assemblage theory nonetheless, is that Latour ascribed equal agency to everything within an assemblage, both human and non-human.[14] The key distinction that Latour makes to enable consideration of agency as being equally attributed to human and non-human is between matters of fact and matters of concern (2007, pp. 87–120). In the context of understanding how we might live, and more specifically how new forms of transformational leadership might be developed, matters of concern acknowledge that there is always more to experiences than meet the eye (p. 109), and that acknowledging the non-human uncovers new understandings of agencies that are shaping the world. Latour gives simple historical examples of stones, rugs, mugs and hammers, as everyday objects which mediate understanding of relationships between humans and their environments. Latour admits that these initial examples relate to the experience of Neanderthals, and uses them to open up the conversation and the question of which other objects might mediate our understandings today? To get to the heart of this, he suggests that we cannot take for granted what we think we know as matters of fact, and notes that

> the discussion turns to the good when one introduces matters of concern ... highly uncertain and loudly disputed, real, objective, atypical, and above all, interesting agencies ... it is livelier, more talkative, active, pluralistic, and more mediated ... the solution [is] to learn how to feed off uncertainties, instead of deciding in advance what the furniture of the world should look like. (2007, pp. 114-15)

So the task is to map what is happening in these different spaces, agonize over the flows of difference, wrestle with them, and reject the temptation to make premature claims of unity, while not dismissing those who we are not yet, or maybe don't foresee ourselves becoming, united with. Without a predisposition to matters of concern we will lose our patience with and lose track of the careful mapping of the realities of what is unfolding and could fall victim to the final principle of rhizomes, decalcomania, taking what we think is there and covering up or dispensing with the realities of the relationships and affects territorializing an assemblage (Deleuze and Guattari, 2016, pp. 11-16). Returning to the reference from the sermon on the mount in Chapter 3, if we are known by our fruits, then the question of decalcomania from Deleuze and Guattari is more akin to offering up a plastic apple from a fake fruit bowl than it is sharing a rich juicy Braeburn from the food pantry. It might do something to feed your imagination, but that is it. The importance of this sense comes into its own when we consider, for example, what we root our hopes in or indeed how leadership practice might be formed.

A final consideration regarding assemblages is the role of agency. Latour (2007) notes that within ANT agency is equally attributed to gathering the different and creative potential of human and non-human actors. However, once we have acknowledged the social and material as including all humans and non-humans, then the collective vocabulary shifts from agency to affect. What this means for assemblages is that there are no subjects and objects within them, there is simply capacity to affect and be affected. Affect is the driver for change within the assemblage, or affects are the becoming of assemblages (Deleuze and Guattari, 2016, p. 299). This is non-linear, or what has previously been discussed as rhizomatic (p. 7), so its affects can take us in multiple directions and can infer that anything within the assemblage can potentially be linked to anything else at any time. As a result, affect can cut across multiple levels of analysis within the assemblage. We must be open to the possibility that assemblages comprise things from different levels: micro, meso, macro. These affective flows are not top-down, or bottom-up, or linear in any other way. They are simultaneously, already and always connected. To consolidate my meaning here and to begin to relate this new materialist exposition back to the wider discussion of hope throughout this book, I will refer to Pope Francis in his 2023 encyclical *Laudate Deum* where he characterizes the nature of the response to the climate crisis and other crises in terms of the way we relate to both the human and the non-human within a connected ecosystem: 'What happens in one part of the world has repercussions on the entire planet. This allows me to reiterate two convictions that I repeat over and over again: "Everything is connected" and "No one is saved alone"' (Pope Francis, 2023).

In this section, I have set out new materialist grammar for mapping differences and creative potential. This grammar offers means of mapping the affective flows of content and expressions of our day-to-day lives within liminal spaces. Deleuze and Guattari's assemblage theory and the associated grammar provide a foundation for my task in the way T. H. Green's work did for Temple. I have been considering and testing this philosophical framework since 2016 in north-west England, with faith-based organizations responding to different crises locally understood. Now I will turn to three practical contexts that map stories of transition and hope, and offer a basis for transformational leadership with which I will move forward into Chapter 5.

Stories of transition, hope and transformational leadership

I will now set out three different ethnographic sites in north-west England. Ethnographic methods enable the unearthing and exploration of rich stories and lived experiences of people in communities. It is a common method for anthropologists and it is no coincidence that Victor Turner was a common proponent of it. The ethnographic sites were aware of the Spaces of Hope movement that was taking place from 2016 to 2019. So this gave a context of four years from which stories emerged from these sites.[15] While they had not necessarily had a formal role in the movement, for example hosting a gathering, people from these sites had been part of it. With this in mind, the stories use pseudonyms rather than the real names of people, places and organizations. The sites were characteristic of terms of reference from the movement, that is, liminality, difference and shared values. These included partnerships engaging across differences in the spaces between faith and public sectors. These partnerships offered hopeful expressions of care and community action in response to a variety of matters of concern and experiences of living with liminality and transition, from poor mental health, to unemployment, food poverty and social division catalysed by Brexit. These partnerships were also ecumenical in nature and were explicit in their pursuit of Christian unity. Some in the partnerships were also acutely aware of the limits of their own existence as an FBO and feared for their own relevance and for their role in serving communities in the future (Barber-Rowell, 2021, pp. 134–41). In terms of demographics, the sites were made up of respondents between the ages of 18 and 80, split roughly two women for every man, in majority-white working-class communities. Only 42 of the respondents were employed, with the others either retired or unemployed. Respondents were either Christian (79%) or non-religious (21%) (Barber-Rowell, 2021, p. 163). Site 1 was a Free Evangelical estate church called Beacon Community, offering multiple independent social action initiatives and a connectors' network on an estate that was, statistically speaking, one of the most depressed places in the UK. Site 2 was Mustard Seed, a partnership-driven social enterprise cafe that operates in an economically poor community on a high street that was experiencing ongoing decline. There is also a second cafe called Seed cafe, which bookends that high street with Mustard Seed. Seed Cafe came into existence due to relationship breakdown with the owners of Mustard Seed. Site 3 was Old Town Church. The church had strong civic links and hosted annual civic prayer breakfasts. There were also a number of faith-based and secular partners. These included Local Values, a life-long learning charity for people with specific learning needs who ran the cafe and offered training opportunities at Old Town Church. Also, the Heritage Association worked out of the church which was also seeking wider strategic engagement with the Local Authority in much the same way a cathedral might in a city. Across the three sites, a set of common themes emerged. These themes were present in all the sites and gave common but differentiated vantage points from which to make sense of lived experiences and stories of hope across the different spaces.

These themes were: (1) types of relationships with place, expressed as service and understood as a source of transformation; (2) leadership, which was incarnational and negotiated between formal and informal leaders who were both generalists and specialists, and expressed different roles and responsibilities; (3) sources of motivation, which were emergent and contextual, as well as related to deep-rooted foundations, that is, different world views, and formed shared values; (4) interface with the public space, comprising communications including both prayer and dialogue, initial welcome and then ongoing care for others, and the professionalization of services; (5) stories, which both had a prophetic character and served to authenticate experiences; and finally (6) administrative and relational flows, including the group or organization finding the flow of the context it is in, forming partnerships in the form of networks, movements or alliances, and then recognizing the need for change, counting the cost of change and then embracing it.

These six were both distinct and simultaneously interdependent characteristics that map the affective flows of difference expressed across and between different spaces. The flow of these differences was not linear, it was rhizomatic, so it looked different in different spaces. As such, any of the six common themes could become a guiding influence for the others. For example, in this book my focus is leadership and what I will refer to as transformational leadership. Transformational leadership is derived from the affective flows of the other five themes, that is, types of relationships with their transformational component, sources of motivation as the deep wells and driving forces that we draw upon to guide what we do, interface with the public space which sets out how we express ourselves, stories which offer an authentic account of our experience, and administrative and relational flows which set it all in a wider context. It is expressed in its own terms as incarnational and negotiated roles and responsibilities. I will offer some definitions for these terms before I set out stories of transition, hope and transformational leadership from Beacon Community, Mustard Seed and Old Town Church.

Incarnational or incarnation is the same word used with respect to Temple's work in Chapter 2. There incarnation was characterized as a philosophical exercise focused on the mind as the centre of our conception of incarnation.

> The whole process of that revelation which has been going on through nature, through history and through prophets, comes to complete ful-

filment in the Incarnation ... Only in the life of Christ is this manifestation given. What we see in Him is what we should see in the history of the universe if we could apprehend that history in its completeness. (Temple, 1919, pp. 317–18)

Here I am presenting something quite different. Here incarnation is the change from possibility to reality within and between affective flows and immanent assemblages in urban spaces. Using the grammar of assemblage theory, this is referred to as 'actualization' (Bonta and Pretovi, 2006, p. 49). This sense of incarnation can become more clearly understood as a process of the potential within a given space becoming actual or concrete. This distinction is drawn by Deleuze and Guattari in *A Thousand Plateaus* as the difference between *puissance* (potential) and *pouvoir* (concrete). To understand this process of incarnation – of the potential becoming concrete, within the gatherings, spaces or assemblages that are being curated within faith-based organizations, and to go beyond the abstract grammar of new materialism, and for the language of incarnation to become related to lived experiences within liminal spaces – we can turn to the stories from those spaces as a means of mapping and opening up leadership. Alongside the incarnational character of leadership there is negotiation. This accounts for the affective relationships between flows of difference within liminal spaces where normal rules of engagement are suspended. This process of negotiation is based on broad characteristics in that it can be enacted in either formal or informal ways by either generalists or specialists, and can be expressed through a wide variety of different roles and responsibilities. These in turn open up the transformational potential on offer within liminal spaces and transitions. I will turn now to three stories of transition and hope that bring transformational leadership to life.

1 Local trusted organizations

Beacon Community was established in 2011. It had been present for seven years when I encountered it. Beacon were based in a building that had been used as a church in the past but was vacant prior to their arrival. Beacon was planted by members of a Free Church fellowship with support from Counties UK, an evangelists' network. Beacon was led by their pastor, Mark, who was initially supported by seven others as they worked to reterritorialize the vacant community space. The model being used at Beacon was oriented to numerical church growth. Mark saw his vocation as a specialist. He was an evangelist seeking to preach the gospel. The Beacon team supported Mark with youth work and musical worship. Over time, Beacon opened a number of community projects including a toddler group and a faith-based franchise cafe.[16] In 2015, an English as a second language (ESOL) class was opened as a response to the affective flows of immigrant communities into the local estate. A foodbank was in operation with support from a local foodbank franchise. There was also a youth initiative that Beacon ran in the community, funded by the Brighter Futures Fund. Brighter Futures Fund was a community fund worth £10 million over ten years to that community. This funding was deployed through what was characterized as a community-led board and governance process, which was overseen by a local trusted organization, that is, a third party who were deemed to be trustworthy to broker resources for all in that community. I will return to the question of trust below.

As the number of people coming through the doors at Beacon grew and the number of commitments Beacon had grown, the nature of the roles and responsibilities held by leaders at Beacon changed. For example, over time Mark generalized to become what he characterized as 60% pastor and 40% evangelist. Other leaders at Beacon did not have identifiable roles and responsibilities and found it hard to reconcile. It was just a case of mucking in together to respond to the changing experiences in the community. This led one couple to leave Beacon. This left a team of six leaders. When I encountered Beacon, Mark and his wife were the only two leaders remaining from the original eight. A new team had formed around Mark and his wife, made up of members of that community. This breaking down of the team and organizational structure was initially seen as a crisis, but it became a pivotal transition for the transformational leadership at Beacon and their role as a trusted organization in that community. The emphasis had shifted away from numerical growth and towards 'blessing' the community (interview with Mark). This marked a key transition and the reterritorialization of Beacon's narrative. At Beacon Community, various respondents noted that day-to-day life was hard. People's lives were characterized by homelessness, unemployment, drug use and highly chaotic lifestyles, resulting in them having been turned away from other places. The story of Beacon recognizes that the well-intentioned inclusion of these local residents was taking place at the exclusion of the rest of the community. The first two years of being open were described as beyond expectation as to how wild and crazy and difficult it could be. Mark noted:

No one was going to come when those [people] were there ... I think in the beginning the community saw that we were here to serve the community and they were quite happy that we were dealing with these people, but they didn't want to join us ... It was just beneath or beyond their expectations of how crazy and wild and difficult it could be ... they would literally come to anything we did, but it started to be that they would destroy anything that we did. (Interview with Mark)

Those who volunteered at Beacon noted a desire to 'seek God'. This was exemplified by 1 Thessalonians 2.8: 'Because we loved you so much, we were delighted to share with you not only the gospel of God but our lives as well.' It was understood that there was a difference between a stated theological or doctrinal standpoint and the lived reality. Taking inspiration from this verse, emphasis was placed on counting the cost of sharing lives with people, however hard that might be. This was exemplified most clearly by a relationship Mark formed with one community member called Nina. Nina's presence established a visceral, challenging and ultimately transformational transition for Mark and his support team, leading to the deterritorialization of his team as they were called to count the cost of embodying the passage from Thessalonians 2.8. Mark was willing to do it. Others were not. Nina was characterized as a 'little old lady who was very anti-God and very anti-church'. Nina's lived experience had meant that suspicion and distrust of everything had built up over time. She brought this distrust into new encounters with others. Mark recounted that he developed a close but professional relationship with Nina that was eventually reciprocated. Over time, that relationship did become characterized by the word 'trust'. Nina measured this amount of trust that was present using a visual illustration between her fingers. As trust grew, the distance between her fingers would grow also, to show Mark that her trust in him was growing. Over weeks, the distance grew so that Nina used the gap between her outstretched hands to illustrate it. Eventually she put her arms fully outstretched to show how much her trust had grown. However, it was also noted that, in between times, others were questioning the nature of the relationship between Mark and Nina. Colleagues of Mark were suggesting that Mark was wasting his time with Nina. This created division and suspicion. The division in the team was a result of both the apparent preoccupation that Mark had with Nina and the fact that other leaders received profoundly negative reactions from her:

This lady [a church leader], whenever she approached [Nina] with her gospel, because she wasn't sharing her life, but she was sharing the gospel ... when she was sharing the gospel, [Nina] was putting her hands over her ears [and going] 'La la la la la la la'. Literally that's what she did until [the church leader] went away. [Nina would] give her a dirty look until she went away.

But she didn't do that with Mark. Mark's experience was not an uncritical one. He noted that he listened to his colleagues and prayed privately. He said that he asked God whether he was wasting his time with Nina, or whether it was the right thing to be doing. The account describes a costly experience for Mark. He noted the response he received to his prayers:

God gave me a real, sort of a real rebuke in my soul. I mean I didn't hear any words particularly, but I know God was saying, and expressing to me, don't you dare! Don't you dare! You know one of these little ones. ... He said to me, if I keep you there, who do you think you are [to question me]? If I keep you there to the end of your life, that one soul! You stay there! So, I said, OK. (Interview with Mark)

It was after this episode that leaders left. In the years that followed, the leadership team became reterritorialized by local people who volunteered and then became employed at the church. Nina became a Christian and died a couple of years later from persistent ill health. Before she passed away, Nina said that she not only trusted Mark, but that she trusted Jesus too. She had become a Christian. Before she died, Nina and Mark prayed together. When Nina died, hundreds of people from the wider community came to the funeral at Beacon. Nina was well known in the community. Interviewees noted that the content of the relationship between Mark and Nina expressed the character of Beacon as a local trusted organization. This was based on God being loved and the community being loved too.

One example that I observed while I was there took place in a drop-in cafe/foodbank assemblage. At one end of the room there was a kitchen with an open counter from which hot drinks were served. In the middle of the room there were sofas in a square facing each other. At the far end of the room was the foodbank offering parcels to people. I saw a man walk into the room and go to the counter. He received a drink and began talking with Mark who was there to welcome people.

> A gentleman has been talking with Mark for maybe 10 minutes now. The conversation has moved from the drinks counter to the second space, with sofas. The guy has been polite to everyone he has spoken to. This included when he accidentally spilt a drink by walking into someone. As he sat down on the sofas the guy has begun to cry. I can see that he also has foodbank bags with him. The man, whilst crying, has begun to have a nosebleed. There is a dialogue developing between 3 people sat around the man, one said, 'Get it all out'. Mark said reassuringly, 'We are not easily embarrassed here.' (Fieldnotes)

As the man transitioned from the cafe space into the sofa space, his circumstances appeared to dawn on him. As he sat down, his emotions came to the fore. This was something that Mark had clearly seen many times before. He noted later that he would encourage the transitions through the three spaces in that way, as it led with welcome and relationship and showed that someone cared for the people who were there. Later I saw the man, who was smiling again. He had his bags of food and was on his way. In 2019, nine years after Beacon opened, I was speaking with a Local Authority officer named Olga. She had worked in that community for eight years and could see the transformational leadership at Beacon Community:

> [Beacon] just opened the doors to anybody, offered a cup of coffee, a listening ear sure and just invited anybody in ... I'm just thinking of especially one lady who's been quiet, I think, probably be fair to say struggled with personal hygiene, you know people with mental health issues where they would not look after themselves really well and there wouldn't be any judgement ... and never any pressure of, uh, having to become a Christian. You know that's never been around. They just welcome people ... [they] look after them ... to still be here and flourish I think is a real testament to their perseverance and commitment to the place ... I've just seen I suppose one determined man go from strength to strength and church has grown. They have had baptisms, weddings now, which is absolutely fabulous. I think the numbers looks really healthy ... and everything around it is growing. He's just opened doors to everyone, doesn't matter what age or race or background. So, you just say strength to strength. (Interview with Olga)

The question of who is trusted and how that trust is discerned in a given community is highlighted when the account of Beacon is set alongside accounts from the Brighter Futures Fund who were named as a local trusted organization in the same community. Local trusted organizations can be a wide variety of things, including housing associations, parish councils, local businesses, charities, voluntary groups, community voluntary services, community foundations, trusts and other funders, community groups, schools, credit unions, churches or a GP surgery (Local Trust, 2019). In this case, the local trusted organization was a regional infrastructure organization who worked with a representative from the Brighter Futures Fund and a committee comprised of community members.

This committee was presented as the decision-making body for the Brighter Futures Fund; in other words, all applications to the fund would be heard by this committee and decisions made by it, subject to due diligence, would be final. While I was journeying with Beacon Community, the local trusted organization received and rejected a funding bid for a two-year social prescription project competitively costed at approximately £80,000. The local trusted organization, in consultation with the employed representative for the Brighter Futures Fund, claimed in writing to the applicant that the decision to reject the application had been made by the committee of community members. In reality, evidenced by conversation with around half of the community members on the committee, this was not the case. Committee members had not been presented with a funding proposal at all. As such, the decision to reject the bid was taken unilaterally and in an unaccountable way by the local trusted organization themselves. I noted in my observations:

> I encountered some of the Brighter Futures Fund committee members at a local drop-in. I asked them about the decision not to move forward with [the social prescription] proposal. One of the members I saw [at the drop-in] was known to me. She told me that she was not present for the meeting, [although] she was in favour of the proposal, so not being present was detrimental ... However, of greater concern, two other committee members who were present at the meeting had no knowledge of the proposal being discussed at all [at that meeting]. I had brief conversations with them, who consented to being recorded. They set out clearly that they had not seen or heard about [the] proposal. I was shocked. [One] chaired the meeting in question, [and] had no knowledge of a discussion taking place. [The other], who has been a long-standing committee member, detailed what she would have expected to see, had she been pitched a proposal, and she had not seen any of it, so could not have made a decision. (Fieldnotes)

I sought to make known these points to an accountable body related to the Brighter Futures Fund. It became apparent that the accountable body was the Brighter Futures Fund representative and the local trusted organization themselves. So where a concern was raised about them, they had set up a system where they decided for themselves whether or not anything should be done. This meant that untrustworthy practices could flourish. Following my submission of information to the Brighter Futures Fund on behalf of the community, they simply returned to me to tell me that the critical points, based on evidence from their own committee members, were not acknowledged by either the Brighter Futures Fund or the local trusted organization. However, some time after this submission and response, structural changes to the Brighter Futures Fund were implemented, with members of staff withdrawn and new ones put in place, to ensure greater accountability and to enhance trustworthy governance processes. I do not know if these changes were directly due to the dishonest brokerage of public funds that was highlighted to the Brighter Futures Fund, or simply a coincidence.

In the cases of both Beacon Community and of the Brighter Futures Fund the question of trust was central to the stories and to the accounts of transformational leadership. The rhizomatic principles of cartography and decalcomania offer a guide through the different affective flows from each. Where Beacon Community was tested, their trustworthiness was authenticated and their relationship with the community they were in was enhanced. They mapped carefully what was going on in the community and responded accordingly. They were called to count the cost of living out their values and they were seen to do so through Mark's encounter with Nina and many others like her. In contrast, the local trusted organization carried the label 'trusted' but when this was tested they were found to be untrustworthy, falling foul of decalcomania; presenting themselves as trustworthy but not authenticating it with their substance.

2 Scattering seeds

This story is rooted in the life of Margery 'Seeds' Bennett, who passed away in the late 1990s but whose story inspired a vision for and the incarnation of social action work by the next generation of people in the community she lived in. This story details the emergence of not one but two projects: Mustard Seed and The Seed Cafe, from the vision inspired by 'Seeds'. Seeds, as she was known, spent many of her days walking the main high street in that community, meeting with people to talk, often gathering on a particular bench outside the shops. She is rumoured to have sat there all day to pass time with people. She was a Christian and was characterized as 'gossiping the gospel'. The name Seeds came from imagery found in Matthew 13.1–23 in the parable of the sower, where seeds were scattered in different environments: some shrivelled in the sun, others grew and faded, and others set roots and grew into trees.[17] When Seeds died, hundreds of people attended her funeral at the local Baptist church, and there was a clear desire to honour her life through some sort of community project. A woman called Janice, who was interviewed as part of the research, attended the same church as Seeds and undertook to honour Seeds' legacy. Janice held a vision for new acts of service in the community where Seeds spent time. This vision was nurtured and interpreted over decades. As I will go on to explain, this vision began as one, and due to affective flows of power and money and unaccountable leadership practice, an asignifying rupture[18] or a sudden and seismic shock took place in the Seed Project assemblage. This in turn led to the Seed Project also becoming reterritorialized through a second project at the far end of the same high street, resulting in two Seeds projects. These were called Mustard Seed and Seed Cafe. Seed Cafe was the realization of the original Seeds vision and was the second to open. Mustard Seed was the first of these projects to open and over time illustrated the limitations experienced when the underpinning story is inauthentic and the rhetorical motivations are at odds with the lived experience. I will explain.

Mustard Seed opened as a commercial venture in May 2014. There were several groups of people representing different churches and community partners involved in Mustard Seed, including Janice who was holding the Seeds vision. The project group identified a community cafe as the best means of honouring Seeds. The project group identified a premises. They secured investment from a local Christian philanthropist. However, as the project came closer to the date of opening, the philanthropist unilaterally imposed multiple conditions on the project in exchange for the release of the cafe to the community members who had nurtured the vision. These conditions were:

- The project should adopt the model of governance and practices associated with a specific charismatic evangelical faith-based social action infrastructure body that was based in the region to which the philanthropist had close ties,[19] called the National Charismatic Social Action Network (NCSAN).[20]

- The Patron insisted that NCSAN must also have members on the board of trustees and that they should maintain a veto power to override decisions made that contravened NCSAN values or might damage their brand.
- The narrative and values within Mustard Seed should be characterized by 'unity'.

In terms of the narrative and values base of 'unity', this is a particular narrative and source of motivation within free charismatic and ecumenical Christian networks and partnerships which was particularly strong in the area. It is a value and a motivation that has a long and rich tradition, which I have talked about in Chapter 2. The sense of unity in the data was drawn from multiple places in Scripture including Psalm 133.1, 'How good and pleasant it is when God's people live together in unity!', and Ephesians 4.1–3:

> As a prisoner of the Lord, then, I urge you to live a life worthy of the calling you have received. Be completely humble and gentle; be patient, bearing with one another in love. Make every effort to keep the unity of the Spirit through the bond of peace.

These scriptures were presented as the basis for the relationships with Mustard Seed. This narrative appears in the data along with the imposition of the NCSAN governance processes and the conditions set by the philanthropist for the use of their resources. A founding trustee for the Mustard Seed project reflected on unity as follows:

> When we dwell in unity there is great power in that. And so that was very much a message at the beginning when we reached out to all the local churches to take part in establishing Mustard Seed here in the community. And I think we've continued to do that. I think our trustees represent a number of churches in the area.

The treatment of differences – mapping or cartography as Deleuze and Guattari (2016) describe it – of the affective flows of relationships across Mustard Seed open up the lived experiences of the assemblage to scrutiny. This allows the different content and expressions of the assemblage to act as a formational part of what is being identified, or to become incarnated. So where language of unity was used in the data, it did not appear to be an authentic value emerging from the story at the heart of the project. The imposition of an ultimatum prior to opening, which was also accompanied by a narrative of unity that felt inauthentic, caused a rupture in the Seeds Project assemblage. The imposition of the unity motive felt autocratic in this case. A Free Church leader in the area raised a question during the research about what unity actually meant in practice, as follows:

> There's an ethos of exchanging of information and ideas and agreeing with each other, but it stops [at a] pretty perfunctory level. [We] should be sharing lives with each other. If you look at the early Christians. Everything was in common ... They were in each other's houses. They were glorifying God when they suffer for Christ. They were rejoicing and they were they were supportive [of each other]. Their whole lives were intertwined.

This assessment encourages a higher standard for the invocation of the unity motive. This quote from one church leader does refer back to biblical texts as sources of wisdom for people to refer to and to use to scrutinize the differences and creative potential on offer. In terms of scrutinizing the other conditions set in place by the philanthropist, NCSAN were included because they offered a proven governance model. It was recognized across the UK. However, Jackie, a local community worker involved on the board of trustees, reflected on this period and noted that while NCSAN did offer a governance model, the people from the Seed Project who were going to be trustees were bringing significant governance experience of their own. This called into question why NCSAN were needed. To compound the impact of this, the 'Seeds' vision was compromised too. The term 'Seed' was included in the name of the new cafe, but it was adapted from the original meaning, to Mustard Seed, and took on a new meaning that deterritorialized the original story and motivations behind the project. In fact, the legal name of the Mustard Seed charity does not have reference to 'seed' in it at all. Instead, it is the NCSAN Centre. In terms of the staff team, Janice, who had identified the 'Seeds' vision in the first place and carried it for two decades, sought to remain united, and volunteered at Mustard Seed under the management of NCSAN for a couple of months after it opened. However, Janice reflected that Mustard Seed simply did not represent a realization of the vision she had held and was not reaching the people that her vision was for, people who were marginalized.

> I realized that I could take [people] in for a coffee but then when we'd drunk our coffee that's it, it's over with. You have to move on. Where-

> as here [the Seed Cafe], people can come and sometimes are here at 10 o'clock and we have to throw them out at 4 o'clock. If they come from a cold home and they're lonely and obviously they can take advantage of a warm place and a free coffee and plenty of company and support. And so, we've developed this, The Seed Cafe, branching out from the original seed concept. (Interview with Janice)

Janice stopped volunteering at Mustard Seed, as did others. A new project, The Seed Cafe, the manifestation of the original Seeds vision, was taken forward by Janice and others from the original project group and was opened in 2015 at the far end of the same street as Mustard Seed. The two Seeds bookended the high street. Jackie, one of the trustees of Mustard Seed reflected that it appeared as if these two projects were in competition with one another and there is clearly historic tension over this episode. However, she also noted with a gracious and reconciliatory tone that 'God honoured both of those visions' (Interview with Jackie). There is a sense from Janice (the original vision-holder) that she had been able to honour the memory of Margery 'Seeds' Bennett by realizing a reincarnation of a simple and faithful vision through The Seed Cafe. It was also acknowledged that in spite of the 'broken and sinful nature' being described within the episode, there is evidence of forgiveness and reconciliation.

> We don't have a blame culture at all, it is all about supposed redemption. It is very much about second chances and moving people forward and strengthening things rather than knocking things down ... And I know a lot of that is because you serve one Lord ... we are all one in Christ and we are all part of that family whether you're in the church or not. We are also part of God's family. (Interview with Jackie)

An epilogue to this account must give due attention to a cafe manager called Jane.[21] Jane was present during the first five years that Mustard Seed was open, and while she was personally aware of much of the discord that deterritorialized the Seeds narrative and staff team, she offered multiple examples of transformational leadership which enabled Mustard Seed to grow and flourish. These examples included the execution of everyday responsibilities within the cafe, from serving customers to completing stock checks and orders, to making food and drinks, to training others. But she also illustrated a deep value of people she served and worked alongside. The way Jane worked honoured the simple and effective origins of the Seeds vision and gave an authentic account of unity that sat at odds with the rhetoric of unity that was imposed. An example that stands out was the way Jane supported a volunteer, Emma, who had autism. Jane sang songs with Emma from the musical *Annie* into a mop handle because that created the rapport necessary to enable both Jane and Emma to do their work well. Jane attended to the details of what was important to people and then worked with that. It was evident in other ways too, such as knowing customers' orders before they had asked for them. Her colleague reflected:

> Jane and I have worked together from the beginning ... We've always been very clear that yes it's a business, but we don't want to run it as a business at the expense of losing sight of all the other aspects of what we're doing. So I think that's been real common vision between Jane and myself and a natural friendship and a trust in one another ... We work around each other's little foibles and the things that make us different ... we work hard to kind of communicate [a] love to one another and make allowances for one another ... five years in, that theme runs really deep through Mustard Seed and through the management.

Jane announced that she was going to leave Mustard Seed in 2019. She was moving out of the area and into a new phase of her life. Jane was one member of staff, but she had become an essential part of the make-up of Mustard Seed, to the extent that her departure was a substantial rupture.[22] Jane's departure really did test the fabric of Mustard Seed. A trustee noted:

> Jane, our lovely Jane, one of the cafe managers is moving to pastures new. She's a very tiny person physically, but she really is going to leave an absolutely massive hole to fill. We 100 per cent bless her in her new experiences ... but we are finding it a challenge to look at how we're going to fill that spot ... we're all praying very hard contacting lots and lots of church contacts and we've put things up on the Christian job website ... We're sort of giving it to God and from prayer chains and things trying to get the right person in. The whole future of the cafe is in this post really. So yeah it's challenging times.

Jane's departure speaks to the continuity she offered and the quiet yet transformational leadership that she expressed. The effect of Jane leaving speaks to the fact that she embodied what would have been seen locally as the Seeds vision and was a unifying figure. This brief account also highlights the limits of the structure that was implemented by the patron at the outset. A rhetorical narrative of unity is one thing. But its limitations were highlighted across Mustard Seed through an existential crisis as one staff member, albeit one excellent staff member, left.

3 Uninvited and unexpected

This story identifies the prophetic influence of a homeless man within multiple gatherings associated with Old Town Church. The story became characterized as the 'uninvited and unexpected'. My use of the word prophetic here is in the sense offered by Walter Brueggemann:

> In both judgement and hope, prophetic articulation – in elusive poetic form – voices the interruption of the known controlled world that is dramatically other than the world managed by the totalism. The prophets voice a world other than the visible, palpable world that is in front of their hearers ... a new sociopolitical, this-world emergence beyond the capacity of the [totalizing] regime. (2018, p. 129)

The elusive poetic form was a homeless man called Eric. He transitioned in and out of the different gatherings that comprised Old Town Church from 2016 to 2019. In so doing he brought a dynamic, gritty, often insightful, sometimes volatile (but never violent) punctuation mark from the margins of the spaces, which affected judgement on the contrasting forms of leadership that were present. Eric was first characterized as the 'uninvited and unexpected' by the Area Bishop in April 2017, during a public gathering at the church. She said:

> The uninvited, perhaps rather unexpected, maybe even disruptive people who just wandered in ... they forced us to, to stop our thing in itself and make space for them. To be present and to be heard and to participate, albeit in a transitory way, that may prove to be the more important space of hope. (Fieldnotes – conference proceedings)

This quote connected Eric's transition through shared spaces with the concept of Spaces of Hope, and in these pages I will share the extent to which that truly was prophetic wisdom. I will do this with examples from two different churches which utilized the same space. These were Old Town Church and House Church, a Free Church plant supported by the Planting Network which was planted into Old Town Church. Old Town Church was in interregnum, a period of transition between the end of one vicar's incumbency and the introduction of a new incumbent.

This interregnum lasted for three years. This is a long transition and was indicative of a search for a plan for the future of the Anglican church in the town. A sense of the search and the plan was offered by the Area Bishop:

> I just want to share with you, I went to the reopening of the Whitworth Art Gallery in Manchester [which] included an exhibition by an artist called Cornelia Parker. One of the things that struck me really powerfully was that she made moulds of the cracks in the pavement. And then cast them in bronze. [They] spoke very powerfully to the places that she made those moulds from; some very evocative places, but, just creating beautiful art out of the cracks in the pavement just spoke to me about where those Spaces of Hope can be found. One of our dangers is that we walk over the cracks in the pavement without paying attention to them. It was really valuable to have the attention drawn to the spaces between things, which helps to see the things themselves more clearly. So that's a way of saying, I think, perhaps the most hopeful spaces are those spaces that we are ordinarily inattentive to, that we disregard, that we are blind to. And I think one of the things that I personally and that faith communities and my church as an institution needs to be reminded of is that too often we think of our ourselves, as myself, as the thing itself. That 'hubris' means that we become blind to the more creative spaces in between.

The Revd John Wright had been seconded to the church not as vicar but in order to help out and to explore the spaces for connection and creativity in the parish. John supported the establishment of a number of partnerships in the town and in particular the launch of an initiative called House Church, which was a free charismatic church, meeting in Old Town Church. It was one of a number of Planting Network satellite gatherings in the region at that time.[23] John noted that permission for House Church to exist within Old Town Church sits right on the legal limit of what the governance of its parent body, the Church of England, would allow:

> The House Church connection I think is significant theologically in all sorts of ways, it really rides on, sits on, the very limits of what we can do legally in an Anglican church – probably actually steps over the line. It's really the Bishop's interpretation, which she feels is OK, so that's OK with me. But there is no formal agreement between the Planting Network and the Church of England. So, it's very much an

experiment but to me it seems to be the way that Christianity in this country should develop. (Interview with John)

In addition to hosting House Church, John acknowledged that Old Town Church was also a host for gatherings by multiple expressions of the Unity Network that was prominent in the town. John noted that, in terms of their capacity for engagement, Old Town Church was down to 'ground zero', so simply hosting events and activities was as much as they could do (Interview with John). However, this limitation was tempered by the fact that Old Town Church held patronages for a variety of churches in the region, so with that in mind, Old Town Church was also noted by John as a potential key player in the area. This insight was borne out by his description of Old Town Church as the 'ballast of the ship', even if it is not the 'rudder' or the 'sails' (Interview with John). John's sense was that these contributions would come from churches that were part of the Unity Network such as House Church.

Eric was often intentionally other than what one expects. Julia, a volunteer at Old Town, noted that at one time he might have had a good job. He was a consistent presence in the data; known by interview respondents and present in observation data, including at House Church.

There are examples of different responses to the presence of this uninvited and unexpected guest in the data and this gets to the prophetic relationship between Eric and forms of transformational leadership. One elderly member of Old Town Church, Julia, said, 'He put the wind up me' (Interview with Julia). However, over time she, along with Joan, one of the wardens, learned how to interact with Eric. They kept being attentive to the different ways he expressed himself. This was one of a number of measures Old Town Church used to support homeless people in the area, including links with the mobile support service Daily Bread and signposting to The Hub, a longstanding and well-respected homelessness support service, kitchen and foodbank near Old Town Church. This meant it was possible to make space for Eric in a way that worked and, where it was needed, to signpost to further support.

A contrasting example came from House Church. I observed Eric entering a worship service when sung worship was going on. There were maybe 20 people in the room. The space was relatively open. He stood to the rear of the space. Eric was encouraged to join in with the singing by an older man. He chose not to do so. The sung worship carried on and the older man chose to begin a confrontation with Eric. The older man moved towards Eric and faced up to Eric and put his head into

Eric's face. Eric was forced from the building. As Eric left, the senior pastor declared, 'The presence of God has returned' (Fieldnotes).

Eric did not return to House Church during the research phase, but he was seen elsewhere in the Old Town Church assemblage. This interpretation of this interaction might be received as circumstantial or as a one-off. However, I was aware of violence on two other occasions. Once when a senior elder kicked a box so as to indicate clear anger at something while engaged in discussion with a junior member of the congregation. A second occasion was when the senior pastor spoke of using anger as a means of getting people to follow his leadership. Other data spoke to this theme. One respondent from House Church wrote responses that were critical of their host church, Old Town Church, after a request to mount monitors on the interior of the building was turned down. The response noted: 'Is the purpose of this hub to introduce people to a family? Sometimes felt like building prioritized over visitors' (Survey respondent).

Another respondent from House Church indicated a particular perspective on the status that they felt House Church should have. 'There are two main bodies that comprise this hub. It has not been possible to provide the correct answer for each' (Survey respondent).

The data shows that Old Town Church was a multifaceted hub with many worship and public gatherings each week (of which House Church was one), two resident partnerships – Local Values, who ran the cafe, and a Heritage Group who ran a permanent heritage centre at the church – and civic and strategic significance in the town. House Church was in its second year of operating. It held a worship service each week and had begun to explore some town centre outreach activities, which comprised the core team of four handing out fliers in the high street.[24] These responses reveal a sense of status that House Church expressed relative to the others which was entirely consistent with their treatment of Eric.

In April 2019, Old Town Church appointed a new rector, Clarissa. New parish boundaries were also agreed for Old Town Church, so that it included a community in the top 0.1% of depression statistics in the country. This represented an expansion of the commitment by Old Town Church to people living in transition and to encounters with the uninvited and unexpected. Clarissa brought substantial knowledge and experience for engagement with marginal people and places. She had experience of living and working on outer estates and had also built a career as a senior leader in the third sector before becoming ordained. Clarissa was interviewed as part of the research and she acknowledged the quiet and transformational leadership of the volunteers during the interregnum and sought to bring about 'fresh expression' of that during her time as Rector. In November 2019 I was made aware by the Old Town Church churchwarden that House Church had ceased meeting as a congregation in the church building in order to reassess their vision. I understand that attendance had dwindled, and members of the leadership team had left. There is no direct causal link between the treatment of Eric and the fortunes of Old Town Church or House Church. But there was a clear prophetic word shared at a public gathering in that space about the affective flows of prophetic judgement and hope that Eric could bring. This then could be seen within the liminal contexts of the interregnum, which authenticated the presence (or otherwise) of transformational leadership.

In this chapter I have set out the theological and conceptual foundations for the Spaces of Hope paradigm and methodology. I have done this through dialogue with interdisciplinary literatures relating to faith-based organization, political philosophy, sociology of religion, social policy and continental philosophy. These literatures have offered a basis for mapping expressions of transformational leadership that I will now take forward into the rest of the book. I turn next to the Covid-19 pandemic, as a crisis that accelerated and intensified lived experiences of liminality and transition and therefore heightened the need for transformational leadership.

Notes

1 I recognize that this terminology will rightfully receive attention from those who do not identify their work as part of a 'faith'-based organization but also may feel included somehow in this introductory paragraph. This apparent discrepancy in terminology will be ironed out and made clear as the chapter progresses.

2 While Esping-Andersen's typology provides an overarching typology for welfare regimes, more work is required to define the role and significance of FBOs across different regimes globally. This is beyond the scope of this book but is certainly of interest for the future. As I will set out next chapter, there is also a transition taking place within welfare contexts following the Covid-19 pandemic, but this is something that I will return to in Chapter 5.

3 The FACIT project concerns the role of faith-based organizations in matters of poverty and other forms of social exclusion in European cities. The project took place between 2008 and 2010 with partners from six nations across Europe: UK, Germany, Netherlands, Spain, Sweden and Turkey.

4 Woodhead notes a 'stickiness' to no religion, that is, once you are a none, you are likely to remain a none, and identity as a none is likely to pass from one generation of a family to another (2017, p. 250). This is contrasted with those who identify as Christian, where the chance of them becoming a none, or going

through 'nonversion' (Bullivant, 2017), is 45%, and with regard to young people who have nones as parents there is a 95% chance that they will remain nones too (Woodhead, 2017, pp. 251–2). The increasing population of nones in the UK is coupled with an increasing number of identities being acknowledged within non-affiliation too.

5 Context is given to the rise of the nones by studies such as the 'Understanding Unbelief' project (Lee, 2016). The study highlights that 'non-religious' cannot be seen as anomalous or 'a vague or marginal population, but a large, often committed and heterogeneous one that should certainly be accounted for alongside religious ones' (Lee, 2016).

6 May (2005) notes that within British and American philosophy, questions that focus on our lives have, to a large extent, been lost to meta-narratives and emphasis on method.

7 Numerous examples of this sense are found in Chapter 2: in the 'There for you' section, where I look beyond the logo and the label that projected my identity to others. A counter example is offered in the 'Hope and despair' section where police officers refused to look at the details they were presented with and instead became complicit in the oppression that was being perpetuated. This approach to difference was then highlighted in the 'By their fruits you will know them' section where different gatherings explored the differences that created a shared sense of being and affinity as people pursued hope together.

8 This first understanding of assemblages is in itself an illustration of the Deleuzian concept of rhizome. The first understanding is found on pp. 375–6, or about halfway through the book. Within the first pages of the book, there are discussions of how the book itself is an assemblage, which they then go on to describe in terms of rhizome (Deleuze and Guattari, 2016, pp. 2–5). Using a rhizomatic understanding it is perfectly reasonable to offer the first understanding of something halfway through in this way.

9 These are: (1) everything is potentially connected; (2) everything is characterized by heterogeneity; (3) heterogeneity or differences are found within a multiplicity; (4) asignifying ruptures can disturb *multiplicities* and change them at any time; (5) cartography or mapping is essential for understanding the details of multiplicity; and (6) decalcomania is a caution against taking for granted what we think is going on and an encouragement to look properly (Deleuze and Guattari, 2016).

10 In this way plural assemblages are multiplicities and also establish connections between certain other multiplicities (Deleuze and Guattari, 2016, p. 25).

11 It is noteworthy that multiple understandings of assemblage have emerged. McFarlane reflected that they are 'not well elaborated' in terms of a consolidated tradition within the literature (2011, p. 204). However, this is not a concern in itself; as each application is developed it can be tested and the emergence of tradition can either follow or not.

12 The work of Manuel DeLanda (2016) on assemblage theory is relevant here. He has developed a framework for the development of assemblage theory and organizations, which my work here could be set in dialogue with as a progression following this volume and as part of further research into curating Spaces of Hope within organizational contexts.

13 Anyone familiar with the cartoons from the Naked Pastor could find examples of sheep of other colours that would also work here.

14 This is a point that I will pick up in greater detail in Chapter 7. The prin-

ciple of affect will point us to the nuances of the things we do and remind us of the socio-material significance of the relationships between the human and the non-human as we seek authentic and hopeful leadership.

15 The ethnographic research comprised 27 interviews, 114 surveys and 90 hours of participant observations that were set in dialogue with the references that had emerged from the movement.

16 The rationale for the faith-based cafe franchise was that the brand the franchise was associated with gave confidence to secular groups that the local expression was trusted. The brand acted as a stamp of approval and authenticity.

17 The names in this account have been changed to protect the identities of the people and the communities in which the research took place. The derivation of the name 'Seeds' is also changed, but it is coterminous with the rationale for the real nickname of the person and the subsequent names of the social action projects concerned.

18 An asignifying rupture is the fourth principle of rhizomes set out by Deleuze and Guattari following connectivity, heterogeneity and multiplicity. Asignifying rupture refers to a sudden or unanticipated and substantial, potentially catastrophic or existential threat occuring. Within Deleuzian grammar, this kind of change is greater than an affect or a deterritorialization.

19 The close connection between the philanthropist and NCSAN was highlighted by respondents within the data and was also made clear to me by Gail, the philanthropist, directly. She did this by introducing me to the Founder and Director of NCSAN in 2017 when we met for coffee. We met multiple times thereafter.

20 This is a pseudonym to protect the identity of the national organization in question.

21 This is a pseudonym.

22 Rupture is a term used by Deleuze and Guattari to illustrate not just the change expressed by deterritorialization, but an unexpected and substantial shock that would test the resilience of the assemblage.

23 Eric attended a gathering I was also present at hosted by Cinema Church, which was also supported by the Planting Network. This gathering was some months later from the one being described above and was a 'vision night' for Cinema Church which was advertised across the research area. I observed the period the homeless man was present (about three minutes), from entering through the door to leaving again. He entered the building, was objected to by members of Cinema Church, and was immediately confronted by the leader of Cinema Church and told to leave. My observation was that he had done absolutely nothing wrong. He simply entered the space, as per the open invitation to the event. However, he was rejected from it without explanation. I was asked afterwards by another member of the gathering who appeared to be an elder within the gathering what I had seen. I reported what I have said here.

24 For the sake of clarity, my personal view is that it is a very good thing that House Church sought to plant at all. It is a sign of commitment to something to establish a new church. Indeed, I led sung worship at House Church for 12 months before the research phase of my PhD commenced, so I was committed to the project working. However, according to the accounts within the data, there are clear distinctions to be drawn between House Church and Old Town Church.

5

A Movement of Hope

From 2020 to 2022, the Covid-19 pandemic was experienced by all around the globe as a pervasive and deadly new virus to which there was no natural immunity or vaccine. In the UK approximately 180,000 people died due to Covid-19 between April 2020 and July 2022 (Raleigh, 2022). In response there were also lockdown measures designed to limit the spread of the virus which intermittently and unequally limited individual freedoms. In this way, the Covid-19 pandemic provided a universal and prolonged experience of liminality, which accelerated and intensified the conditions mapped during Chapters 3 and 4. The pandemic also had the effect of increasing collaboration across the UK between people and organizations responding locally to the pandemic. This was taking place alongside unprecedented strain on the NHS and state apparatus, characterized in *Preventable* by Professor Devi Sridhar as 'total systems failure'[1] (Sridhar, 2022, p. 127). In terms of the local responses, the 'Keeping the Faith' research commissioned by the All Party Parliamentary Group on Faith and Society (cited in the text as APPG), for which I was a researcher, offers insights from across the UK. *Keeping the Faith* (Baker, 2020) engaged all 408 local authorities in the UK in the research. 194 valid survey responses were received from local authorities (47.5%) and 55 in-depth interviews were conducted with local authority leaders and coordinators of faith-based projects across ten sample local authority areas which were chosen for their demographic and geographic diversity (p. 3). The research found that critical provision of food and financial support, mental health and well-being support, and vaccine rollout support was undertaken. Of local authorities, 91% describe their experience of partnership-working during the pandemic as either very positive or positive (p. 6). Regarding food, 66% of local authorities were already engaged in this kind of provision before the pandemic. This rose to 78% during the pandemic (p. 6). Health and well-being services rose from 43% to 48% (p. 8). Of local authorities surveyed, 93% indicated best practice in coproduction between community partners as either 'very important' or 'important' to them

(p. 8). This point was reinforced by observations from faith leaders in the north-west of England. They highlighted specifically the role that digital spaces played in opening up and radically democratizing the decision-making process. This shift to hybrid working facilitated greater participation. This happened by broadening access to community partners and empowering them to speak. One respondent who represented faith communities in Greater Manchester noted digital spaces flattened the structure of meetings and therefore shifted the meeting dynamics so that voices could emerge from multiple places simultaneously, as opposed to the order and hierarchy of a boardroom table with people in power at the head of the table to which the discussion was directed. Across 2020–22 the experience of pandemic response was broadly characterized as 'rescue and emergency' and then 'building back better' (APPG, 2022, p. 3). The research highlighted a new appreciation for faith groups and an increased trustworthiness that had surprised local authorities. There was also a resourcefulness and innovation present, demarcating a more radically open space whereby citizens are not merely co-implementers but co-initiators, as well as co-designers (APPG, 2022, p. 43). Stephen Timms MP characterized this as a source of positive challenge in the public sector,

> Local authorities had become much more aware of what faith groups were doing, and how well they were doing it. The success of the partnerships had deepened dialogue and strengthened relationships. Many of the collaborative initiatives at the start of the pandemic crisis had been highly innovative. Respondents were reflecting on how the same ethos and approach might now be applied to tough, longer term challenges. (APPG, 2022, p. 2)

The question of how the ethos and approach from the pandemic might be applied to tough long-term challenges stands in the context of whether faith-based organizations are an asset to be harnessed or a problem to be solved. During the pandemic, Jeff Levin from Baylor University conducted a longitudinal study into the role of religious groups in the pandemic in a global context. He reflected:

> The mixed track record of the faith sector in addressing the COVID-19 pandemic includes some religious groups' deliberate disregard of public health measures to control transmission, mitigate damage, and promote vaccination, plus the 'infodemic' of misinformation spread from some pulpits. Troubling, too, is anxiety created

by apocalyptic speculation about the virus and misinformation about face masks and social-distancing guidelines originating from some clergy and religious leaders, often advocated in the name of religious freedom. (Levin, 2022)

Levin's analysis finds that while the hindrance offered by faith groups cannot be underplayed and has in all likelihood contributed to the loss of lives in some contexts, it should also be read alongside positive contributions of pastoral role, messages of hope, emotional and tangible support through food and shelter for those made jobless and homeless by the pandemic, and worship practices as a means of reducing isolation and building a sense of community. This more hopeful message chimes with the prevailing view of the *Keeping the Faith* research in 2022. Following on from there, in a UK context the Bloom Review (Bloom, 2022) offered a more tempered perspective on the role of faith-based organizations in post-pandemic policy-making, which takes into account some of the problems historically associated with faith groups, including terrorism fuelled by extremism and fundamentalist teaching. This sets the call for cocreation, coimplementation, coinitiation and codesign advocated by the *Keeping the Faith* reports in further context. Nonetheless, there is a role for citizens of different world views at different stages of partnership, policy and practice. With this in mind, there are questions of terminology and emphasis that I will now consider.

The role of citizens

The general idea for involving citizens in the production of public service outputs is found in the work of Elinor Ostrom from the 1970s. Her research considered the extent to which relational approaches to policing would improve the quality of policing in Indianapolis (Ostrom and Whitaker, 1973). The evidence base for the use of this kind of approach has dramatically improved since Ostrom's initial work, including the internationally recognized volume *Co-production and Co-creation: Engaging Citizens in Public Services* (Brandsen et al., 2018). The terms coproduction and cocreation are often used interchangeably in practitioner and policy circles, but they are theoretically different, possessing different applications in different disciplines. Coproduction finds its roots in Ostrom's work looking at public service design including the input of citizens. Cocreation is a term derived from the commercial business community and has only recently become synonymous with public and social policy contexts (Brandsen and Honingh, 2018, p. 9). Further, it is also recognized that the terms are not unified under one body of work, instead they are represented by separate bodies of work that scholars have sought to link (see Voorberg, Bekkers and Tummers, 2015; Brandsen and Honingh, 2018). For example, Brandsen and Honigh offer three ways of understanding the relationship between the two terms: (1) coproduction and cocreation mean roughly the same and refer to any kind of citizen input in public services; (2) cocreation is the more encompassing term, referring to all kinds of citizen inputs in services, whereas coproduction has a more specific meaning; (3) cocreation and coproduction have distinct meanings, referring to different kinds of citizen input (2018, p. 10). It should be noted that cocreation is considered to be the 'newer and more slippery term' (p. 10) while also being characterized as a more strategic or early-phase input by citizens compared to coproduction (p. 13). With this distinction in mind, I will take forward the second understanding, that cocreation is the more encompassing term, referring to all kinds of citizen inputs. My rationale for this is twofold:

1 The nature of the research I am drawing on for this book is interdisciplinary. As such there is no standardised definition of the terms (cocreation or coproduction) that has been applied across the different literatures used thus far: faith-based organizations, belief in social policy, urban geography, or sociology of religion. So in order to recognize the use of non-standardised but related terms, I will opt not to tighten or limit arbitrarily the definition of terms at this stage.
2 The context here is citizen responses to the liminal transition created by the Covid-19 pandemic where normal rules of engagement were suspended. With this in mind, citizens were characterized as early-stage coinitiators and codesigners in response to unprecedented and immediate changes in working practices, which points more to cocreation as the appropriate (albeit more slippery) term.

So, having established terminology of cocreation for citizen action, I will turn to post-pandemic Spaces of Hope gatherings that took place between 2022 and 2024. These gatherings served dual purposes. They were space and time for those involved to reflect on their experiences and to consider hopeful ways forward in the future. These gatherings were also a learning process through which the Curating Spaces of Hope approach defined in earlier chapters was applied and tested such that a movement of hope has been cocreated by some 500 or so citizen leaders across a further 26 gatherings, in addition to the approximately 1,000 people who contributed to around 40 gatherings across 2016–19. It is from this movement that the transformational leadership approach at the heart of this book has been developed. I will turn to that further in chapters to come, but first I will consider the social movement literatures.

Social movement

The 'concept' of social movement has been around for 100 years or so (Chesters and Welsh, 2011). The roots of social movement studies can be found in the visibility of collective action in response to common problems experienced by different groups. Some historical examples include: the Student Christian Movement, founded in 1889, with whom William Temple had a strong association, and with whom I am pleased to have published through SCM Press; the Environmental Movement, founded following the publication of *Silent Spring* by Rachel Carson (1962) and spearheaded today by David Attenborough and others through the likes of the Earthshot Prize; the Civil Rights movement in the USA, symbolized by the Revd Dr Martin Luther King Jnr among many others; the British Labour movement in the early twentieth century inspired by Methodism and, to a lesser extent, Marxism provides one UK-based example. The anti-fascist movement in Italy in the 1920s led by Antonio Gramsci also stands out. While there are a great many more examples, my intention here is to trace parameters for social movements offered by social movement studies. This will provide a basis for understanding the movement of hope characterized in this chapter on its own terms, rather than limiting it to comparison of individual examples. For this I will use a typology of 'old', 'new' and 'networked' movements.

Old, new and networked social movements

I will begin briefly with 'old' social movements. These are derived from the Marxist theoretical tradition relating directly to positionalities defined in terms of class struggle (Chesters and Welsh, 2011, p. 126). This simple definition can be contrasted with new social movements, which are characterized with respect to a foundation other than class struggle. From my discussion in Chapters 3 and 4, the Spaces of Hope movement is not defined in terms of class struggle. It does not exclude discussion of class, but the idea of class struggle is simply not there in the lineage of the work, so it would be wrong of me to claim otherwise. The Spaces of Hope movement is a response to different experiences of crises: poly-crises and meta-crises. To make more sense of this, I will turn to new social movements.

New social movements (NSM) are part of a school of thought developed in European contexts by Alain Touraine (1977, 1981, 1983), Alberto Melucci (1980, 1985, 1989), Claus Offe (1985), Jürgen Habermas (1976 and 1987), and Ernesto Laclau and Chantal Mouffe (2001) who develop the case for NSM within a radical democratic tradition of politics, drawing on the work of Antonio Gramsci. NSM emerged in response in part to the limitations of Marxist theory to speak to emerging collective phenomena and sought to address struggles other than class struggle. Instead NSM addressed more specific concerns: the environment, student experience, women's rights, oppression experienced specifically by black and/or ethnic minority groups, gender or sexuality, or unemployment. The definition of old and new can be contentious in that it could be seen to dismiss 'old' in favour of 'new', or indeed characterize chronologically more recent movements as distinct from chronologically older movements, when in fact they are broadly conceptually similar (see Calhoun, 1993). Further, the choice of either old or new can mask the blurring of categories within the etymology of a movement; for example there might be a movement that is both underpinned by class struggle *and* a further category, for example, gender, race, environmentalism, etc. To this end, Bert Klanderman's (1991) typology can be used to understand elements of 'newness'. He sets out constituencies, values and forms of action. By *constituencies*, he identifies that new social movements look beyond the proletariat, and are made up of groups that might be considered to be newly marginalized by circumstances beyond their control. By *values*, he does not mean to prescribe one value or the other, but does identify what is being responded to as undermining the quality of peoples' lives, which opens up a question about what it is that they value. By *forms of action* he means that autonomous action originating outside of established groups within civil society could be characterized as 'new'. These are 'anti' or 'non' hierarchical and might be but are not always antagonistic to institutions.[2]

A final consideration are 'networked' movements. This is a relatively uncontested term within social movement theory, which offers three further characteristics: the *virtual* (mailing lists, websites, social media, etc.); the *situated* (physical spaces and places of encounter that enable connection and trust building); the *textual* (information and knowledge that circulate both about the movement and the outward-facing engagements the movement participates in) (Chesters and Welsh, 2011, pp. 120–1). Pragmatically, these three are commonplace in our world today and the relationship between the virtual and the situated was emphasized and accelerated during the Covid-19 pandemic. I will take these parameters forward, along with Klanderman's (1991) typology: constituencies, values and forms of action.

With these literatures in mind we can locate Spaces of Hope as a new/networked movement. This is in evidence in Chapter 3 through its emergence from 2016 to 2020, during which time Spaces of Hope drew on multiple constituencies, responding to a multiplicity of concerns, engaged in a search for value that was open both to deep sources of inspiration from theology, philosophy and everyday life, and emerged from community contexts that, far from being antagonistic to institutions, offered a critical friend perspective that called for and embodied change and offers (in this book) a means of exploring that change further. With this in mind, I will set out the movement that has emerged post-pandemic.

Spaces of Hope as a new/networked movement

Chapter 1 positioned Spaces of Hope as responding to poly-crises and meta-crises, which are intensifying and accelerating conditions of liminality set out in Chapter 3. These conditions, for which Curating Spaces of Hope was made, moved me to issue a call to action for different constituents to gather to explore their experience and to find hope together (see Barber-Rowell, 2022a, 2022b and 2022c). In the two years that followed, from January 2022 to April 2024, over 500 people convened across a global movement that became centred in the city of Liverpool. The different connections emerged via X (Twitter), via LinkedIn, in response to blogs and journal articles, and in person as one gathering led to the next. The gatherings emerged on three of the four sides of the public square: in educational contexts, in grass-roots politics and in civic and faith contexts. While there was a call to action, there was no clear plan about how the movement would emerge, if it did at all. I will turn now to the gatherings, mapping the rhizomatic emergence of dialogues that opened up diverse concerns and understandings of transformational leadership from citizens across society.

Liverpool Hope University

Liverpool Hope University is a unique higher education institution. Hope was founded by both the Anglican and Roman Catholic Churches from three theological colleges based in the city of Liverpool, Notre Dame College, St Catherine's College and Christ's College (two Catholic and one Anglican). These colleges were noteworthy in their own right for their pioneering education of women before there was a right to education in Great Britain.[3] This contributes to a rich institutional heritage of over 175 years. Hope was formed within a wider culture of ecumenical partnership in Liverpool that was established by Bishop David Sheppard and Archbishop Derek Worlock in the 1970s and 1980s. Their friendship and pursuit of the common good was a notable change in the response to poverty, sectarianism and wider social unrest in the city. Their legacy and presence is enshrined in the Sheppard Worlock Library which is named for them. Liverpool Hope University College was incorporated in 2003 by Chief Executive Professor Simon Lee who named the institution 'Hope', sourcing inspiration from colleagues, Sheppard and Worlock and Hope Street, which runs between the Anglican and Catholic cathedrals in Liverpool city centre. Hope was also leant to Hope Park, the university campus in Childwall. In *Serendipity of Hope*, edited by Lee and Professor Ian Markham, perspectives from numerous former colleagues and students reflect on the formation of Hope. The volume reflects back on lived experiences of hope at Hope, 25 years after it was established.[4] In Lee's chapter he reflected on the university as John Henry Newman did, with theology as the queen of the sciences at the heart of the institution, and the university or 'Alma Mater' understood as a source of nourishment or nurture through a formative phase of life (Lee, 2023b, p. 4). Lee also defined 'serendipity' not in the terms commonly associated with the word, a random happenstance or a stroke of luck, but as attentive to the details of things, 'Using wits, senses, spirit, and talents, and powers of observation to spot clues and opportunities on [the] journey that others might miss but that might make the difference to someone else' (p. 3). In this sense, hope is in the details and serendipity is how hope is made real. These two points reoccur in chapters from staff and students alike from that founding generation at Hope. Different accounts map hope as a diverse learning journey, a personal odyssey, within pedagogies and strategies that shape student experience, in community projects – Network of Hope, Communities of Hope and Hope One World – as well as the institutional culture characterized in terms of 'collegiality' ongoing day to day. This sense of hope is captured in another Newman quote, from the hymn 'Lead kindly light' (1833): 'I do not ask to see the distant scene; one step enough for me'.

In early 2022, Cardinal Michael Fitzgerald was welcomed to Hope to deliver a keynote lecture and to convene a dialogue in the Senate Room. Cardinal Fitzgerald is a world expert on dialogue between those of Christian faith and those of Muslim faith. The lecture was on inter-religious relationships, inspired by the *Document on Human Fraternity*. This letter was cosigned by Pope Francis and the Grand Imam of Al-Azhar, Ahmad Al-Tayyeb. It explored a basis for building relationships between groups of different world views, and opportunities for living more closely together. Following this lecture, those gathered were encouraged to explore opportunities for dialogue between different groups in the city. This move to dialogue between people of different positions in the church and in society was taking place at the same time as the worldwide synodal process in the Catholic Church. I provide this backdrop as it is this document and the Spaces of Hope that followed that formed the evidence for me being admitted to Hope as an Honorary Fellow, and provided a positionality on the periphery of the university and the city, to call for change on behalf of staff, students and residents alike. I turn to this below.

In July 2022, I convened a gathering with lay and ordained leaders from St Vincent de Paul Catholic church in the Baltic Triangle, a post-industrial area bordering Toxteth within Liverpool city centre. This church is also where Cardinal Fitzgerald served. We connected with ecumenical colleagues from other churches in the city. The pandemic was very much in the forefront of people's minds, national lockdown restrictions and subsequent tiered lockdowns had taken place and networks of support had proliferated across the city. However, little time had been given to reflecting on the pandemic experience both of ecumenical activism and the activists themselves. This dialogue drew inspiration from the parable of the good Samaritan, and provided space and time for people to reflect, each from their own perspective, on things that offered hope, challenge and ways forward. Those gathered noted a desire to serve all comers, from Ukrainian refugees fleeing war to the Traveller/Roma gypsy community that had settled in the neighbouring Anglican parish. However, there was a sense of reticence from those gathered, because there were examples of the people being welcomed in ultimately 'taking advantage' of the goodwill on offer. Nonetheless, there was a conviction to continue to be welcoming. It was felt that a hopeful culture was needed within the parish and within the archdiocese. Key to this was partnership working with other churches and secular agencies. This dialogue had an emancipatory quality to it. It was the first time that those gathered had met together in this way, and it pointed to the need for further gatherings of that kind.

Hope by name and hope by nature?

The gathering in the Baltic predated my role as an honorary postdoctoral fellow at Liverpool Hope University. However, it was pivotal evidence of the contribution I could make to the university community. Subsequently, I submitted an application that was considered by Vice Chancellor Professor Pillay FRSA, and I was granted an honorary fellowship later in 2022.[5] I was subsequently invited to conduct similar such dialogues across the university. They were reframed for the purposes of the academic community. The question that guided the gatherings was 'Are we Hope by name and hope by nature?' Dialogues engaged academic and non-academic staff from all levels of the institution, external partners from elsewhere in the UK and internationally, as well as students. The spaces used for dialogue varied. For example, one took place in the chaplaincy room at Hope Park, situated in a physical space, visible to anyone passing by, in the middle of the campus gardens. Another was hosted in a virtual Zoom room, drawing participation from partners across the Hope Ecumenical Network, including from Ukraine, the USA and India. A thoroughfare or transitional space between two canteens – Our Place, and Fresh Hope – was also used, so that rather than the dialogues being perceived as an exclusive or formal gathering to which one might be invited and for which one would set aside time, they also constituted a moment in time, in transition between other activities. Brokerage of space for dialogue in this way resonates with the heritage of the university. The dialogues utilized the theme of hope as a means of opening up the subjectivities of those gathered, including a spiritual dimension alongside the social and material nuances of the environments people share, the aesthetics of the campus grounds and gardens, and the empowerment gleaned from interpersonal relationships in response to managerial pressures. Responses highlighted the negative effects of micromanagement and included claims of bullying. Conversely, solace was taken in others. The words of Albert Camus were quoted: 'There is more to admire than despise in the human.' The metaphor of 'little platoons' found in the work of Edmund Burke was used, coalescing with stories from spaces of resistance and resilience found in departmental teams. Beyond disputes over working practices, others invoked natural spaces on campus as a reminder of home:

> I love sunflowers and so the grounds here remind me of my favourite flower. It is beautiful. Sunflowers give me a sense of hope and so I see hope here when I am here [in the gardens and grounds]. It gives me a real boost.

Respondents also highlighted the juxtaposition of experiences with technology. The impact of social media on student outlook and on their sense of their environments: 'The use of social media and its replacement of relationships among many of our students. Inability to share our experiences due to the pressures of time that come with work.'

Beyond social media was the perceived threat of artificial intelligence (AI). Innovations taking place in AI, for example through ChatGPT4, were featured in the press in November 2023. This prompted seminars on the future of AI and higher education and the impact on student experience and people's jobs. Other views on virtual spaces were shared too. They were seen as valuable to students separated not only by the pandemic but also because they were forced to leave their homes due to the war in Ukraine. One respondent summarized:

> In relation to international Christian HE, what gives me hope is the shared mission we at Hope share with our international Christian HE partners. To see, hear and experience how the individual's lived experiences connect and integrate to form part of a wider community is continually inspiring.

However, these dialogues took place against a backdrop of concern for the future of humanities subjects in higher education. Different respondents highlighted this point and its impact on campus culture:

> There is a culture of pessimism [characterizd by a] human 'stain'; blindness, wickedness, self-assertion and the ideological cancel culture movement, [perpetuated by] weariness and exhaustion and fear and anxiety permeating the post-Covid climate [and] the limitations of a Christian vision occasioned by institutional failures.

This sense was echoed in other gatherings on campus: 'There is a lack of collegial living and living in conversation. [There is] refusal by people in power to listen or learn exhibited in politics and government policies. We are experiencing a functionalist secular view of the purpose of education.' A participant from the University of Cambridge who joined the Zoom gathering for Hope and its partner networks also echoed this sense of the sector, lamenting the situation they find themselves in:

> I often lament these two barriers I see: (1) dualistic world views that prohibit Christian postgrads from seeing the public/intellectual implications of their faith on scholarship, and (2) not enough staff and funding to respond to the high level of student interest in Christian higher education.

The concern over the finances of the university was also seen as a barrier to hope. This point was set in the context of the university as a vocational endeavour, echoing the sense of nurture found in Newman's view of the university and linking it to the experiences of technology too. One respondent noted:

> [There is] a perceived positive linkage between the economic outcomes of university education and learning itself. Christian learning is about discovering God's world and your calling within it. Vocation of calling is broader than economic return on educational investment. Further, technology for all its enablement is also a barrier to hope when we daily experience global crises through our phones.

During the period of research, strike action was led nationally by the UTU and taken locally by the Hope branch of the UTU. There were disputes over pay and conditions which had implications for the working conditions of the staff at Hope and their remuneration. As an honorary fellow, I had no pay nor any conditions to speak of and was not being remunerated. Therefore, while those who chose to strike did so and told me why it was in my interest that they did, I took the only option open to me and continued to work as an unpaid, honorary postdoctoral fellow and early career researcher. I met with those who *were* present and gathered their perspectives. This sense of juxtaposition of different positionalities and perspectives within university culture came through in the dialogues:

> We are giving opportunities and money to the 'past' more than the 'future'. Second, the sense of community is declining and the 'me' is prevailing on the 'us': it is so difficult to find hope if you are alone; hope is something shared and found, not created by yourself.

The tensions within the culture of the university and within the staff team were named explicitly within the data. Deep frustrations came through about colleagues:

> I am not naming individuals but I think some staff are quite weak. I think some people in positions of power are not competent. I don't want to be personal about it. I have experienced staff in the past who have been very proactive at helping students but felt they were banging their head against a brick wall and have subsequently left.

Tensions between different strata of the organization notwithstanding, there was an opportunity presented to me after this research was compete to share the outcomes and recommendations for change with the Mission and Values Committee of the university, which was staffed by the senior management of the university and was chaired by the new Vice Chancellor, Professor Claire Ozanne. These included but were not limited to recommendations for investment in staff well-being, and the cocreation of a contextual theology of hope for Liverpool Hope University which could be used to guide a theory of change. This sense of opportunity was captured by one respondent who talked about how we journey on together:

> We overcome barriers by sustained conversation with each other about the barriers and how to create new/different practices and structures to overcome them. People need to talk, develop tangible cooperative relationship, and go the second and third mile in addressing a problem. Many solutions are possible in Christian higher education when we slow down and focus on how a specific problem also creates an opportunity.

This would enable the story of the institution to be told and developed through a theory of change based on the world views at the root of the university, which in turn nurture a culture of collegiality within the university and across its networks. This sense of a way forward was consolidated through this recommendation by one respondent:

> I can always remember that not everyone is capable, or will destroy your hope. The world is a social world. Interdependence is as important as competition. For me to survive, others need to survive and vice versa. Hope comes from knowing we are all in this together, We all feel the same things, want and need the same things, etc. People look

to me for hope, as much as I do for them. This is an ingredient for building trust, and with trust comes a sense of security, confidence and hope! I just need to overcome generalizations and be a bit more open-minded.

Hope and the public square

In December 2022, a gathering took place at Blackburn Cathedral entitled 'William Temple and the Rebuilding of the Public Square in Post-pandemic Britain'. This gathering was hosted by Liverpool Hope University Scholar and William Temple Foundation Trustee, Dr Yazid Said, with whom I had begun to work closely at Hope. The gathering, hosted in a diocese Temple created, picked up the theme of dialogue across different world views and explored dialogue between Christian, Muslim and Jewish faiths. This was in the spirit of Temple's work noted in Chapter 2, including establishment of the Council of Christians and Jews in 1941. This gathering was concerned with activities in north-west England, and deployed dialogue as a means for cocreating or curating citizen leadership. The relationship between these two terms, curation and cocreation, was raised at the gathering by Cardinal Fitzgerald who was present once again. The simple answer is that both speak to a way of citizens contributing. Cocreation is broadly about when citizens begin to contribute. Curation is a question of how that is done. However, I will make this distinction explicit and the means of curating much more specific in Chapter 7. This gathering served to open up space for a new meta-narrative that could consider not just higher education institutions but other public institutions characterized by new forms of partnership in the public square. Former Archbishop of Canterbury, Rowan Williams, reflected on this theme from the church's perspective and noted the need for emancipation and accountability:

> It is a delicate balance. The church asks for freedom, not to defend its territory, but to discharge its task of 'giving space' – creating 'Spaces of Hope' in the resonant phrase explored in one of these essays. Yet its demands for freedom can – in a society powerfully focussed on public accountability – sound like a plea for exemptions from anything that affects its conduct. (Williams, 2023)

Williams related this point explicitly to the issues for which the church has become known in recent years: provision for the ordination of women; the legalization of same-sex marriage; and the failures relating to safeguarding in the church, which have been highlighted so vividly through the Makin Review (2024) and the resignation of the Archbishop of Canterbury for the first time since the fourteenth century. However, Williams found some hope in the way that Temple worked through the challenges of his day. This was in Temple's leadership across difference, in ecumenical and inter-faith settings, in his strategic leadership on social issues shaping society, and in his method. Williams continued:

> Temple, I think, is inviting us to reflect on what the liberties are that are specifically bound up with our ability to go on being a place in which society can find room for its hardest debates and most awkward vulnerabilities without the fear of being pressured into an ideological framework. I suspect that he would have resisted as a tempting short-cut any idea – whether from inside or outside the church – that secular legal process could be invoked to accelerate desired changes in the Christian community, not least because he was aware (as who could not have been aware in the 1930s and 1940s?) of which malign political forces might want to take advantage of any precedents in this respect. He would have wanted to be sure that the pedagogy of sacramental participation in the self-forgetting love of God in Christ was not being sidelined or surrendered. He would readily have stood alongside other religious communities in denying that they existed only by franchise of an all-powerful sovereign polity. He would also have been cautious about too frequent resort to tactical alliances, 'co-belligerence' on specific questions of public morality that seem to threaten traditional positions – largely because of the risks of looking for solutions simply in terms of political pressure rather than cultural consent. In short, Temple offers not only a theology and ethic of public engagement for the church but a theology and ethic of its method of engagement. There is not much point in speaking about self-forgetful love if the methods used to support ethical ideals are coercive or manipulative. (Williams, 2023)

William's point is set out at length as it speaks to the complexity of the test the church faces. There is a need for emancipation and accountability, to hold space for addressing the differences people and communities are wrestling with, and the responsibility of leadership to address this in a way that gathers consent for what follows.

While Williams found these themes in the church, it is not the only faith-based organization interested in contributing to the public square, nor, as evidenced in Chapter 4, is it the only world view. Our gathering was joined by Professor of Islamic Studies at the Muslim College at the University of Cambridge, Tim Winter. Winter is also a British-born Sunni Muslim known as Shaykh Abdal Hakim Murad. Winter cited a current example of the Issa Brothers from the north-west who work internationally, and founded EG Group which owns the Asda Supermarket chain and the EG Petrol Station chain. Looking to the future, Winter reflected:

> The idea of a holy company, a commercial 'space of hope', rooted in traditional Islamic ideals of mercantile piety [might] perhaps represent a distinctively Muslim contribution [to] the intermediate space in society ... [I]n the corporate neoliberal world, where identity is increasingly bound up with company affiliation, this may serve to add an additional dimension to the postsecular settlement as it continues to shift and evolve. (Winter, 2023)

The process of ideating or cocreating a different shape to the intermediate institutions that make up civil society, and the means by which they operate or curate, is a rich source of hope, which is explored further in this chapter as part of the emerging movement of hope.

The Dialogue Society

In order to understand who the Dialogue Society are, I must first set out the Hizmet movement (*'hizmet'* meaning service). Hizmet is an international Islamic movement founded by Muhammed Fethullah Gülen – a traditionally trained Islamic scholar of Turkish origin from within the Hanafi school of Sunni Islam (Weller, 2022). The Hizmet movement established a presence in the UK in the early 1990s (p. 67). It is characterized as

> A network of congregants, recordings, books, sobhets (or meetings) that has developed in interactive engagement with the emergence of Fethullah Gülen as a figure who has religiously inspired, intellectually articulated and practically initiated a distinctive action-and-reflection-oriented hermeneutic of Anatolian and Sufi-inflected Sunni Islam into a dynamic and organic set of networked initiatives including dormitories (often known as 'lighthouses'), schools, businesses, media

enterprises, business and other initiatives that have a relationship with one another in terms of mutual engagement, learning and challenge. (Weller, 2022, p. 28)

The Hizmet movement is oriented to overcoming three key challenges: ignorance, conflict and poverty. It works to eradicate these three in broad terms by establishing schools, civic peace and unity and social action. It does so through subsidiary organizations such as the Dialogue Society. July 2016 is a key date in the history of the Hizmet movement. It met with substantial controversy when it was accused by the Turkish Government of instigating a military coup. A coup did take place and it was quelled. Hizmet and followers of Gülen were labelled as terrorists and a terrorist organization by the Turkish government led by President Erdogan. It is acknowledged that there were individuals involved who were part of the Hizmet movement; however, the claims that Gülen or the Hizmet movement instigated the coup are widely contested and are not recognized by the UK government or other governments around Europe, including Germany (see Weller, 2022, pp. 107–13). In the light of the coup and the controversy surrounding it, the Hizmet movement and its adherents have been exiled from Turkey and those who stay face persecution and imprisonment within the country.

The Dialogue Society is a daughter or subsidiary organization of the Hizmet movement. While the Hizmet movement is characterized in explicitly religious terms and is openly associated with a prominent Islamic leader, the Dialogue Society in contrast does not publicly recognize its own religious roots, instead seeking to position itself as non-religious: 'From its origins (1999), the Society projected its self-understanding as being neither a religious nor an ethnic organization. It aims to facilitate dialogue on a whole range of social issues, regardless of any particular faith or religion' (Weller, 2022, p. 68). This description sits at odds with the demonstrable religious roots of the Dialogue Society in Islam. Weller's work was supported using funds granted through the Dialogue Society, so one must assume it is accurate. The choice to adopt a public-facing position that is non-religious as opposed to religious has curious resonance with the secular narrative that was prevalent when the Dialogue Society formed itself in the UK. This choice to present themselves as non-religious also does not appear to add up when considered alongside activities the Dialogue Society has undertaken. These include the development of inter-faith dialogue from 2004 to 2007 and the establishment of a mosque in London in 2008. This is to say nothing of the community Iftar model that the Dialogue Society deploys uniformly across its different branches in the UK, in Bristol, Durham, Hull, Leicester, Manchester, Northampton, Oxford and Liverpool.

In 2021, refugees from Turkey who were part of the Hizmet movement arrived in Liverpool, seeking asylum in the UK. In early 2022, I was approached by Paul Weller to convene a gathering for the recently arrived refugees. Weller is an editor of the *Journal of Dialogue Studies*, with whom I published an article in 2021. Weller also wrote the first account of the Hizmet movement since July 2016, *Hizmet in Transitions: European Developments of a Turkish Muslim-Inspired Movement* (2022). I initially met with the national directors of the Dialogue Society, before then meeting on Zoom with 13 members of this new community in Liverpool.

Through our Zoom gathering, we explored themes including the safety and education of children, loss of loved ones, the limitations created by a language barrier, and the stress and insecurity of being in an unknown city. One respondent noted that this was the first opportunity they had had to reflect on their journey. They asked for the opportunity to write down their feelings and their experiences, as it would give them time to translate their thoughts from Turkish to English. Those gathered expressed a deep resilience to overcoming barriers, supported by the small actions of others, a phone call from a friend in Turkey or a cup of tea from a fellow community member in Liverpool. The group noted that they had lost work (in business, science and education) but gained a sense of togetherness and common humanity, which they said was not limited by their own preconceptions and world views, but defined by finding common ground with neighbours. Within this gathering there was no explicit discussion of suffering in Turkey, nor was there explicit reference to 'July 2016', which is the acknowledged shorthand for the coup attempt that took place in Turkey.

In the 12 months that followed, the group of refugees began to identify as volunteers of the Dialogue Society, and a new local branch was set up and a new coordinator identified. I was asked to support the fledgling branch to coconvene a community Iftar in Liverpool in April 2023, to thank the community the Dialogue Society volunteers were now part of. About 25 local residents and people who worked in the city met alongside around 100 people from the Turkish Muslim community who had recently had their asylum status granted. The Iftar included some notable figures from the city: the Chief Constable of Merseyside Police, senior members of the Fire Service, and Metro Mayor for the Liverpool City Region, Steve Rotherham. My perception was that a gathering with senior leaders of this kind would have represented something to celebrate for this group who had recently been granted asylum. However, these honoured guests were greeted and entertained not by the new Branch Coordinator, but instead by a person who identified himself as the Northern Director of the Dialogue Society. It was noteworthy that the Liverpool Branch Coordinator was now identifying himself as the Branch Director. This was brought to my attention via new business cards being handed out. The role of the Branch Director on the night appeared to be to coordinate the gathering administration. This included fixing the technical issues that arose with the Dialogue Society promotional video which sought to showcase the national network and their flagship programmes. Other elements of the gathering were not as anticipated either. For example, I thought I was asked to coconvene the gathering on the basis that I was developing dialogue gatherings in the area and my work might be of assistance. Instead, I was pressed by the Branch Director to find funds for them, source musical entertainment, and invite my networks to the gathering which included academics, faith and community leaders. In and of themselves, these details are innocuous enough, but suspicions rose when I was not given sight of an accurate events schedule and was also pressed in my WhatsApp exchanges with the Director to find an event host for the evening whom they characterized as 'beautiful'. This didn't sit well. I immediately queried this terminology noting that this was not a characteristic for an event host that I was comfortable with and I wasn't prepared to identify someone based on that criterion. I did make myself available to host the event if that was acceptable to them. However, instead of dialogue about this, the Director disengaged from me. Notwithstanding these increasingly bewildering circumstances, I attended the Iftar to share the story of the Turkish Muslim asylum seekers I had met with in 2022. While the plans from previous months appeared to be in disarray, sharing this story is what I had initially agreed to do for a group who were in an existential transition to a new life in a new city. However, even this was not straightforward. On arrival, I found that a female lecturer from the university I was at had been lined up to host the gathering alongside a teenage girl from the Turkish Muslim community. This showed me that the organizers would do what they needed to do to achieve their aims, and that I was seen as disposable and of nominal value to the Dialogue Society. In speaking with my colleague, I found that there was a prepared script for the event, which on inspection bore no relation to the discussions I had had in previous months and was clearly a standardized script for all the Iftars run by the Dialogue Society branches across the UK that year. This copy and paste script did not include space for any local contributions such as the one I had been asked to provide. In the minutes before the gathering began an adjustment was made to provide space to share the authentic story of hope that had been gathered at the Zoom meeting the year before.

In response, those who had gathered did come together to share their own hopes for their community and their future. Respondents noted different sources of hope including their relationship with their God, and the opportunity to gather together at all, such as we were doing that evening. Hopeful responses included, 'To give thanks to Allah every day', 'Spread peace', 'Witness to the unity of humanity "we are all one"', 'Work to overcome the barriers – welcome to refugees', and 'Hope is gained through connection, through the divine, self, family, friends, and of course with those in our communities and society'. These views were contrasted with reference to the evils the Hizmet movement seeks to end, people's ignorance, or 'ignorance by innocence' as it was put in the responses. Narratives of fear and government corruption were present, stated in terms of 'Ideological unwillingness to address the problems of ordinary people', and, 'The rise of populist and hateful figures given space in media to incite hatred'.

Following this dialogue came the call to prayer, to mark the end of the fast for Ramadan. While the marking of Ramadan through the Iftar was in itself a meaningful cultural exchange and a clear and authentic expression of the Islamic faith, and the dialogue about hope that had taken place had surfaced revealing expressions of hope and fear in the room, I was left deeply uncomfortable by the experience overall. On the one hand, there was the incarnational narrative of the trials of asylum seekers and their transition into a new city. On the other hand, there was imposition of a transactional approach to leveraging local support, the presumptive, bordering on aggressive, approach to accessing resources, the apparent sexism and cultural insensitivity expressed in the search for a local host, the uniformity of the template event plan, and the obvious strategic positioning and political manoeuvring at play evidenced by the presence of senior political and civic figures as honoured guests. What was presented to me as an emergent gathering of active citizens seeking to learn the local context and become integrated with groups of different world views via a relational approach to building links with community members and local activists of modest status such as myself, was replaced by something more concerned with developing influence and credibility for an established regional and national network with international backing, which had a singular and clearly articulated Islamic world view. A point that typified this experience was that I received multiple approaches from someone who shared very few details about themselves to co-author a publication with them to espouse the virtues of the Dialogue Society and to champion their role as a source and broker of social capital. I declined these approaches.

Research set out in *Hizmet in Transitions* sets the experience I had in a clear context. It highlights clear issues being experienced by Hizmet in a variety of European contexts. First, there is what I hear as an entirely understandable experience of 'woundedness' by the Dialogue Society volunteers. This refers to the legacy of July 2016 and the experience of seeking asylum in other countries. 'We are trying to start new projects [but] … we still need a couple of years to get those emigrants adapted … it is clear that we are still not fully back to our game yet, that we still have wounds' (Weller, 2022, p. 245).

Holding space for the group of asylum seekers to work through these wounds, to the extent I was able, was a privilege. Sharing their story as a means of opening up a new narrative of hope for the group was also a privilege. However, this is set in the context of the jarring, inauthentic and coercive importing of influence, structures and identikit scripts and a contextless methodology. Weller reflects:

> For any continued distinctiveness and vitality of Hizmet in Europe, the creative way forward will likely not be one based on any combination of … Gulen's inherited teaching, pregnant though that remains … or the 'copy-pasting' of historical Hizmet initiatives, as valid and important as they have been for their contexts and times. [Heeding instead a] dynamic methodological call to continuously renewed and contextualised engagement with religious and spiritual sources that are centred on love and on the human. (2022, pp. 245–6)

I have sought to engage with the Dialogue Society branch in Liverpool since this iftar in a spirit of reconciliation and partnership, inviting their Branch Director to share their story and experience at a gathering at Liverpool Hope University. The invitation was declined; however, they did seek to build a relationship with another colleague of mine in the same department. My colleague, who was aware of my work and my experiences, copied me into the communications and they ceased contact. This experience with the Dialogue Society highlighted the pitfalls of working across difference, albeit with one specific organization and one specific branch in one city. It also highlights the issues that have emerged from the transition the Hizmet movement are working through. There are always opportunities for misunderstandings, for different cultural norms or political manoeuvring to become barriers, or legitimately traumatic lived experiences to shape events adversely. This is the case with all partnerships and it speaks to the question of how difficult it might be or otherwise to find deep unity between groups of different world views. However, none of these are reasons not to continue seeking out hope across differences in the public square. I am in touch with the Dialogue Society team at national level regards the experiences I have set out here, so there is still hope as transition continues.

The Royal Society of Arts (RSA)

I became a Fellow of the Royal Society of Arts in 2017 as part of the social movement work I did in South Manchester. The RSA is a non-religious public institution which has been contributing to the public square in Great Britain for the last 270 years through its organizational support and its network of Fellows. The fellowship numbers approximately 31,000 Fellows around the globe. Through the centuries it has included a breadth of pioneers, innovators and entrepreneurs, including Adam Smith (economist and philosopher), Karl Marx (father of Communism), Prue Leith (restauranteur, TV presenter and university chancellor), Dame Judi Dench (actor), Bernardine Evaristo (author), Isambard Brunel (civil engineer), Vivienne Westwood (fashion designer), David Attenborough (broadcaster and biologist), Deborah Meaden (entrepreneur and investor), Colin Powell (politician), Tim Berners Lee (scientist), Nelson Mandela (politician and campaigner), May Rose Craig (author and activist), Shirley Manson (musician and actress) and Sarah Mason (charity leader) (RSA Journal, 2024). The most recent biography of the RSA, *Arts and Minds: How the Royal Society of Art Changed a Nation*, uses its opening pages to indicate the breadth and scope of the RSA. The dedication reads simply 'to the public spirited'. The introduction continues:

> [The RSA] is by its nature difficult to define. There is no other organisation quite like it, and nor has there ever been. It is in a category of its own. For almost 300 years the Society has essentially been Britain's voluntary, subscription funded, national improvement agency. (Howes, 2020, p. xi)

Since the Society was established by William Shipley in 1754, Fellows have gathered in coffee shops and public spaces to discuss how they might respond to challenges of innovation and social concerns. This has produced shared solutions for the betterment of society. At its best, the RSA has exhibited this culture through the centuries. There have been recent renewals of this culture. One example was the 'Coffee House Challenge' for the 250th anniversary of the RSA, and renewal took place once again under former CEO Matthew Taylor. He is attributed as seeking an open and inclusive culture that nurtured an active fellowship; 'a ready-made social movement' (Howes, 2020, p. 308). While he was not the first Director of the RSA to do so, it was his influence in my period as a Fellow (2017–present) that offered space for young public-spirited people seeking to contribute to society. Taylor characterized the fellowship as follows: 'While many fellows have achieved recognition for their contribution in a particular field, this is not the defining criterion for becoming a fellow. Our ethos is inclusive; we value all who positively impact society' (Taylor, in Howes, 2020, p. 310).

A culture of gatherings at the RSA is also accompanied by RSA publications. In fact, Taylor's vision was one of combining the publications of the RSA think tank with space for the membership to meet and mobilize (Howes, 2020, p. 307). This culture, continued by the new CEO, Andy Haldane, meant that during the pandemic, virtual coffee houses were also convened. On the final page of *Arts and Minds*, Howes reflects, 'Just as in 1754, and ever since, its usefulness to the public will depend upon the public-spiritedness and initiative of those who choose to be involved' (Howes, 2020, p. 318).

I found ways to utilize all three mechanisms (physical and digital gatherings and publication) for engaging the fellowship. In May 2022, I presented the Spaces of Hope movement at the virtual Northern Coffee House gathering hosted on Friday lunchtimes. There I connected with Fellows with interests in unionizing and leftist politics, as well as a leader in the movement to reduce preventable suicides in the UK. In June 2022 I convened a fellowship gathering at Mother Espresso Coffee House in Liverpool, where I met a trustee from Liverpool Charity and Voluntary Services. I also published a blog hosted on the RSA Comment pages. Following this I received a response from an advisor at the European Innovation Council who recently founded the Global Collaboration Institute, and from the convenor of the Antonio Gramsci Society UK who is also on the board of 29 fellowship councillors who support the running of the RSA. I will now turn to each of these connections and the fruit they produced.

Hope in the Coffee House

In early 2022, I shared my plans to gather Fellows to talk about hope with the Northern Manager of the RSA. Together we convened a gathering to explore how Fellows might renew relationships post-pandemic and work together to respond to some of their shared social concerns. These included a housing crisis, mental health epidemic, heritage and civic space, ecology, sustainable development, community activism, and eradicating poverty. Those gathered acknowledged a vulnerability created by social isolation during the pandemic and the need for a renewed sense of joy. They imagined opening the city back up through festival-like encounters in physical spaces such as the 'bombed-out church', a cultural space curated by the Anglican parish of St Luke in the City. This was tempered by a sense of worry. Digital spaces had created distance and alienation for some; it was easy to anonymize oneself by going screen off. There was a sense of anxiety at returning to gatherings in real life. This was in addition to inequalities exacerbated by the pandemic. There was acknowledgement of the need to open up further spaces to share stories and to work together to develop hopes for the future.[6]

Liverpool Charity and Voluntary Services (LCVS)

As a result of the initial Coffee House gathering, a member of the board of LCVS approached me to curate Spaces of Hope gatherings for them and their members. LCVS wanted to establish a new vision and strategy for eradicating poverty in the city, which might be mobilized as a social movement, with partners from the community, voluntary, faith and social enterprise sector in the city. LCVS is the oldest charity and voluntary infrastructure organization in Great Britain, founded in 1909 to eradicate poverty in the city (Morris and Russell, 2010). LCVS has had different names over the years: Liverpool Charities Council was used in the formative stages; Liverpool Council of Voluntary Aid from 1909; Liverpool Council of Social Services was used from 1930 to 2005; Liverpool Council for Voluntary Service was added in 1974 for uniformity with the CVS movement nationally. In 2005, the name changed to Liverpool Charity and Voluntary Services (LCVS) (Morris and Russell, 2010, p. ix). To understand the task LCVS had it is important to understand something of the city of Liverpool. In *Rooted in the City*, published by LCVS themselves in 2010, John Lansley, a Methodist preacher and social policy lecturer at the University of Liverpool, described Liverpool as a heterogeneous city characterized in terms of rapid growth, mercantile heritage, divides between rich and poor, separate churches, religious division, and expressions of both innovation and consolidation (pp. 1–11). In terms of the city as a whole, Lansley described Liverpool dispassionately as a 'place with an 800-year history [but] no particular significance until the end of the 17th century' (p. 2). From 1790 to 1880 there was a tenfold increase in population from 54,000 to 611,000 (p. 3). This spike in population related to the merchant activities of the city through the slave trade, and complex sectarian Protestant–Catholic relations spilling over from Ireland (p. 7). These mercantile commitments brought wealth to the city which was used to build city institutions by a group of influential families, but this was also tempered by a rapid increase in poverty levels (pp. 8–9). Lansley cited sectarian divisions as slowing the pace of the social support being developed in the city (p. 10). His challenge in 2009 was this:

> Liverpudlians were noted for their cheerful giving. This is true ... But is it true of the city as a whole, and do we need to find new ways of being independent in our patterns of support for others – and more importantly, for each other? (Lansley, 2010, p. 11)

In 2021, there were over 3,000 voluntary sector organizations in Liverpool, employing around 10,000 full-time equivalent employees, which comprises 43% of the voluntary and community sector workforce across Liverpool city region. LCVS operate on behalf of these organizations and engage regularly with around 250 of them (locally understood as member organizations), who are self-selecting through frequency of their activity, as a broker of relationships with other anchor institutions in the city, such as the city council and the Chamber of Commerce, on matters of community engagement and resources, policy and practice. The Spaces of Hope that we curated were varied depending on the nature of the leaders involved. Seventy-seven people participated from three main cohorts:

1 Senior strategic leaders from the city representing the 'Marmot Partnership Group' in different sectors across the city: political, faith and community, health, commerce and policy. This group was convened in response to the Marmot Reviews (2010, and 2020) which set out the experiences of poverty and inequalities in the UK. This group seeks to find holistic solutions to shared issues shaping the city based on the pioneering work led by Michael Marmot.[7]

2 Local leaders from communities and member organizations across the city, from church leaders to charity CEOs, to community organizers, to volunteers, to social entrepreneurs, to public sector and public health officers.
3 Representatives of LCVS who were seeking to take the movement forward.

Gatherings were convened in both virtual and situated settings in order to establish a vision, strategy and calls to action that provoke a movement of hope across the sector and the city. The provocation begins with the stories of poverty in Liverpool. It is described as an intergenerational one. Poverty was characterized as 'compacted and grinding'. Liverpool is the third most deprived city in England in terms of health and disability, fourth most deprived in terms of income, and fifth most deprived in terms of living environment (Index of Multiple Deprivation statistics). Of Liverpool residents, 60% are in the 20% most deprived nationally; 47% of residents are in the 10% most deprived nationally (Liverpool City Region 2019 data). The city was described by one of the city leaders as 'a poor family within a poor family'. Poverty in the city is compounded by global factors, for example the historical legacy of slavery and post-industrial decline. There is a legacy from the global financial crash (2008) and Brexit (2016) and exacerbated social divisions. The Covid-19 pandemic (2020–22), climate crisis, cost of living crisis and energy crisis are all delivering material impacts on the city, its people and the sector. With this in mind, one member of the Marmot Group reflected:

> It actually never ceases to amaze me, because in theory we should be so depressed, that we can't, you know, we as a civic life, we shouldn't be able to get out of bed, but we do so. Poverty, the language of poverty, doesn't necessarily equate to poverty of civic life, engagement and carefulness and kindness. But obviously, it's really hard and it's depressing. And … it's just really demoralizing.

Other respondents noted the complexity of the situation. They identified that Liverpool appears beset by a dependency on external resources and relationships on the one hand, and a clear narrative of independence on the other. This resonates with Lansley's challenge from 2010. There was consensus in the data that the scale of the challenge faced by the city requires external support. However, the independence narrative was characterized defiantly and with pride, by phrases such as 'the Republic of Liverpool' and 'not part of England'. On the one hand, the independence narrative infers a comradeship that serves the city well in some respects. A prominent example from the last few decades is the long fight for justice for the 97 who died as a result of the Hillsborough disaster. On the other, unless interdependence is acknowledged, respondents believe that ongoing issues such as cycles of poverty will continue. The history of sectarianism, slavery and division in the city pointed to by Lansley (2010) speaks to this point. But this is not a new source of concern for the city. Regarding slavery, one respondent noted:

> We were the last place on earth that continued to support slavery ... we were still a Confederate state when there were no others in America. Historically we set ourselves apart from something important, like that sort of social change ... we don't want to hold our heads high about that. I think we do recognize that ... it's both absurd and notable.

Respondents pointed to twentieth-century concerns too. The effects of world wars, the Thatcher government in the 1980s, riots in the city, and multiple other concerns that compound over time.

> You've got social deprivation, the depression between the wars, then you have the Second World War, and the city was bombed to shyt, wasn't it ... As a city we moved a lot of our high functioning individuals who were our workforce out of the city and into other parts of our region. So lots of people move from the city out to Kirby, Knowsley and Sefton and various other places that people were moved to strategically to keep them safe. And ... it changed the nature of the city. So the grinding deprivation and poverty is not, you know, can't blame it all on one government in the 80s.

This is experienced in unequal ways across the city too. Respondents pointed to the wards of Woolton and Walton. They are three miles apart and they have a differential in life expectancy of 12 years. Wavertree and Picton are neighbouring wards – they have a life expectancy differential of 14 years. The codirector of public policy at the Heseltine Institute rejected the idea that these variations are not given the respect they are due:

> People like to divide Liverpool to north and south. But there's a lot of variation in between and you can't compare one neighbourhood

in North Liverpool to another neighbourhood in North Liverpool, you've got to be aware of different dynamics in different areas, so if you are doing any work in areas to address, you know, some of the poverty issues you've got, you've got to be mindful of that in terms of how you tackle it.

These differentials are seen through visible rough sleeping, begging in the streets, and the increased likelihood of disability in specific localities. People wear darker clothes in poorer communities. It was noted that this saves on washing and helps clothes look newer for longer. This was contrasted with brighter clothes in more affluent communities. The nature of work is an indicator too. For example, otherwise aspirational people are taking whatever jobs are going: working as a sales assistant in a shop for example, before finding it tough or impossible to move on to 'better' employment, becoming trapped in poverty. There is a mismatch in terms of the jobs being sought, the number of people seeking them, and the type of jobs available. The chief executive for the Chamber of Commerce said:

> In micro economic terms, there's a huge challenge ... it manifests itself through obviously crime statistics, through skills, attainments through health inequalities, access to health care, and fundamentally access to jobs and the ability to generate a fair wage, a sufficient wage ... I think where we are at the moment in Liverpool ... we have generations of worthlessness, by definition of poverty, we've also got a massive challenge around in work poverty ... we don't have sufficient numbers of jobs at a particularly well-paid level [relative] to all the cities in the UK, not just Manchester, which is usually the easy comparison, [but] Newcastle, Bristol, Nottingham. It's not unique to Liverpool ... [although] Liverpool is unique in terms of perpetuating some of these issues ... So poverty has a substantial impact on [people being] physically and mentally well, capable of undertaking work at a level that they want to.

It would be wrong to give the impression that there is not genuine collaboration in the city. A city councillor who had been active in different senior leadership roles in the city for a number of decades reflected the general sense of how things can work:

> Some of the people who had power in the community worked with others who had the power to build relationships, then we had different

kinds of transformation stuff [going on]. It's a bit of Gramsci, not Alinsky. It's not that adversarial stuff, you know, it's doing the long-term stuff together.

Saul Alinsky was a community organizer in the 1960s and 1970s – the reference here is with respect to his *Rules for Radicals*, which has wide reach and influence within community organizing internationally. The rules offered are gleaned from Alinsky's experience in lower-class urban spaces in Chicago. In the first chapter of *Rules for Radicals*, Alinsky initially set out his purpose as follows:

> The life of man upon earth is a warfare. (Job 7:1)
> What follows is for those who want to change the world from what it is to what they believe it should be. *The Prince* was written by Machiavelli for the Haves on how to hold power. *Rules for Radicals* is written for the Have-Nots on how to take it away. (Alinksy, 1971, p. 3)

This sense of othering and adversarial engagement is born out throughout the rules that underpin Alinsky's work – the language of ridicule, targeting, weaponry and polarization is promoted and encouraged. The point being made by the councillor is that they believe the tactics deployed within any new movement should move away from this kind of destructive and adversarial engagement towards other strategies drawn from the work of Antonio Gramsci, which focus on other forms of power, including the role of folklore and storytelling in gaining consent for change. I will turn to Gramsci later in this chapter and Chapter 6 onwards.

In terms of the Liverpool context, there are new narratives of hope emerging. They show up in different ways. Liverpool throws a great party. City-wide festivals and cultural events capture the identity of parts or all of the city, drawing out specific facets of the heritage. For example, the Capital of Culture award (2008) and the Giants (2018) speak to cultural and creative expression, while AfricaOye (annual) and Eurovision (2023) speak to musical heritage, diversity and unity. This was so much in evidence that, following Eurovision in Liverpool, the song contest permanently changed its strap-line to the one exemplified by Liverpool: 'united by music'. It is not just a case of having a party, though. These gatherings are understood rightly as important affinity spaces not only for cocreating a new narrative but also for building local resilience. These spaces do not fix poverty, but they do galvanize people while trying to respond to deeper issues. These spaces are not only found at large city-wide gatherings, but rather in small local gatherings that nurture relationships, values, ideas and local leadership in the city. Local leaders offered their perspectives too. They issued a call to action for a new generation of leaders to rise up to overcome the failed bureaucracy and corruption that they believed to be blighting the city. This was after the 2020 arrest of the former Mayor of Liverpool and a number of his colleagues. The *Liverpool Post* reflected recently on this situation after it was raised in the House of Lords. They quoted Lord Heseltine speaking in the House of Lords:

> The mayor of Liverpool, Joe Anderson, was arrested on various charges, including fraud and bribery. That was three years and four months ago. He lost his job, his reputation and his income. No charge has been placed since then. I would just like to ask the minister: does he think that's justice? (*Liverpool Post*, 2024)

In the aftermath of Anderson's arrest, government inspectors were brought into Liverpool City Council to oversee a change in the way the city is run. In June 2023 a faith leader in the city noted:

> The hope of the government inspectors staying for a bit longer is that they may actually see that story out. Do you know what I mean? As in we might actually see some of that emerging. I really, really hope our elected members, I think Liam Robinson [the leader of Liverpool City Council] can pull this off. You know, I think that that this could be a real turning point. But for our elected members. We'll wait and see, hey? We've been here before.

In March 2024, the government inspectors began to leave their roles with Liverpool City Council after sufficient improvements had been seen in the way the council was operating. An independent board would support the transition the council is continuing to work through, up to March 2025 (Coleman, 2024). This episode prompted many in the city to call for a new leadership culture where people live the values they espouse. This included a commitment to the different sectors in the city becoming more integrated, and also integration taking place with other places across Liverpool City Region, as well as other cities in the northwest of England. Respondents noted that there should be an emphasis on power sharing, driven by lived values symbolized by the recurring and somewhat paradoxical phrase, 'We need to learn to do ourselves out of a job.' There was a call for anchor institutions to facilitate this hopeful and emancipatory movement, while promoting transparency and accountability. What should follow is freedom from excessive bureaucracy, enabling people to work together, share skills and knowledge across generations. The impact of this should be a reduction in service-user numbers, an increase in food security, and an increase in the quality of mental health and well-being. If this can be realized, then individuals will have the capacity to consider their own futures, what it means to them to proposer, and what it looks like for them to get there, while contributing to the health and wealth of the city. One respondent noted that by eradicating poverty, there will also be personal and civic transformation in the city.

Following the initial connection with an LCVS board member in mid-2022, the vision and strategy for the eradication of poverty in the city was delivered to LCVS and its members in October 2023. Two notable recommendations beyond the different areas discussed above were: (1) the review of fundraising strategy across the city – in early 2024 this began through a consultation to cocreate grant-making processes in the city; 2) the establishment of a volunteering hub in the city at LCVS HQ, and in the region, which lobbies for changes to volunteering rules for those receiving benefits – a new hub opened in early 2024. The scope is there for responding in further ways that bring hope in the face of grinding poverty and support and nurture the conditions for civic renewal and a new culture of leadership. For this vision to be realized, it will need to become a city-wide story of change adopted by transformational leadership from everywhere.

Global collaborative leadership

In November 2022, I issued a publication through the RSA Comment Blog. My piece told the story of the emergence of Spaces of Hope and set out some ideas around leadership. One of the respondents was an advisor from the European Innovation Council who was developing a collaborative vision for global leadership, based on 20 years reflecting on the different things that might contribute to leadership practice. Through a series of three gatherings, we worked together to use Spaces of Hope as a means of curating further understandings of leadership practice. Where previous gatherings were oriented to storytelling, cultural change and local action, this gathering was focused on ideation and developing a global collaborative leadership approach:

... behaving as one responsible humankind, acting when we feel the need. In principle, all those that want to do the work that needs to be done are welcome, no matter what they think. What is important is the freedom to love, a willingness to speak truth to power to challenge the status quo. And when each of us aligns our individual power with the collective one, we can perform miracles ... the results of what genuine love can deliver, putting back the well-being of all at the centre of the system.

Leaders involved in this ideation process were from different countries and professions including policy-makers from the EU institutions in Brussels, a tech entrepreneur from Toulouse in France, a business consultant from the Austrian Alps, an education advisor from Pakistan, a consultant from Portugal, and from numerous cities in the UK, including a retired civil servant from Germany living in Northumberland, a content creator and social entrepreneur from Manchester, an academic from Liverpool and a senior policy advisor from London.

The first dialogue focused on ourselves. There was agreement that this was an existential exercise as we are on a journey. We have identities that are adaptive and context dependent. This is opposed to a view put forward belligerently by one senior policy-maker and participant, that the idea of changing identities was just symptomatic of schizophrenia. Examples of identities mentioned were maker, doer, adventurer, Anglican, academic, journeyman, son, fellow. Our dialogue brought a deep sense of self into close proximity with others. Who we are is formed inwardly and shaped outwardly, but, in that, there is a risk involved. That risk was based on the fact that if we do not have self-respect, then others will not respect us either. There was a sense that some people will try to overpower and control other people to get what they want. So the caution was made that we must have a clear sense of who we are so that we can both fulfil our role as a leader and be wise to and guard against the coercive influence of others. This was characterized by the phrase, 'We want your talent but we don't want you.' To respond well to this, it was suggested that we look at the details of things, the origins, roots or etymologies. For example, the idea of sacrificial or servant leadership might not be reciprocated and can be reduced either to a transaction or to us becoming a slave to the desires of others. One delegate said:

In terms of etymology – service is linked to servitude and slavery so it is not a word people like – service is associated with work and people are paid for services – distinct from volunteering, which is a choice and something that people opt into.

So the motivations that leaders draw on matter and shape service. Service in turn might be seen as a concept that is adaptive and pragmatic and expressed differently at different times. The sense in the dialogue was that as people we first have to look after ourselves and our basic needs, but then consider who or what we are faithful to. One respondent summarized, 'We must find the object of our love and go from there.'

Following these gatherings, the Global Collaborative Leadership journey continued on and in 2024 the Global Collaboration Institute launched, taking forward with it the ideas for leadership we had worked on, and in turn their sense of transformational leadership is shared here.

The Gramsci Society

A final set of dialogue gatherings that emerged from the RSA fellowship was with the Gramsci Society. This followed my RSA Comment Blog in 2022, where synergies between my discussion of leadership and that of Antonio Gramsci were identified. In Chapter 6, I give an account of who Gramsci was and some of his key ideas. I was invited to share Spaces of Hope with the Gramsci Society via Zoom to establish what if any conceptual resonances there might be between Spaces of Hope and the thought leadership of Antonio Gramsci. These dialogues opened up a fresh frontier that I had not explored before, within political theory. One respondent critiqued Spaces of Hope as follows: 'What you appear to have made is the socio-psychological cure for combatting the fascist movement that the system is imposing on us. What you have done, putting freedom and hope at the centre of it, is so important.'

Another, addressing the applicability of our dialogue to social movements they had knowledge of, said:

> You seem to have gathered a structure and a way of finding meaning and it reminds me of a friend who spent time in Guatemala with guerrilla insurgencies ... don't get them around the campfire and start reading the Communist Manifesto [he said], but do start speaking bitterness and what they have been through and the consciousness begins to raise ... Also, there is the Women's Movement in China, 'Half of China' they're called. When the men in the village were treating their wives poorly, the movement would mobilise and visit the

husbands and ask them to stop 'otherwise half of China will be on the doorstep'.

The dialogue turned to more explicitly Gramscian ideas with one respondent querying whether I had thought about party-building as a way of applying Spaces of Hope. From the accounts in Chapters 3 and 4 you will see that while I had thought about forms of organization, I hadn't thought about party-building in an explicitly political sense. This question related to Gramsci's theory of the modern prince:

> Gramsci was trying to find ways to build an effective party that was democratic and organic and vital, and solved the kind of problems you are talking about. Gramsci was attacked for wanting a party of school teachers, whereas others wanted a party of people who could carry out orders. Anyway, my question is, do you ever think of yourself as party-building, building the revolutionary instrument we need to change the world order?

There were many teachers in the gathering,[8] and there was consensus from them that there is very little space for disruptive or divergent thinking akin to what I was talking about. They queried whether this was something I had considered also, including whether Spaces of Hope could be used in the classroom? These questions might point to new horizons for the movement. The dialogue was incredibly rich and spoke to the opportunities that could come from conversing with Gramscian theory. We met again in summer 2023. I had convened multiple gatherings from those described in this chapter and shared them with the group. These included within educational settings at Liverpool Hope, although not in a taught context, with the Dialogue Society, and as part of a movement for change to eradicate poverty in the city in Liverpool. This time new elements of the dialogue with Gramsci's work came through. One person who had attended both sessions reflected:

> In the first session it felt hopeful in an organic way, and this time you have given us something about how things are working on the ground suggesting that sometimes hope differs depending on the realities we face in activating or eliciting hope in physical spaces.

A senior local authority officer from York was on the call and they queried how the work I am talking about might work in response to the negative externalities that shape people's lives. 'People may feel empowered to take control of their lives, but there are externalities that mean what we want to do, for example eradicating poverty, make that almost impossible. What do we do about that?' There was a recognition of time and the need for time to be respected. For example, eradicating poverty quickly won't happen. But what can be done is empowering people with a sense of purpose, and recognizing that different people are on the same side of these broader concerns and crises. Opening up the spaces of that kind is a necessary starting point, but not the whole story. These are both small spaces, 15–20 people, and also larger gatherings, city-wide gatherings, national gatherings, international gatherings, so that gatherings at difference scales can interrelate.

Another highlighted the synergy with what I was talking about taking place within the mill town they lived in outside Pittsburgh in the USA. This example came from two people from Australia who came and lived in the town for a while. They were inspired by the work of the Church Army, which the respondent described as a liberation movement within the Anglican Church. They noted that the Church Army as they understood it did not base their faith in cathedrals, but found it in the slums of London. Their example was a cafe set up in the Mill Town in Pittsburgh which was supported by a number of local partners including churches. The cafe was called Uncommon Grounds and they held an open space and a safe space for dialogue, including open-mic nights for rappers, hillbillies and anyone else that wanted to come. This grew to a bookshop and a community garden and began to spread hope in a city of despair that had been destroyed by the steel mills closing years before. The cafe planted seeds of hope that opened up into other things. The respondent noted the value of the outsider coming in with a different perspective. One person said:

> This is a Gramscian approach, captured in the role of the 'organic intellectual', which invests autonomy and power to improve the agency of others in a 'place responsive' way. This can be especially important in a city where a diversity of people does not always mean integration or interaction in ways that you would hope would happen when there are so many. This resonates with your idea of 'freedom for others'.

This sense was developed in terms of how culture in a place is stored and developed. There was a recognition of formal and informal education, of lifelong learning, speaking to the culture of the place, and thus the hegemonic forces at work within education speaking to the ways in which culture is either being opened up or limited in society at large. A function of large networks and organizations that was highlighted as a negative influence was the 'long arm affect', that is, where it was clear that decision-making was not being taken locally and decisions in that place were being directly influenced by those outside it who were not willing to be present and available; this was disempowering and structurally problematic. This sense of the relationship between individual contributions, cultural relations and structural concerns mediated within and by institutions is where we concluded.

Radical hope in an election year?

In April 2024, the gatherings from the previous two years were brought together into a roundtable dialogue, which sought both to reflect on emerging matters of concern for the movement, emerging practice from the movement, and also to consider the movement in a context of elections taking place in the UK and in 82 other nations around the world in 2024. The gathering took place at Liverpool Hope University and we were grateful to Vice-Chancellor Professor Clare Ozanne for her support of this event. In addition to my ongoing association with Hope, this roundtable saw the return of former Rector, Professor Simon Lee, and former head of theology and now Dean of Virginia Theological Seminary, Professor Ian Markham, who in 2023 published *Serendipity of Hope*. The edited volume reflected on experiences from Liverpool Hope University from the roots of the university 25 years ago and the relevance of those agendas for today. The gathering sought to address two questions: (1) What is Radical Hope? and (2) Where might Radical Hope come from?

Strategic leaders from the region gathered to explore answers to these questions. In addition to myself, Canon Dr Said and Professor Lee from Liverpool Hope University and the William Temple Foundation, it was a privilege to gather with Professor Markham; Bishop John Arnold from the Catholic Diocese of Salford and lead for the environment in the Catholic House of Bishops in England and Wales; the Revd Canon Grace Thomas, Diocesan Environmental Officer for the Diocese of Manchester and Canon Missioner for Manchester Cathedral; Professor Guy Cuthbertson, Head of Humanities at Liverpool Hope University; the Revd Professor Steven Shakespeare, Professor of Continental Philosophy at Liverpool Hope University; the Revd Julia Pratt, Anglican Chaplain at Liverpool Hope University; Professor Peter McGrail, head of Theology at Liverpool Hope University; Dr Natalija Atas, convenor of the Poverty Research and Advocacy Network (PRAN) in the northwest of England; Professor Edward Abbott-Halpin, Emeritus Professor at the University of the Highlands and Islands; and Dr Hirpo Kumbi, Entrepreneur and Director of Operations for the Xpertis College.

The gathering was opened by Lee, who set out three conceptions of hope:

1 'Running streams of hope', inspired by the quote by Cardinal Suenens, 'To hope is not to dream but to turn dreams into reality', which encouraged a more grounded and determined sense of hope within political, national and institutional life.
2 'Ripples of hope', inspired by the words of Robert F. Kennedy speaking in South Africa during the apartheid era:

> each time [you] stand up for an ideal or act to improve the lot of others, or strike out against injustice, [you] send forth a tiny ripple of hope, and crossing each other from a million different centers of energy and daring, those ripples build a current that can sweep down the mightiest wall of oppression and resistance.

3 'Deep-freezing hope', which took inspiration from Chief Plenty Coups of the Crow People in America, who set down his headdress and coup stick, the symbols of his leadership in his culture, to mark the end of an era in the life of his people, while holding on to the dream they represented for future generations to take up should they wish. This account is given in Jonathan Lear's *Radical Hope: Ethics in the Face of Cultural Devastation* (Lear, 2008). The prophetic challenge in this final conception of hope was for one generation to set down their pursuit of their dream, so that a new generation might pick up the task in a manner that is suitable for it and for them.

We then turned to themes set out in Chapters 1–6 of this book, which I used to locate the roundtable within discussions of the Temple Tradition after Temple, the emergence of radical democratic movements and different forms of leadership that address shared matters of concern in the public square. These concerns included ecology and the climate crisis, poverty and inequality, the role of education, institutional change and grass-roots politics. Bishop John Arnold set out sources of encouragement and hope in terms of global leadership that seeks to address the climate crisis, including Pope Francis through his encyclicals *Laudato Si'* and *Laudate Deum*, the activism of Greta Thunberg, King Charles and

David Attenborough, and the recent publication of an Islamic document called *Al-Mizan: A Covenant for the Earth*, which is a teaching document drawn up by a broad spectrum of Islamic scholars, with language and prayers closely aligned to *Laudato Si'* (Arnold, 2024, p. 45). Bishop John also advocated for the role of new generations of people in the fight for our planet:

> I am so impressed by the concern being shown particularly by young people as they recognise the impact that our carelessness will have upon their lives and future generations. At our Laudato Si' Centre, at Wardley Hall ... we try always to educate the young without employing any sense of fear about the future but rather a celebration of Nature and God's creation. Their enthusiasm is so encouraging. A recent survey of 16–25-year-olds suggests that 75% are either 'very worried' or 'frightened' by climate change. (Arnold, 2024, p. 44)

Professor Shakespeare considered the dialogue from the perspective of hyper-local ecologies and our relationship with all of God's creation, which he characterized as the 'more than human'. For his presentation, Professor Shakespeare walked 450 steps from his front door and examined the pavement to see what was growing in his vicinity. His approach was to locate his philosophy literally in the lived and grounded rather than up in the air. He noticed many plants growing in urban spaces which each told their own stories of how they got there and what they stood for and how understandings of this had changed over time:

> By the side of the pavement, in the wall, in the cracks ... they were: shepherd's purse, wood avens, bitter cress, dandelion, selfheal, herb robert, bellflower, viper's bugloss, foxglove, three-cornered leek, mosses and lichens ... Herb Robert, for instance – a type of geranium – is associated with the St Robert who was an 11th century herbalist and founder of the Cistercians. But that association may not be wholly correct; in any case its name has evolved. Because of the smell of burning rubber it gives off when crushed, it is known as Stinking Bob ... What I saw then was the persistence and opportunism of plant life. In an urban space, the will of nature was being expressed in and through and despite concrete and stone ... I saw the intertwining of plants with folklore, medicine and human history. Nature and culture rubbed up against one another. I also saw the effects of human classification and intervention. Along one wall, miner's lettuce grew in profusion. This is an edible plant native to America, eaten by miners in the Californian

gold rush in order to stave off scurvy. Last year, it was green and lush. When I did my walk this year, it was limp and dying, because someone from the council had been round the streets spraying them with weed-killer. (Shakespeare, 2024, pp. 39–40)

The persistence of things that grow, and the creative ways in which they do so and the stories they tell, was offered as a sign of hope. They prompt 'small revolutions', as it was put by Shakespeare, when we give our attention to them; we encounter otherness. The grounded approach to philosophy encouraged us to reorient ourselves to the world around us: 'I think our habits of action and perception and valuing need to be reoriented. In Christian terms, we need to repent: to turn and face a different direction, with a different mindset, a different openness, a different spirit' (Shakespeare, 2024, pp. 37–8).

This sense of reorientation was present in the paper from Canon Thomas too. Thomas spoke of her own experience of living in poverty as a young mother as a basis for looking differently at the world, and looking differently at where we might find hope. This is an experience that Thomas has brought to the fore in her own strategic leadership in the region. She reflected:

As Conde-Frazier points out, policies based on research that has looked on from afar, rather than from lived experience, tend to be policies that further oppression (Conde-Frazier, 2006, 325). The real learning arises when knowledge constructed through the lived experience of people directly affected by the situations the policies seek to address is valorised. Such knowledge is found when people living in these situations are acknowledged as experts in their field, and where their stories are listened to. (Thomas, 2024, p. 49)

The sources of knowledge and wisdom within the spaces highlighted by Thomas was given nuance and developed by Professor Markham, who brought an international and educationalist perspective to the roundtable. He questioned how movements of social reform are characterized and how they might aid movement on from intractable lived experiences. Markham began with three possible avenues: charity as demonstrated by William Booth and the Salvation Army, revolution advocated for by Karl Marx, and education demonstrated by F. D. Maurice. Markham took education forward and set out three challenges faced in education today: the utilitarian approach to learning and the decline of the humanities; the emergence of culture wars; and the question of the extent students feel 'safe' on campuses that host things with which they disagree. Markham offered three 'untruths' that underpinned these challenges:

1 The Untruth of Fragility: what doesn't kill you makes you weaker.
2 The Untruth of Emotional Reasoning: always trust your feelings.
3 The Untruth of Us versus Them: life is a battle between good and evil people. (Lukianoff and Haidt, 2018).

With these untruths in mind, Markham reflected:

> People are made stronger by encountering different opinions (even deeply offensive ones); people should not assume that if they 'feel' something is wrong or offensive, then it is; and people must not allow the complexity of human lives to be reduced to good and evil … Visiting F. D. Maurice might be a good place to start. Education is part of the solution to the ills of society; however, for Maurice this was within an ideological frame. Institutions need a clarity of focus. Key themes must be the quest for truth, the need for disciplines to be in conversation, creating persons of virtue, the need for a legitimate pluralism of viewpoint to be celebrated, and a recognition that we all live within a world view … a diversity of ideological frameworks for educational institution is good. So, let us have Catholic, Anglican, Buddhist, Muslim, Jewish, and, yes, secular … One strength we enjoy is that in the end the three options of mid-nineteenth-century London remain the main contenders for social change. Given the choice between charity, education and revolution, I still think the majority of people would choose education. (Markham, 2024)

The Revd Julia Pratt addressed these different threads through reflections on her experience as a university chaplain and as a person of mixed heritage from Liverpool. She called on institutions to do more to promote the diversity of world views and heritages that make up the contexts they operate within and to fulfil the role of nurturing students across the whole time that they are with institutions. It was noted that this begins with recruitment and before attendance at the university itself. Pratt noted:

> One of the things I put forward to our recruitment team was the need to get thinking about the lack of young people of minority ethnic backgrounds from Liverpool coming to this university. Perhaps one way

forward is to go out to more of our schools and colleges ... and perhaps to take alumni with them, some of our minority ethnic alumni. I think too we need to encourage all our students ... to aspire to be the best they possibly can ... it just astounds me, when speaking to some third-year students now who are about to finish their studies, that when I ask them about what they are going to do after their studies, I often get the response, 'I don't know'. (Pratt, 2024, p. 69)

Others listened from the margins of the day and offered their perspectives as the day went on, or indeed after, through an edited volume that followed the gathering. Professor Peter McGrail reflected on the day his sense of hope:

Hope is extremely practical, and that has come through very clearly from the various things that we've heard, starting off with, of course, the tiny ripple, but it actually costs. That's a thing that's come through from several of the papers this afternoon, that hope isn't just not a weak word, it's a very costly word. The stories that we've heard today which have been so powerful, of the Crow people of North America, Chief Plenty Coups, that sense of laying down. Matthew's example drawing from Deleuze. I think that those two things are pretty well saying the same thing: that to transition through progressively from one thing to another, each taking up is always at the cost of something being laid down, even if the accumulation of the laying down and the taking up is one which moves you forward. (McGrail, 2024, p. 71)

The significance of the different spaces of the Spaces of Hope movement were highlighted too. Simon Lee highlighted that these spaces across different disciplines and diverse communities are much needed. Lee related these spaces back to the Temple Tradition and the kind of education he and it supported:

In my time here, drawing on the shape of the Metropolitan Cathedral where we held graduations in alternate years, we talked of Hope's mission as being 'education in the round'. By this we meant education of the whole person, in mind, body and spirit. That is also what William Temple and his friends stood for, and what we need in this year of elections and beyond. Thank you to those who have listened, as well as to those who have spoken, at this roundtable. It is a radical act of hope in itself to celebrate a rounded education, to call for a rounded politics and to listen intently to one another around a roundtable. (Lee, 2024, p. 78)

The gathering offered foundations for the future in terms of how to open up spaces that can hear from and speak into local contexts. This gathering was rooted in the north-west of England. Understandably, this brought to the fore considerations that were pertinent to the north-west. This was not a limitation, but a means contextualizing what took place and how it might be taken forward. Professor Abbott-Halpin reflected on this point:

> In the North West, in a church-founded university, it was natural that there would be a focus on faith and education. Yet global themes of poverty, war and peace, and of the environmental crisis, were also to the fore. William Temple himself lived through times of international conflict, through World War One, which was regarded as 'a war to end all wars', and through much of World War Two. He witnessed great social deprivation, and with his friends and colleagues, William Beveridge and R. H. Tawney, sought to address the societal issues with radical responses that originated in his faith. Listening to the speakers, raising my own questions from around the table, and then in the 'margins' during brief breaks talking with them, it was possible to discern the passion for justice. It was possible to see the ripples of radical hope emanating from the work of William Temple, and still now obvious in the work of the William Temple Foundation: the values evident in each presentation in addressing challenges and seeking to deliver hope, justice and fairness, through faith.

A colleague from the William Temple Foundation, who was not involved in the gathering, noted that reports from it conjured the image of a 'micro-Malvern' (see Barber-Rowell, 2024) invoking the gathering Temple held in 1941. This sense of micro-scale also highlighted the importance of a social movement approach which opens up and synthesizes dialogue across multiple spaces and scales, or micro-Malverns, or micro-publics, which can collectively advocate for hope, justice and bring about citizen-led change.

In this chapter I have set out accounts of gatherings that have taken place within the emerging Spaces of Hope social movement. I began the chapter by reminding us of the accelerating and intensifying contexts of crisis which have increased the urgency of a new paradigm of faith-based organization and new forms of leadership in the postsecular public square. The form this is taking is a new/networked social movement, which is able to draw together otherwise disparate gatherings across local, regional, national and international contexts which have evidenced and tested Spaces of Hope as a common paradigm and methodology to offer a synthesis of, in this case, approaches to transformational leadership. I concluded the chapter with reflections on what this movement means for leadership within contexts of radical democracy and change. What this chapter has shown is that as well as synthesizing hope for the future that emerges out of liminal spaces of dialogue in transition, Spaces of Hope can open up dialogue with different disciplines, social concerns, world views and interdisciplinary interlocutors to enrich the paradigm itself. This was highlighted by the dialogues with the Gramsci Society. In Chapter 6 I will turn to Gramsci's political theory to develop transformational leadership further.

Notes

1 This quote is actually attributed to Dominic Cummings, Special Advisor to Prime Minister Boris Johnson during the pandemic.

2 A point that is tangential to this discussion of new social movements is offered by Chesters and Welsh (2011). They note that the effect of new movements is to bring about empirical and theoretical modifications in how the academy thinks about such movements (p. 13). One wonders about the relevance of the Spaces of Hope movement to this point. In Chapters 3 and 4 I have set out the emergence of Spaces of Hope as an expression of the postsecular, theorized by Jürgen Habermas. Cloke et al. (2019) note that social movements are a trajectory for the postsecular. If the Spaces of Hope movement is cocreating postsecular spaces and also has the means to map and learn from them then this is a potentially powerful tool relating to the different disciplines Spaces of Hope relates to, and a movement that can develop with respect to anthropology, theology and religious studies, radical democratic movements mediated through hybrid spaces, the role and understanding of different world views in the public sphere, leadership practice across these different disciplines, the formation of social policy, and the understanding of faith-based organizations.

3 My granny attended Notre Dame in the 1960s and recalled it to me on numerous occasions. Granny's heritage was in Methodist Chapel in Swansea. My grandad was raised in the Church in Wales in Buckley. This meant Granny had experience of theological differences, before then being welcomed by the Catholic sisters who ran Notre Dame. I was told numerous times of the warmth of the welcome received at Notre Dame and the formative nature of the time Granny had there. She became a religious education teacher and later my mum also became a religious education and philosophy teacher.

4 This project and the retrospective it offered began in 2019, 25 years after Lee left Hope. However, the pandemic meant that the final launch of the book took place at Lambeth Palace in 2023 and then again in April 2024 at Liverpool Hope University.

5 There were two avenues that brought me to Hope. The first was a connection with Dr Yazid Said at the William Temple Foundation. He is a senior lecturer in Islamic Studies at Hope and supported me as I sought to consolidate a place for

postdoctoral research. The second was via Vice Chancellor Professor Pillay FRSA, who, following my gathering with the Royal Society for Arts, manufactures and commerce in Liverpool, spoke with me about ways that my work might be supported at Hope and in the city.

6 One of those gathered was on the board of Liverpool Charity and Voluntary Services (LCVS), who developed this initial dialogue with me and also encouraged me to consider whether there were other RSA Fellows in academia in the city that could join us. I looked into this and found Professor Pillay, Vice Chancellor of Liverpool Hope, whom I approached in order to establish the network of gatherings at Liverpool Hope University that I discussed in the last section.

7 The legacy of Marmot's work is centred on eight principles or policy areas which might be seen as a modern-day equivalent to those set out by William Temple. Temple himself saw his middle axioms as indicative and not prescriptive and so may not have invited the comparison I am making. This is for others to discuss. Marmot's principles were: (1) give every child the best start in life; (2) enable all children, young people and adults to maximize their capabilities and have control over their lives; (3) create fair employment and good work for all; (4) ensure a healthy standard of living for all; (5) create and develop healthy and sustainable places and communities; (6) strengthen the role and impact of ill-health prevention; (7) tackle racism, discrimination and their outcomes; (8) pursue environmental sustainability and health equity together.

8 One may also notice from my comments in the margins that teaching is in the roots of my own heritage, along with a passion for organizing, leadership, different world views and shared values. I am confident I have found affinity with Gramsci and the traditional and organic intellectuals who draw on his work.

6

Gramsci's Intellectuals

In this chapter, I am going to set out Gramsci's theory of the intellectuals. In Chapter 2, I considered the question of leadership within the work of William Temple, recognizing its historical significance and its contemporary limitations. In Chapter 3, I began to explore a new basis for leadership in transition, emerging from liminal spaces. In Chapter 4, I offered a set of characteristics for transformational leadership, drawn from ethnographic data in South Manchester. And in Chapter 5, I have set out the gatherings that have taken place post-pandemic where a movement of hope and transformational leadership has been emerging. Here I will develop this model of leadership further by setting it in dialogue with Gramscian political theory and Gramsci's theory of the intellectuals. In the last chapter, a number of ideas emerged from Gramsci's work, mediated through dialogues with the Gramsci Society. These included hegemony, the modern prince, Gramsci's views on education and his theory of the intellectuals. The data from the gatherings speaks to some of the basics of these theories and the potential relationships they have with Spaces of Hope. However, it is Gramsci's theories of the intellectuals that I want to pick up as the starting point. Gramsci's theory of the intellectuals will help to flesh out understanding of the positionality of transformational leaders. To begin, though, I will set out who Gramsci was and where his work emerged from.

Antonio Gramsci

Antonio Gramsci was an Italian Marxist who lived from 1891 to 1937. He was born in Sardinia into relative poverty. He became a journalist and a political leader during the period of the First World War, as he was not fit for military service. During this period he was an organizer within the Turin Factory Movement, a founding member of the Italian Communist Party and founder of L'Ordine Nuovo (The New Order), which offered 'a weekly review of socialist culture' in Italy (Gramsci,

1921). This gave an early indication of the changing thought and political inclination of Gramsci, which included seeking to mobilize factory council gatherings (of which there were 20) in Turin (the most industrialized city in Italy) as a movement to bring about a revolutionary party. Gramsci's approach on the face of it was both emancipatory and highly structured. He recognized what Joll (1977) characterizes as classic concerns of movement building, 'reconciling freedom and authority, spontaneity and discipline' (Joll, 1977, p. 39). Gramsci's rationale for working with the factory councils was interesting too. An assumption was that if the factory councils were on board, then all who worked in the factories would be also. This included those who unionized, those who did not, members of the Socialist Party and those who held other political beliefs (Joll, 1977, pp. 40–42). This desire for unity was set in the context of what Gramsci saw as the struggle to come:

> The present phase of the class struggle in Italy is the phase that precedes either the conquest of power by the revolutionary proletariat for the transition to new modes of distribution ... or a tremendous reaction on the part of the governing class ... they will try inexorably to shatter the organism of political struggle of the working class. (Gramsci, 1920, p. 117)

Gramsci was right about both the timing and the action that was to be taken against the factory councils in 1920. During this period Gramsci was alienated from many in Turin, but it is noteworthy that while clear eyed about the context of his work with the factory councils, he did not see that work as the end in itself. Gramsci saw the value of working with the factory councils as a stepping stone within a wider project: 'The establishment of the councils is only valuable if it is conceived as the beginning of a revolutionary process. The exercise of control (in the factories) has a significance only if it is a stage in this process' (Gramsci, 1920, p. 249).

So Gramsci was willing to commit to both the struggle of the process in the short term and the alienation that followed, because of his longer-term vision and commitment to revolution. His determination during this period meant that he found himself being recognized by Lenin for wrestling with some of the fundamental problems blighting the Socialist Party at the time. Nonetheless, his different thinking and his generalist perspective alienated existing union and party leaders and was a catalyst for a split in the Socialist Party in Italy, and the formation of the Communist Party in 1921 (Joll, 1977, pp. 44–5). Gramsci's thinking during this period set a foundation for what was to come. As leader of the Communist Party, Gramsci was elected to the Italian parliament in 1924, but when Benito Mussolini came to power Gramsci was arrested and imprisoned for his opposition to the Fascist regime. It is from prison that Gramsci wrote what have become known as his *Prison Notebooks*, which are the source of the Gramscian tradition of political theory.

Antonio Gramsci: Selections from the Prison Notebooks was edited and translated by Hoare and Smith (Gramsci, 1971) from collections of unpublished manuscripts that were recovered after Gramsci died, and published between 1948 and 1951 in Italian by Turin publisher Einaudi. This is taken as a foundational text for accessing Gramsci's work in English. *Antonio Gramsci: The Modern Prince and other Writings*, compiled by Louis Marks in 1957, is also recognized, including by Hoare and Smith. These details are relevant for two reasons: first, because of the fragmented nature of the notebooks and, second, because of his intentions for them. He was after all writing from prison and he died before many of the ideas within them were brought together in a comprehensive manner (Gramsci, 1971, p. x). Gramsci was extremely well read. He wrote on a breadth of topics, including philosophy, history, politics and sociology. This can be seen both in the highly original approach to Marxism that Gramsci took – this is evidenced by his emphasis on politics and political action, as opposed to the emphasis on social theory or economics, which is found in historical Marxism – and also in the complex and incomplete nature of a lot of his work (see Gramsci, 1971).

Gramsci's cell

In spite of Gramsci's resilience, his time in prison did take a substantial toll. It was the reason for his premature death at the age of 46 as it exacerbated his pre-existing health issues. The fact that Gramsci was writing from prison was also the reason why it took decades for Gramsci's work to emerge as a distinct resource, available to political theory. In the decade after his death, his work was known only to his comrades in the Italian Communist Party, where it appears to have influenced elders that followed him (Joll, 1977). So while Gramsci's name was known, his work was not known until well after the Second World War. In terms of *how* Gramsci worked, Hoare and Smith (Gramsci, 1971, p. x) and a later volume by James Joll (1977, p. 12) both note that Gramsci struggled with study for its own sake. In one of his letters,

Gramsci wrote, 'Thinking disinterestedly of study for its own sake are difficult for me ... I do not like throwing stones in the dark, I like to have a concrete interlocutor or adversary.'

With this in mind, the isolation of a prison cell, the scarcity of books and resources with which to interact, and his fluctuating health make the existence of the prison notebooks all the more remarkable. Gramsci's experience of his cell was something he reflected on for himself. He describes a special kind of boredom, not as a sense of being idle, but as a result of enforced isolation (Joll, 1977). A letter to his mother in 1929 highlights this point:

> Boredom is my worst enemy, although I read or write all day long; it's a special kind of boredom, which doesn't spring from idleness ... But from the lack of contact with the outside world. I don't know whether you've read the lives of Saints, and hermits: they were tormented by the special boredom, which they called the 'noonday devil' because, towards midday, they were seized ... by a longing for a change, to return to the world, to see people. (Gramsci, 1973, p. 153)

The psychology of his cell is something that Gramsci wrestled with. In a letter to his sister-in-law, with whom he corresponded from prison, he reflected that rather than referring to a 'psychoanalytic cure', implying access to external resources or support (and it is reasonable to assume he is speaking of himself here), 'I believe, therefore, that a person of culture, an active element in society, is, and must be his own best psychoanalyst.' This sense is reinforced later, reflecting on, one can reasonably assume, the conditions he was facing:

> One can arrive at a certain serenity, even in the clash of the most absurd contradictions and under the pressure of the most implacable necessity. But one can only reach it if one succeeds in thinking 'historically', dialectically, and identifying one's own task with intellectual dispassionateness ... in this sense ... one can, and therefore one must be one's own doctor. (Gramsci, 1965, p. 584)

This speaks to Gramsci's resilience, his reflexivity and his commitment to developing his work to the extent that he did. His outlook was one that was critically engaged with the self in respect to the rest of the world. This point is addressed in his prison notebooks:

I mean that one must conceive of man as a series of active relationships (a process) in which individuality, though perhaps the most important, is not, however, the only element to be taken into account. The humanity which is reflected in each individuality is composed of various elements: 1) the individual; 2) other men; 3) the natural world. (Gramsci, 1971, p. 352).

As I will go on to explain, each individual and the way that they make sense of their environment, enables them to understand how they might contribute to a common movement both within their social group and across civil society. With this in mind, it will not be a surprise as I continue, that Gramsci's theory of the intellectuals was a key focus for him and essential starting point for engaging with his political theory. Smith and Hoare (Gramsci, 1971) identify the intellectuals project as a focus for Gramsci in 1927 at the outset of his time in prison. This emphasis is then maintained, as can be seen in a 1931 letter to his sister-in-law, which makes clear Gramsci's continuing aspirations for his intellectuals project:

> My study of the intellectuals is a vast project ... I greatly extend the notion of intellectuals, beyond the current meaning of the word, which refers chiefly to great intellectuals. This study also leads me to certain determinations of the state. Usually this is understood as political society (i.e. the dictatorship of coercive apparatus, to bring the mass of the people into conformity with the type of production, and economy, dominant at any given moment). And not as an equilibrium between political society and civil society (i.e. the hegemony of a social group over the entire national society, exercised through the so-called private organisations, such as the church, trade unions, the schools, et cetera). Civil society is precisely the special field of action of the intellectuals. (Gramsci, 1967, p. 481)

The nature of Gramsci's work means that his theory of the intellectuals was never completed. However, it does offer a recognizable and original foundation for thinking about leadership within movements. His theory is drawn from across *Prison Notebooks* and it exists in what Hoare and Sperber (2016) characterize as an 'exploratory' form. Nonetheless, this exploration is very much in the spirit of Gramsci's work itself, which offers conceptual continuity even if there are inevitable limits to the meaning available from Gramsci's writing.

Gramsci's intellectuals

The first thing to address is terms of reference. Gramsci referred to intellectuals as the people who shaped society. These people are located within different strata or social groupings in society and it is the role of these people to exert hegemony, by means of either consent from or control over others. Gramsci offers two basic forms of intellectual: the 'traditional intellectual' and the 'organic intellectual'. The traditional intellectual is the philosophical and political leader who uses hegemony to supply the system of beliefs, accepted by ordinary people, so that they do not question the actions of their rulers. Examples given of these traditional forms include philosophers, 'ecclesiastics' or clergy, scientists and aristocrats. The organic intellectual is every person who demonstrates in different ways their capacity for different forms of intellectual activity. What appears to be the case from Gramsci's writing, although it is not explicit, is that as one form of intellectual becomes established and transcends its original starting position, it can become the other form. An example of this is the clergy, who originally functioned as bounded to a particular class, that is, as an organic intellectual, but as time went on they established a position of independence from the dominant social group, thereby becoming a traditional intellectual (Gramsci, 1971, p. 7). It is the introduction of a second category that opens up the potential for leadership to come from somewhere other than those in traditionally recognized seats of power who orate and influence. Gramsci offers us a sense of what this shift looks like:

> The mood of being of the new intellectuals can no longer consist in eloquence, which is an exterior and momentary mover of feelings and passions, but in active participation in practical life, as constructor, organizer, 'permanent persuader', and not just a simple orator. (Gramsci, 1971, p. 10)

By offering two conceptions of the intellectual, Gramsci is identifying the significance of interconnectedness and social relations between people and their environments, in the formation of what he refers to as social blocks, and is opening up a new way of conceiving of each of these, with new implications:

> Intellectuals, who are conscious of being linked organically to a national popular mass ... to struggle against... the false heroisms and pseudo aristocracies stimulates the formation of homogenous, compact, social

blocks, which will give birth to their own intellectuals, their own commandos, their own Vanguard, who in turn will react upon those blocks in order to develop them. (Gramsci, 1971, pp. 204–5)

Gramsci is careful to progress his definition of intellectuals across the two different categories he has begun with and across the multiple different social blocks that can be formed. What I mean by this is that he resists, and in fact cautions against, prioritization of one criterion, characteristic or skill set over another. He refers to the temptation to do this as a 'widespread methodological error' (Gramsci, 1971, p. 8). Instead, Gramsci recognizes the wide variety of different skills and experiences that people bring to their position as an intellectual and encourages us to consider them within the complex mix of social relations in which they are taking place. He notes, 'The worker, or the proletarian, for example, are not specifically characterised by their manual or skilled work, but by this work performed in certain conditions, and in certain social relations' (1971, p. 8).

To this end, Gramsci holds open the potential for all people to be intellectuals, while acknowledging that we do not all fulfil that function in society. Simple evidence of this is given by the example that each can fry an egg or sew on a button, but that doesn't mean that whoever does that is then a chef or a tailor (1971, p. 9). This potential is fleshed out further by the claim that the practical and intellectual skills that we each have potential for are interconnected. Gramsci notes:

> There is no human activity, from which all intellectual intervention can be excluded, Homo Faber cannot be separated from Homo Sapiens. Finally, every man, outside his own job, develops some intellectual activity; he is, in other words, a 'philosopher', an artist, a man of taste, he has a conception of the world, he has a conscious line of moral conduct, and so contributes towards maintaining or changing a conception of the world, that is, towards encouraging new modes of thought. (Gramsci, 1971, p. 9)

Gramsci's positioning of the intellectual as both traditional and organic and as practitioner and philosopher gets to the heart of his theory, such that it exists in the *Prison Notebooks*. Gramsci's argument is that each has the capacity to make sense of what they do and how they contribute for themselves and with respect to others, and draw on the resources they have to improve and develop themselves and the social relations that they are part of. This emphasis on individual action which then becomes part of a shared environment is how Gramsci personifies politics in his theory:

> Man does not enter into relations with the natural world just by himself being part of the natural world, but actively, by means of work and technique ... The real philosopher is, and cannot be other than, the politician, the active man who modifies the environment, understanding by environment the ensemble of relations which each of us enters to take part in. If one's individuality is the ensemble of these relations, to create one's personality means to acquire consciousness of them, and to modify one's own personality means to modify the ensemble of these relations. (1971, p. 352)

It is worth noting that Gramsci's framing of the relationship between individuals and social relations and wider environments is primary for him, compared to the relationship between individuals and the means of production within Marxism, for example. As someone who is considered to be a Marxist theorist, this is a notable departure by Gramsci from the priorities within Marx's work, framed as it is with respect to capital, the means of production and class struggle. To this end, Gramsci notes:

> The relationship between intellectuals in the world of production is not immediate, as is the case for fundamental social groups, and relates the intellectuals to two frames of reference; 1) their role in civil society, i.e. the environment that hosts expressions of initially private concerns and forms political action and 2) political society or the state [corresponding to] the exercise of hegemony or [alternatively] juridicial rule. (Gramsci, 1971, p. 124)

This is one of the main rationales for Gramsci's work to be positioned as a political theory as opposed to an economic or a social theory. This broad conception of all people as intellectuals, in Gramscian terms, is the basis for including his political theory in my argument.[1]

The broad approach taken by Gramsci applied to his views on education too. I have set out his theory of the intellectuals and their relationship with social relations. A point that is inferred but yet to be made explicitly is that education, what might be learned and where and how that takes place, is also an important part of Gramsci's thinking. Gramsci promoted a maximal approach to lifelong learning, which recognized social, civic and public organizations as legitimate spaces of education and learning, in addition to traditional and vocational school environments. Interestingly, Gramsci felt that access should be available to a diverse array of learning opportunities in a way that it may not have been:

> The tendency today is to abolish every type of schooling that is 'disinterested' (not serving immediate interests) or 'formative' – keeping at most only a small-scale version to serve a tiny elite of ladies and gentlemen who do not have to worry about assuring themselves of a future. (Gramsci, 1971, p. 27)

Gramsci felt that a broad education combined with vocational activities would support the development of new generations of intellectuals and their contributions to civil society. This would be derived from traditional school settings, but it would also take place in the public space and the institutions that shape it. Gramsci makes reference to deliberative bodies and the way in which they form bureaucracies using different forms of education: specialist or technical contributions that came from experts, and generalists or organic intellectuals engaging in deliberative or political matters. In his *Prison Notebooks* Gramsci notes:

> Undoubtedly in this kind of collective activity, each task produces new capacities and possibilities of work, since it creates ever more organic conditions of work: files, bibliographical digests, a library of basic specialised works, etc. Such activity requires an unyielding struggle against habits of dilettantism, of improvisation, of 'rhetorical' solutions or those proposed for effect. (1971, p. 29)

While brief, this provides a foundation for Gramsci's understanding of how intellectuals are educated. In order to move forward, I need to set out a nuanced view of how Gramsci's theory of the intellectuals relates to religion, and also the different resources that are used to make sense of our social relations. To do this I will turn to Gramsci and the church, before turning to his framing of philosophy and 'folklore' and their role in shaping civil society.

Gramsci and the church

Gramsci was writing in Italy in the early twentieth century. It was in a context where the church was a prominent national institution. As a result, the church, ecclesiastics (bishops and priests), and the Catholic and Calvinist (as Gramsci referred to them) expressions of the Christian faith were present and are subject to analysis in the *Prison Notebooks*. Hobsbawm notes that this is typical for a Marxist thinker, as they do not invent their ideas in the abstract but understand them within the historical and political contexts of their time (2012, p. 316). Gramsci's perception of the church was that it was involved in maintaining the rule of the ruling classes, while being separate from the state apparatus. This ability to maintain order utilized what Gramsci refers to as hegemony, that is, gaining consent from those it seeks to control, not just utilizing coercive force. In his critique of the role of the church, Gramsci notes that this order was achieved, to the extent it was, through the clear emphasis on doctrinal unity within the church, which served to hold together the entire social block:

> The strength of religions, and of the Catholic church in particular, has lain, and still lies, in the fact that they feel very strongly the need for the doctrinal unity of the whole mass of the faithful and strive to ensure that the higher intellectual stratum does not get separated from the lower. The Roman church has always been most vigorous in the struggle to prevent the 'official' formation of two religions, one for the 'intellectuals' and the other for the 'simple souls'. (Gramsci, 1971, p. 328)

But this is not to say that there were not splits between the two levels, the ecclesiastics and the simple souls, as Gramsci put it. And Gramsci's analysis of these splits speaks to the revolutionary nature of his theory of the intellectuals. His theory sets the traditional and organic forms together within the same framework and suggests a movement of organic intellectuals could transform the consciousness of society. However, his project offers this while also observing an alternative approach within the church:

> That the Church has to face up to a problem of the 'simple' means precisely that there has been a split in the community of the faithful. This split cannot be healed by raising the simple to the level of the intellectuals (the Church does not even envisage such a task, which is both ideologically and economically beyond its present capacities), but only by imposing an iron discipline on the intellectuals so that they do not exceed certain limits of differentiation and so render the split catastrophic and irreparable. (Gramsci, 1971, p. 331)

Historically this meant the establishment of religious orders, which were used to control these splits, and in a more recent and contemporary context Gramsci proposes that the emergence of Christian democracy is also used in a similar way (1971, p. 332).

Gramsci's assessment of the church and the role of religion in shaping society is a dispassionate one. He contrasts the approach of the church and his own philosophy of praxis, arguing that the church seeks to keep 'simple souls' in a position of ignorance, whereas the revolutionary movement he presents seeks to emancipate the masses. Notwithstanding Gramsci's view, the Catholic Church in Italy is a prominent theme in his political theory. He highlights the role of the church as a pertinent public institution, and draws examples from church structures and church cultures to aid the formation of his theory of the intellectuals, which offers a sufficient point of reference to take forward.

Philosophy, folklore and cultural hegemony

> All men are philosophers.

This is the starting point for Gramsci's theory of philosophy as it relates to the intellectuals (Gramsci, 1971, p. 323). His view is that philosophy can be understood in two ways, as can the intellectuals. There is traditional philosophy understood as a specialism that he himself expressed along with others trained in the art, through the development of ideas with respect to other philosophers. In Gramsci's case these were Marx, Lenin, Croce, Machiavelli and some others. Then there is philosophy that Gramsci terms 'spontaneous philosophy' which is the philosophy that is generally available to all. This spontaneous philosophy is comprised of three parts: (1) the language we use not simply for basic communication but to denote notions and concepts; (2) common sense and good sense,[2] which are used to establish the assumptions by which people live; (3) folklore, by which is meant religion, superstitions and belief systems that are used to guide how people see things and act (1971, p. 323). The way in which folklore is situated as part of our social relations with respect to common sense, with respect to philosophy, is elaborated and is worth noting here.

> Every social stratum has its own common sense and its own good sense, which are basically the most widespread conceptions of life and of man. Every philosophical current leaves behind a sediment of com-

mon sense; which is the document of its historical effectiveness, [it] is not something rigid and immobile, but is constantly transforming itself and enriching itself with scientific ideas and philosophical opinions which have entered ordinary life. 'Common sense' is the folklore of philosophy, and is always half way between folklore properly speaking and the philosophy, science and economics of the specialists. Common sense creates the folklore of the future. (Gramsci, 1971, p. 326)

As with his framing of the intellectuals, Gramsci once again presents the potential for all to become philosophers and in the premise of his notebook on the subject offers the reader a choice. Is it better to 'think' without critical awareness and simply accept the terms imposed on our environments, or is it better to work out consciously and critically one's own conception of the world 'being one's own guide', with respect to the resources available, language, good sense, folklore? As we begin to answer this question, our own critical awareness and engagement within our environments and across social relations become significant. These relationships are mediated between traditional and organic intellectuals, and the philosophies and folklore that emerge are the means by which this takes place. These inform the prevailing common sense that everyone uses to guide their day-to-day lives. By living with respect to this, our different philosophical outlooks, stories and the common sense they produce, people in civil society are giving consent for society to function in a particular way. This is what Gramsci refers to as cultural hegemony. The closest Gramsci himself comes to a definition offers two sides to the same coin: consent on the one, and coercion on the other:

> The 'spontaneous' consent, given by the great masses of the population to the general direction imposed on social life by the dominant fundamental group; this consent is 'historically' caused by the prestige (and consequent confidence) which the dominant group enjoys because of its position and function ... The apparatus of state coercive power ... 'legally' enforces discipline on those groups who do not 'consent' either actively or passively. This apparatus is, however, constituted for the whole of society, in anticipation of moments of crisis of command and direction, when spontaneous consent has failed. (1971, p. 12)

The question of what informs consent and the way in which world views are treated in the public square, and as a result which ones become dominant, or indeed which approach to world views becomes dominant, is at the heart of this struggle.

Gramsci's intellectuals and a movement from the centre

I opened this chapter with a summary of the Turin Factory Movement and Gramsci's thinking on how it would develop. I finish this section with a further assessment of Gramsci's views on the movement from his prison notebooks. First, in terms of timing. Gramsci's willingness to endure the shorter-term struggle of the Factory Movement as part of a longer-term project spoke to the different senses of time he recognized. In this way, Gramsci drew a distinction between conjunctural movements, which are more tactical or strategic or the result of propaganda, and organic movements, that is, the long-term trends in a society (Gramsci, 1971, pp. 177–8). He advocated an organic movement characterized by the mobility of intellectuals between strata, which emanates from the centre:

> A centralism in movement, so to speak, a continuous adaptation of the organisation to the true movement, blending of pressure from below, with leadership from above … which will ensure continuity and regular accumulation of experience … [this] lends itself to many incarnations. It consists in the critical search for what is similar and what is apparently different. And on the other hand for what is distinct or even opposite in what is apparently uniform. [They are] experimental and not the result of a rationalistic deductive abstract process, which is characteristic of pure intellectuals (or pure asses). (1971, pp. 188–9)

To this point in the chapter I have introduced political theory from Antonio Gramsci. The question of who Gramsci is, including a section on his cell and the psychology of his cell, might feel at odds with what I have set up as a political theory. However, you will notice in Chapter 2 in relation to William Temple, Chapter 3 in relation to myself as the author and anyone seeking to engage with this conversation, and then in Chapters 4 and 5, the route into the argument I'm developing is lived experience and the rich resources it offers us to contribute to understandings and deployment of transformational leadership. As such, Gramsci's experiences representing local workers, alienation from others on the road with him, that is, the Socialist Party in Italy, his emergence as the national leader of the Communist Party and his experience in prison, inform directly how he can shape the transformational leadership developing in this book. There are also clear differences from Temple. While both men were academically capable and involved in reform movements at an early age, Gramsci was doing so from a marginal position in a way that Temple appeared not to be. Gramsci's typology for leaders, his traditional and organic intellectuals, open up the opportunity for this comparison and for debates to go on about this. Which were they, a traditional or organic intellectual? Gramsci certainly makes a clear case for the value of both traditional and organic positionalities and I will consider these now with respect to both the idea of 'curators' of Spaces of Hope and transformational leadership.

Gramsci's intellectuals and curators of Spaces of Hope

Curator is a word that crosses multiple different contexts and spheres of interest. It has conjured a sense of artistry, creativity and design over the nine-plus years that it has been associated with this work. It offers a multiplicity of different positionalities a common term of reference. In the preceding chapters I have used terminology of leader and intellectual. Here I will consolidate these terms so that leader, intellectual and curator can be taken as synonyms within Spaces of Hope.

The function of curators thus far has been to gather contributions to the common cause of unearthing hope and expressing it through transformational leadership. The sense in which I first heard the word used was in relation to museums and art exhibitions and discussed in the 'By their fruits you will know them' section of Chapter 3. This referred to drawing together diverse content and expression that all speak to a common theme. The salience of a sense of drawing together of difference around a common theme will be obvious from previous chapters. The second sense in which curation is commonly used is in relation to the role of clergy in the parish, who have the 'cure of souls', which can be otherwise understood as caring for people at a deep level, at the level of the soul. Given the arguments made in previous chapters, one could reasonably assume the extension of this from an ordained role to one that is expressed by laity as well. So, curators draw together differences and care for others. It was in this sense that I deployed the term curator as part of the social movements from 2016. Spaces of Hope were curated with respect to a breadth of different themes; I referred to these within the new materialist grammar offered in Charter 4 borrowed from Bruno Latour as 'matters of concern' (Latour, 2007, pp. 114–15), examining the details of things and mapping the relationships between them.

Spaces of Hope have been created with respect to a wide variety of different matters of concern since 2016. Across three different gatherings in 2016 and 2017, which we referred to as 'symposiums', we gathered nearly 200 people from across the region around concerns of: (1) finding common cause in disconnected communities; (2) combatting the enemy of isolation in uncertain times: and (3) unlocking the potential for partnerships in the city. These gatherings were first with a group of organic intellectuals, before then welcoming traditional intellectuals in the form of bishops (ecclesiastics, as Gramsci would put it), local authority officers, and professors to contribute to these public gatherings as a means of cocreating what followed. As the movement progressed, more matters of concern have emerged, from social divisions surfaced by Brexit, the impacts of a mental health epidemic, inter-faith dialogue, the climate crisis, grass-roots movements, the church on the high street, just and sustainable transitions, local and urban governance, the Covid-19 pandemic, eradicating poverty in the city, responding to deficits in organizational culture and working practices, the value of and the values informing education and educational institutions, responding to and embracing cultural difference across world views, to assemblage and synthesis of different theological, anthropological, philosophical, sociological, ecological, economic, policy and political voices and ideas. These are to name just a few themes or concerns that you will recognize from earlier in the book.

In terms of the breadth of organic intellectuals that have been involved in this process of cocreation and indeed the formation of principles for curation that I will open up in Chapter 7, there are approximately 1,500 who have contributed to over 80 gatherings during the previous nine-plus years of the Spaces of Hope movement. Just some of these organic intellectuals have self identified as:

> Community workers, family support workers, youth workers, parish administrators, community volunteers, cafe managers, charity trustees, teachers, project managers, health and well-being officers, social prescribers, intelligence and governance managers, citizens advice officers, members of the autistic community who felt the job centre had failed them, education consultants, public health practitioners, the politically disenfranchised, Rector of Liverpool, director of city council department, a public health principal, a working-class mother of two, a Russian translator, foster carers, chief executives, a postgraduate student in international business, partnerships lead for a charity working with the NHS, Liverpool resident, Network development coordinator, asylum seekers, catering team, student, chaplain, hospitality coordinator, scholar in Islamic studies, social entrepreneur, senior advisor,

resident tutor, cleaner, scout leader, Roma Gypsy translator, curate, black activist, journalist, office worker, barista.

This list of 45 different positionalities represents about 3% of those who have participated who can be included in this list, including some people who have been named in Chapter 3 from before 2016 who deserve noting for their support before there was anything incarnated. Some might be crying out that some of those listed have professional titles and senior roles so must be traditional and not organic intellectuals. Good point. However, my challenge would be that it depends. I would argue that our positionality changes depending on our context. In their office, the chief executive is a traditional intellectual. Even sitting at the front of a conference wearing their bishop's hat (as it were), the bishop is a traditional intellectual. But where the conditions change and the spaces that are opening up are curated by others, then positionalities become contested and the nature of the kind of leadership we can each offer changes. A strength of the Spaces of Hope movement identified by the Inquiry into the Future of Civil Society in Chapter 3 was that participation was wide and the make-up of the dialogues was deep – philosophical, theological, sociological, etc. – such that everyone could participate. And so they did, and continued to do as per Chapters 4 and 5. Gramsci left the space for us to transcend positionalities in that an organic intellectual could become a traditional intellectual, so why not flip it on its head through a wholesale paradigm shift and hold space for traditional intellectuals to become organic intellectuals once again? Not forgoing their roles and responsibilities of course, but allowing the lived experiences of the masses to genuinely inform what they do and what their leadership looks like. This is what transformational leadership can offer. What has emerged is a model of transformational leadership which, with the help of Gramsci, can critically assess positionality in terms of limits and opportunities for *all* to offer leadership, each from their own experience, belief base and world view into the cocreation of responses to shared matters of concern shaping the public space and the institutions that make it up. The question becomes then, how do the shared characteristics of leadership set out in Chapter 4 relate to a Gramscian conversation set out here in Chapter 6? I turn to those now drawing on the emerging movement from Chapter 5.

Gramsci's intellectuals and transformational leadership

I begin with a brief reminder of the characteristics I set out for transformational leadership at the end of Chapter 4.

1 Transformational leadership is incarnational. Abstractly, this is defined in terms of the emergence of potential from different spaces and the realizing of that potential. In new materialist terms, it is the 'actualization' of the potential (*puissance*) in shared space, or potential becoming real or concrete (*pouvoir*). I will give numerous practical examples below from both organic and traditional intellectuals alike.
2 Transformational leadership is negotiated or cocreated. In new materialist terms, this is drawn from the idea that there is no meaning without one being in a relationship with the other. This sense of negotiation takes place within all assemblages, gatherings, territories or spaces, based on the different and creative potential that is being contributed. This connects with Gramsci's sense that we all have something to contribute because we are all philosophers, we are all storytellers, we are all intellectuals, or at least we all have the potential to be. So the emergence or incarnation of something is meaningless without this second element. Earlier in Chapter 5, I discussed the general idea of cocreation. This idea was central to the discussion during the Covid-19 pandemic and remains prominent within policy conversations. But, as one crisis dissipates, the temptation is there to revert to type and to redeploy old ways of working. I would urge us to resist this temptation and to recognize the context of poly-crisis that we are living in. This is not a case of doom mongering. It is a case of learning from the lived experiences of transition and uncertainty that enable us to grow into our lives and become more hopeful and resilient. It is a personal test of our own leadership to maintain an open stance to negotiating and cocreating whatever comes next. Gramsci's journey offers the example of his work with the factory councils. By all accounts, this was a failure and saw him alienated from those around him. But he also knew the risks, and he took them anyway, because he recognized that a failure in the short term opened up opportunities in the long term. He saw what he was doing as part of a wider, revolutionary goal. And in terms of this revolutionary movement itself, he noted that it takes time. So the point is that leadership should be incarnational, that is, emerging from context, and also cocreated, which means a willingness to fail and to learn afresh what is important.

3 We each have different roles and responsibilities, formal and informal, generalist and specialist. Gramsci highlighted this in his pursuit of a general conception for his intellectuals project by saying that it was a methodological error to be too specific or to prioritize one type over another.

So we have common ground between Gramscian political theory and the typology of transformational leadership from Spaces of Hope. It begs the question, what does all this look like and how does it work? I will turn to examples now from Chapter 5 to set up what this can look like, and then in Chapter 7 turn to principles for how transformational leadership can work.

Liverpool Hope University

At Liverpool Hope, affective flows of dialogue and emergent folklore can be mapped across at least eight gatherings from February 2022 to November 2023. There are classically Gramscian conceptions of traditional intellectuals within these spaces too, for example Catholic ecclesiastics: Pope Francis via his encyclicals, and Cardinal Fitzgerald through his presence and leadership. I would imagine that Gramsci's view of the church might have been challenged by the narrative being promoted, that is, seeking new forms of human fraternity inspired by a papal encyclical, and the fact that, at the same time as the dialogues at Hope, there were also dialogues taking place across the Catholic Church as part of their worldwide synodal process where the church sought to engage the 'simple souls',[3] as Gramsci would refer to them.

The affective flows of hope into the city, following the Cardinal's message and the deterritorialization of people out from the Senate Room, set the context for the gathering of organic intellectuals in the Baltic Triangle at St Vincent de Paul's Church (see p. 112 above). Gramsci would characterize organic intellectuals as those who have emerged from their context to take up leadership roles and responsibilities. Those gathered at St Vincent de Paul's were a self-selecting group who wanted to share stories of their contributions as volunteers during the pandemic. This gathering unearthed both the ways in which those organic intellectuals supported refugees and the homeless through a cafe, foodbank and clothes bank, and surfaced a shared sense of fear of being taken advantage of. Emergent from this gathering was new folklore for inspiring and nurturing transformational leadership as the group continued in their work.

The gatherings that followed later at Liverpool Hope turned their attention to the institutional culture, working conditions and the role of hope (the value) in shaping Hope (the institution). As an Honorary Research Fellow, I was curating this series of gatherings from the periphery of the university. This juxtaposed my positionality, paradoxically, as both a traditional intellectual as an academic deploying my work, and as an organic intellectual emerging from a disparate set of peers from across the university. The 51 others who participated were experiencing the same paradox, participating in both situated and virtual spaces, and becoming spontaneous philosophers, as Gramsci puts it, as they exchanged views on what gave them hope, the barriers they foresaw, and what they wanted to take forward to be presented to the Mission and Values committee of the university as recommendations for change. The affective flows of dialogue sought to make good sense of the experiences of colleagues, as part of a possible return to a culture of collegiality that sits within the folklore of the institution.

While substantially smaller in scale, these gatherings find resonance with Gramsci's role in the Turin Factory Movement in terms of his approach to gathering and organizing people. He saw the opportunity to gather people during a period of uncertainty for the work force, in a way that was not universally well received, as it stood at odds with the policy of the unions. The dialogues I ran took place at a time when strike action was going on. As someone who was not unionized, nor able to benefit from any deal that might have been reached through the action, I was left with no choice but to find an alternative way forward. In this way, I both delivered work and brought the views of the workers to the traditional intellectuals at the head of the institution. Gramsci's words in *L'Ordine Nuovo* resonate here. These gatherings at Hope, such that they gathered affective flows of hope and reterritorialized them as good sense and folklore for the traditional intellectuals, only serve a purpose 'if it is conceived as the beginning of a revolutionary process' (Gramsci, 1920, p. 249). Time will tell. And if there is hope at Hope, then what hope might there also be for other Christian and Islamic institutions, as per the reflections from traditional intellectuals Archbishop Williams and Shaykh Murad?

The Dialogue Society

In 2022 it was my role as a traditional intellectual to curate a digital space for the volunteers of the Dialogue Society, to open up the authentic stories of hope and despair experienced by the group of Turkish Muslim asylum seekers in their transition as refugees from Turkey to the UK. The story that emerged can be understood in Gramscian terms as of the philosophy of this group being discerned from their particular outlook inspired by the Hizmet movement. Key concepts and ideas were opened up that enabled good sense to be taken and folklore to be produced. In the intervening period, from the group that gathered, an organic intellectual emerged who became the Coordinator and later the Director of the Liverpool branch. They were joined by a traditional intellectual, the Northen Director, from the Dialogue Society at the Iftar in the community hall in Liverpool in 2023. During this intervening period the role of traditional intellectual had been reterritorialized by the Northern Director of the Dialogue Society and the process of cartographic mapping which had been used previously had been deterritorialized through the copy-paste strategy noted by Weller (2022) and exhibited in the experiences set out in Chapter 5. Regrettably, this movement from above by the Northern Director served to undermine the public narrative of unity espoused by the Dialogue Society. This was indicative of what Deleuze and Guattari describe as 'decalcomania' (2016, pp. 11–16), which I colloquially characterize as the Ronseal Test, that is, does it do what it says on the tin? (It did not.) Regrettably also, the emergence of the folklore of the organic intellectuals who had become incarnated in Liverpool was also deterritorialized by the affective flows of narrative propaganda symptomatic of the conjectural movement by Hizmet-aligned groups. This example offers a case of where the characteristics of transformational leadership can be found, but it is a case of where it has not been adapted.

The Royal Society of Arts

Ten gatherings took place with RSA fellows and their networks between May 2022 and July 2023. These gatherings began with other organic intellectuals from Liverpool, the Gramsci Society UK, and the Global Collaboration Institute, who either attended a gathering I had called or responded to pieces that I had written for the RSA Comments Blog. The local, national and international strata on which these gatherings took place would be recognized conceptually by Gramsci, as with the other case studies.

The methodology of Spaces of Hope resonates with the folklore of the RSA in that the RSA is rooted in local gatherings in coffee shops of Fellows seeking to respond to social issues of the day, each from their own positionality. These gatherings raised the consciousness of Fellows to the RSA's recurring commitment to see the fellowship as a social movement. There was recognition from those within the Gramsci Society that the gatherings being opened up did territorialize a sense of movement for them. They were reminded of the 'Half of China' movement, which mobilized in response to ruptures in family life due to spousal abuse. Also, the Guatemalan guerrilla movement who gathered and 'spoke bitterness to one another' to 'raise the consciousness' of what was happening and to gather a sense of what should be done. This was an authentication of the diversity of organic and traditional intellectuals within the gatherings with RSA Fellows, and spoke to the potential for a centrist movement akin to what Gramsci envisaged:

> a continuous adaptation of the organisation to the real movement, a matching of thrust from below with orders from above, a continuous insertion of elements thrown up from the depth of the rank and file into the solid framework of the leadership apparatus which ensures continuity and the regular accumulation of experience ... [this] can be embodied in many diverse forms; it comes alive in so far as it is interpreted and continually adapted to necessity. (Gramsci, 1971, pp. 188–9)

Three incarnations of this movement manifested, through the RSA Fellow-inspired gatherings, as a means of mapping possibilities for the future:

1 a provocation to end poverty in Liverpool, beginning by deterritorializing the folklore of the city, where existing narratives ignore the reasons for inequality in the city, historic sectarian division, and an unwanted attribution of longer engagement with the slave trade than the last confederate state in the USA;
2 a global network of policy-makers and educators seeking new ideas and approaches to share love and work together through collaborative leadership practices in an increasingly divided world;
3 a relationship with the Gramsci Society and Gramsci's own political theory, to explore means of reterritorializing it through transformational leadership practice within Spaces of Hope.

These are just three of the many examples on offer.

In this chapter I have set out the Gramscian theory of the intellectuals and brought it together with the concept of the curator from Chapter 3, characteristics of transformational leadership set out in Chapter 4, and synthesized them with the Spaces of Hope movement from Chapter 5. This provides the basis for Spaces of Hope to be understood as a movement of transformational leaders who are both organic and traditional forms of intellectuals who can curate Spaces of Hope. In Chapter 7 I will turn to principles for *how* this curation or transformational leadership can be made real within the many incarnations that Spaces of Hope has had and can have in the future.

Notes

1 I will note briefly that Gramsci discusses intellectuals in terms of urban and rural subtypes (Gramsci, 1971, p. 9). However, I see this as symptomatic of the 'exploratory' nature of the theory noted by Hoare and Sperber (2016) and do not feel that they are helpful binary categories in addition to traditional/organic, nor do they fit within the new/networked framing of social movement I set out in Chapter 5. This approach is not new or unique to me, although my rationale is obviously distinct to me. This approach is also found in Marks' (1957) translation *The Modern Prince and Other Writings*, where he translates sections from the Prison Notebooks relating to the intellectuals, but leaves out the section on urban/rural subtypes completely from the publication.

2 This is helpfully translated and contextualized by Smith and Hoare (Gramsci, 1971). Where Gramsci refers to common sense, he is referring to something that is often incoherent and about assumptions held in general in a society. Where he refers to good sense, it is 'practical empirical common sense in the English sense of the term' (Gramsci, 1971, p. 323).

3 I use the term here as a means of mocking Gramsci. While he obviously felt animosity towards the church, a position he is completely entitled to hold, his rhetoric was patronizing. I wonder if he was being doubly provocative by using the term, in so doing also inferring that ecclesiastics were being patronizing to the 'simple souls'? As a member of the laity myself and therefore one of the simple souls he is referring to, I don't agree with his characterization. Further, the group gathered at St Vincent de Paul included people who were anything but simple, some of whom were indeed traditional intellectuals in their own professional contexts. This points us to the nuanced and contextual reading of positionality being discussed.

7

Principles for Transformational Leadership

In this chapter I will set out principles for guiding transformational leadership, namely freedom, relationship, service, affect and authenticity. To derive these principles I will draw inspiration from across the interdisciplinary sources used so far: the work of William Temple (Chapter 2); the pre-pandemic social movement (Chapter 3); stories of local trusted organizations, scattered seeds, and uninvited and unexpected (Chapter 4); the post-pandemic social movement (Chapter 5); and the work of Antonio Gramsci (Chapter 6).

Deriving principles

The social principles offered by William Temple, set out in Chapter 2, were freedom, fellowship and service. He began with personal freedom, the importance of the role of the individual, and their place relative to family life and communities, the intermediate groups that make up civil society, and the state and the way that that is ordered. His outlook is captured in the famous phrase that bears repeating, 'the art of government in fact is the art of so ordering life that self-interest prompts what justice demands' (Temple, 1976, p. 65). Temple recognized the self-interest of individuals, the contributions that individuals can make to questions of justice, and the relationships and the strata that can be found in between. This includes the selfishness and limitations of individuals, which Temple characterizes as freedom 'from' others. It also includes the interdependence that individuals have with their contexts, and that that is an enriching thing for both individuals and those they're in association with. Temple considered his principles as being for both current and future generations. But most importantly for Temple is that his principles were rooted in every person being made in the image of God. He checks himself on multiple occasions, noting that the book he was writing was about social order, not Christian mission. Nonetheless, he recognized the importance of freedom only being truly realized through relationship with God. In a country that is no longer a majority Christian one, and particularly in a work that draws on multiple different world views from across the public square, including non-religious and Muslim world views, it is not sufficient simply to require people who don't share my world view to adopt it in order to engage with the principles I'm going to set out. As such, within the transformational leadership characteristics I have set out in Chapter 4 and then applied to diverse contexts in Chapter 5, the space is left for the different world views that leaders hold to be considered on their own merits as their leadership potential is realized. This in the spirit of public and contested understandings of world views found in the postsecular debate in Chapter 4 and in the work of Gramsci, which sees world views as a key influence on leaders and on the consent that is given within civil society for us to function. So this represents an approach that I believe to be in the spirit of Temple, albeit using a paradigm fit for purpose for the twenty-first century.

Before I move on to the principles themselves, I should note that taking Temple's principles as a starting point is not unique to me. Others have tried this in the past. Baker (2015) reframed fellowship in a contemporary idiom of solidarity, where fellowship was deemed to be an outdated term. As a Fellow of the William Temple Foundation, a Fellow of the Royal Society of Arts and a Fellow of Liverpool Hope University, I would suggest the term 'fellow' and the associated term 'fellowship' are still very much in use. Temple himself queried whether his three principles should be joined by a fourth. He identified self-sacrifice as a possibility, but dispensed with it on account of world views other than Christianity not requiring adherents to be self-sacrificial (Temple, 1976, pp. 76–7). Lucas (2018) argued that Temple might have included the principle of 'equality' and seeks to develop Temple's thinking with notes on liberty and equality in *The Human Condition* by Hannah Arendt:

> ... the given world depends, in the last analysis, upon the fact that men, not one man, but men in the plural inhabit the earth ... The equality attending the public realm is necessarily an equality of unequals that stand in need of being 'equalised' in certain respects and for certain purposes. (Arendt, 1998, pp. 9, 215)

However, I don't believe that Temple himself would have agreed with Lucas or Arendt, because, while he believed in equality of worth before God, he did not reflect this in his view of society. He wrote:

> People are born with different capacities and gifts, and if you insist on the principle that everyone must be free to develop their own, the emphasis will be on liberty, but not equality; whereas if you begin with the insistence that all must be counted alike, however different their gifts and powers, then of necessity, you will put greater restraint on many citizens and possibly on all. (Temple, 1925, p. 80)

Beyond Temple's view on equality, I don't think it is a useful principle here. Within the gatherings in Liverpool, for example, the rhetoric of equality was substantially at odds with the reality of inequality in the city. This is especially the case when there are historical issues that are yet to be resolved. One example from Liverpool stands out: it was identified as the last stronghold of the slave trade, even after confederate states in the USA had outlawed it. Principles which speak to false hope or even rhetorical falsehood are not helpful. This kind of critical evaluation of the principles is not new within Spaces of Hope either. One example of this was the subtraction of the principle 'honouring identity' from the set of seven used in 2018/19. You will see from previous chapters that the importance of different identities, and indeed identities formed from our differences and creative potential, is very much recognized. However, in terms of its use as a principle, language of identity conjured adversarial notions of identity politics, which people felt excluded by. Ultimately it led to misunderstanding and didn't add positive value in addition to the principle of authenticity which was also present.[1] With this in mind, I will turn to five principles for transformational leadership. These principles emerged from the initial social movement, which drew inspiration from Temple's work. They were then tested within liminal spaces in urban contexts in north-west England where they were mapped within the stories and lived experiences of leaders across these spaces. These principles have been developed alongside the characteristics of transformational leadership discussed in previous chapters. They are freedom, relationship, service, affect and authenticity.

Freedom

Temple identified freedom as a distinctly personal quality. He noted, 'One of our first considerations will be the widest possible extension of personal responsibility; it is the responsible exercise of deliberate choice, which most fully express personality and best deserves the great name of freedom' (Temple, 1976, p. 67). These two parts, personal responsibility and personality, point to the considerations that we make based on the content of a heart and the context that we find ourselves in, and the way we express things that we do. Temple is clear in his advocacy for bringing our whole selves into the world. A poignant example that he gives is the way that Jesus did not prevent Judas from speaking and acting when he went to betray Jesus. So freedom is an emancipatory foundation for all, even those we disagree with and with whom we might reasonably be existentially opposed because they seek to do us harm. Temple argues that freedom is found in different ways in different generations, and that with each new generation we have an opportunity to go about seeking freedom, the right way. He is clear that the responsibility to exercise freedom well belongs to all of us.

Throughout our lives, the different conditions that we find ourselves in directly shape the experiences that we have and our ability or otherwise both to take responsibility and to express our personality. These are liminal experiences, rites of passage or transitions that we need to consider our freedom with respect to. They are both challenges and opportunities. The liminal period is described by Turner as 'a process, a becoming ... even a transformation' (1967, p. 4). Liminal experiences can be disorientating. On the one hand, they are the antithesis to the ordering structures that we often seek in our lives, but they are also the source of them all. Turner notes that liminal experiences are 'a realm of pure possibility whence novel configurations of ideas and relations may arise' (Turner, 1967, p. 7). If we accept that we live within liminal contexts then our freedom is available to different degrees at different times. At times it will be limited and will be subdued or brought low. At other times, we will become emancipated, elevated and transformed.

This was evident at Beacon Community. The freedom to establish a group in that place was there for the leaders of Beacon. However, their first two years were completely wild and beyond any expectations that the leaders had. This was both in terms of people seeking to do damage to what they were trying to do, and in terms of the challenge that was being faced within their own team. Making sense of freedom within these conditions led to some of the original leaders choosing to be emancipated from the project all together and it led to a complete transformation in the way Beacon Community itself was run. The scattered seeds story offers other examples of freedom in terms of the vision holder, Janice, taking responsibility and carrying the vision for over 20 years; it was then brought to fruition in a way that honoured the personality of Margaret 'Seeds' Bennett. However, a contrasting example is given by the local philanthropist, who utilized her freedom to impose strict limits on others in a way that was coercive and cost them. The implications of this were seen later. There is also the story of Old Town Church. While the church has been present in that place for substantially longer than most other local institutions, it was going through an extended period of interregnum, which surfaced an existential crisis for the church, while also asking the volunteers who were faithfully present and offering informal leadership during that time to be resourceful and welcoming in a way that was personally costly to them.

One might reasonably ask how to interpret these examples for our own contexts. For this, we need the capacity to map liminal spaces and experiences so that we might understand each from our own positionality what freedom means. In Chapter 4, I set out new materialist grammar drawing on the work of Gilles Deleuze and Felix Guattari, and Bruno Latour. This provided a way of mapping the differences and creative potential that flow through and between different spaces, the relationships between these differences as they transition out of or become deterritorialized from these spaces, and the affect that they have on one another. I also set out a set of characteristics that make practical sense of these differences, relationships and affects, which I have developed in Chapters 5 and 6 in terms of transformational leadership: incarnation, negotiation or cocreation, and roles and responsibilities. Massumi, in *Politics of Affect*, helps us to locate freedom within this abstract grammar. He notes that freedom is the vague sense of potential (*puissance*) which is then made real or concrete (*pouvoir*) or incarnated (Massumi, 2015, p. 5). Freedom is the 'wriggle room' (p. 6) we find to do anything at all as transformational leaders. Freedom is our starting point, and how we express it is our point of difference.

A key question is, what inspires us to use our freedom in any given way? Transformational leadership and the world views that underpin it are incarnated and made real through lived experience. As such, the world views that inspire the way in which we use our freedom are made real and made sense of within our shared gatherings, assemblages, territories or spaces themselves. As such, in order to understand what it means to be free, we need a clear and open dialogue about our different world views; the way that they motivate us, the context in which we use them, the foundations we draw on to make sense of them, and the values they express. Examples of this are found within the gatherings in Chapter 5: at Liverpool Hope University, an institution which is itself defined by two different Christian world views; the Dialogue Society, an organization characterized by a Muslim perspective; and the Royal Society of Arts, which has no religious affiliation. These world views make up approximately 90% of the world views in the public square in the UK. Gramsci refers to different sources of motivation as our philosophy, as our religion, and as folklore, which allow us to make good sense of how we realize our potential and how consent is secured for the development of a functioning civil society. In terms of how we do this, Gramsci notes:

> The active man modifies the environment, understanding by environment the ensemble of relations which each of us enters to take part in. If one's individuality is the ensemble of these relations, to create one's personality means to acquire consciousness of them, and to modify one's own personality, means to modify the ensemble of these relations. (Gramsci, 1971, p. 352)

In this way, freedom is to take responsibility and to express our personality, with respect to and in response to the different environments we find ourselves in, inspired by the different world views that we hold. We do this each from our own positionality, based on the potential that we have and wiggle room we can create to do something. However, freedom is in relationship with everything around us, so I will turn to this now.

Relationship

The second principle for transformational leadership regards how we might direct our freedom and to what. Temple reminds us:

> No man is fitted for an isolated life; everyone has needs that he cannot supply for himself; but he needs not only what his neighbours contribute to the equipment of his life but their actual selves as the compliment of his own. Man is naturally and incurably social. (Temple, 1976, p. 69)

Our incurably social nature, as Temple puts it, is based on relationships with our families and our communities, and what he characterized as intermediate groups within civil society, which are where our freedom is nurtured and our personality grows. In Chapter 2, I set out Temple's differentiation between freedom *from* others on the one hand and freedom *for* others, on the other. To express freedom for others is to participate within these different associations. It is possible to take some inspiration from Temple here, but how we conceive of these associations has changed. Reddie (2023) vividly contrasts the associations experienced by Temple and his contemporaries from Balliol with three black women on a park bench in Handsworth in inner-city Birmingham. This calls much needed critical attention to the impact of social relations on transformational leadership.

In Chapter 3, I argue that we are living in transition. The global financial crash of 2008 was one cause of transition that opened up this question of how we use our freedom. The influence of colonialism and global geo-politics in the Democratic Republic of Congo also brought into sharp focus the impact that can be had on civil society, and those who are most vulnerable; in that case, it was children. However, accounts of transition and vulnerability are not limited to the lived experiences of others elsewhere in the world, as significant as they are. These transitions are something that we all go through in our own lives too. As such this second principle draws attention to how we submit to the conditions we find ourselves in, how we conceive of our relationships and where they take place and with respect to what, as we transition through life.

At Beacon Community, the scope and significance of being in relationship with others, and using one's freedom for others, was highlighted in multiple ways. A brief but powerful example is offered by Pastor Mark supporting a man who was faced with his own reality in the foodbank. A more significant example for Beacon Community itself was the distinction between leadership that sought simply to share the Christian gospel with people, and sharing one's whole life. Where relationships had integrity, trust was formed and lives were changed. In the story of the scattered seeds, the philanthropist was not motivated by using her freedom for the originators of the Seed Project, so much as she was motivated to establish a franchise of her favoured faith-based infrastructure organization, NCSAN. This action was one of freedom from others, as opposed to freedom for others, and it was masked by a stated motivation of 'unity', which was imposed. I will return to what it means to be united with others in Chapter 8.

At Old Town Church, the significance of the principle of relationship was set up by the presence of Eric, a homeless man, who became characterized as the uninvited and unexpected. These were not designed to be disparaging characteristics, but rather a challenge to those occupying spaces to be attentive to and welcoming of those transitioning through the spaces. Key to these brief examples is that relationships are shaped by everything in our environments and the way each expression of freedom is made. This is a point developed most clearly in Chapter 5. It is the relationships between the different things that make up our environments that enable us to form meaning. Further examples can bring this sense of negotiation to the fore.

The Covid-19 pandemic changed the way that we relate to one another in our local communities and around the world. Both physical and digital spaces opened up to mediate our relationships in a wide variety of new ways, some related to pandemic response, others seeking fresh hope out of circumstances that were unprecedented. The gatherings from Liverpool Hope University opened up the lived experiences of staff and students alike across the institution, and highlighted the extent to which the rhetorical values of the institution were actually being lived out. The question of whether we are 'hope by name and hope by nature' drew attention to where leadership across the institution had fallen short, but also where opportunities were for relationships to flourish. The gatherings with the Dialogue Society highlighted the inherent risk in forming relationships across difference, the misunderstanding that can take place, particularly within relationships punctuated by trauma. Freedom for others means finding ways of caring for them. In order to give relationships the greatest chance of succeeding, we need to develop a shared understanding of what has gone before, and discern ways of moving forward into the future. A related point was highlighted by the gatherings with Liverpool Charity Voluntary Services, which noted that if it was possible to be more open about experiences of inequality in the city, and also the roots that the city has in the slave trade, there would be a better opportunity for finding hope for the future. These themes were brought into sharper focus still in the dialogue about radical hope. Bishop John Arnold and the Revd Julia Pratt both highlighted the significance of new generations and called into question how we might relate to them. Professor Markham emphasized that relationships across difference are not necessarily going to be safe. However, there is hope in that if people and institutions are able to make sense of their own world views, then they will be better equipped to relate to others, and, as Professor Shakespeare put it, relate to the more than human world. Gramsci's thought helps to consolidate this sense of relationship:

> One must conceive of man as a series of active relationships (a process) in which individuality, though perhaps the most important, is not, however, the only element to be taken into account. The humanity which is reflected in each individuality is composed of various elements: 1) the individual, 2) other men, 3) the natural world. (Gramsci, 1971)

Service

The third principle is *service*. This is the point at which the potential that we have is incarnated, in negotiation with our environments, and becomes words and deeds. Temple advocated that service was expressed through our contributions to civil society through intermediate groups or faith-based organizations. But he also called us to consider service as a vocation, or something that we commit our lives to. Temple makes it clear that he thinks each new generations should be trying to develop their lives in a way that is in service to others. He calls us to consider what one is able to sacrifice, or how we might each share from what we have through the things we do.

From my own experience, it can take time to make sense of what one has to offer, and what one can do, or as a young person, how one can realize the potential that we have in an uncertain world. This sense-making is ongoing. It is a deeply valuable part of growing up, and can also hurt. When we think of service, we could be forgiven for simply thinking of public services. Many examples of intermediate groups offering these kinds of services are present in earlier chapters. These ranged from foodbanks and money management courses to community festivals, to well-being, support on a narrowboat, to a Pana-football cage project that responded to antisocial behaviour, a connectivity hub within the local Methodist church, and environments such as a not-for-profit market and the 'Well-being High Street' offering innovative ways to access local services. Then there was Night Church, which supported people engaging with the night-time economy, and even bereavement support such as Elsie Ever After. Friendly Fridays was coproduced around the five ways to well-being, and 'the space' was open for people with disabilities to drop in and connect. Service was in evidence via social prescription networks and community enterprise cafes, as well as homelessness provision and support for refugees. However, the principle of service here is not limited to projects that stand in the gap left by the withdrawal of the state, as deeply valuable as they are. The principle of service is a call to an embodied expression of the deepest resources that we have available to us, in whichever spaces we find ourselves. At Beacon Community, this looked like Mark's prayerful commitment to Nina, which came at the expense, in the short term, of the team around him. Within the story of the scattered seeds, Janice chose to serve the seeds legacy by establishing a new seeds project. And at Old Town Church volunteers expressed service through their response to Eric, going along with him and seeking to make him feel welcome, even though at times he made them feel uncomfortable.

A reasonable question to ask is, can service have a dark side? Might it descend into servitude? When do the good intentions and sacrificial nature that people have stop being productive and turn into something that might be exploited? For Gramsci, this is the exercise of hegemony within civil society (Gramsci, 1971, p. 124). The incarnation from freedom and relationship can therefore have two forms: service in the sense Temple talks about it, or a more coercive form, which is servitude. If service in this sense is an emancipatory or liberating act to some extent, then servitude is the opposite. Massumi says:

> Servitude, as much of oneself as of others, servitude to structures of power at whatever level, is energetically, collectively desired. In the 1930s the 'masses', Deleuze and Guattari say, were not ideologically duped into submitting to fascism. They positively desired it. They actively affirmed it. Fascism emerged from the bare-active stirrings of a mode of collective affective attunement tending towards ressentiment, which it amplified and reinforced, organized and returned to, then fed off in an infernal cycle. (Massumi, 2015, p. 104)

While the connection with fascist regimes in the 1930s might seem distant or far-fetched, it is not. Both Temple and Gramsci understood this at that time. In times of crisis we need to be vigilant to prevent history from repeating itself. The juxtaposition between service and servitude as an outworking of our conceptions of freedom and relationships, and how they affect the different spaces and organizations that make up civil society, is a pivotal one. This juxtaposition can look different in different contexts. At Liverpool Hope University, service was understood in terms of looking after one another's well-being and ensuring that the gardens on campus, as a source of beauty and inspiration, were attended to. Service was working in teams and departments to empower one another. The contrasting experience was one characterized by micromanagement, disempowerment and bullying from above. The Dialogue Society is associated with a movement, the Hizmet movement, characterized by service. At its best it looks like gathering together, engaging in conversation, sharing food, developing educational opportunities and so on. But at its worst, it is implicated by the spectre of a failed coup attempt by some of its members oversees, characterized by expressions of cultural insensitivity, and guilty of seeking to exploit others for their own ends in a new city. This is compounded by the fact that members of its own community appear to be left to deal with their own woundedness from the existential transition they are going through.

The Royal Society of Arts gathering also spoke to the tension between service and servitude. The legacy of slavery in the city of Liverpool was characterized as both absurd and notable, as 'we were still a Confederate state when none were left in America'. Good sense says that the city should deterritorialize that folklore due to the legacy of servitude it speaks to. However, this is not at all straightforward in a context where generations of citizens are trapped in grinding poverty, while there is also recognition of a crisis of leadership in the city which threatens to deterritorialize the city of its organic intellectuals. However, there is hope as the gatherings unearthed expressions of leadership that embodied service, characterized by a culture of 'learning to do ourselves out of a job'. The etymology of service came through within the Global Collaborative Leadership gatherings, which provided space for ideation. One participant offered their interpretation, which they related back to slavery. A sense of self-respect was highlighted, that is, if one is to avoid servitude then they should respect themselves to avoid being taken advantage of. Within the Gramsci Society gatherings, Spaces of Hope was framed as a 'socio-psychological cure for combatting the fascist movement' characterized in terms of insurgent manoeuvres responding to the bitterness of what people have experienced, such that their consciousness begins to rise. If that is the case, then the principle of service will speak to whether this is an emancipatory movement or not. To make further sense of this I will turn to the principle of affect.

Affect

The fourth principle for transformational leadership recognizes that we are living in inherently uncertain times. In the introduction to this book, I referred to the storms identified by Justin Welby, or risks highlighted by Hans Rosling, or poly-crises defined by the World Economic Forum, or even meta-crises introduced using the work of Jonathan Rowson. In Chapter 3, I have offered the conceptual lens of liminality as a basis for understanding transitions that take place in response to these crises. I highlighted the global pandemic in 2020 as an experience that impacted us all globally and accelerated and intensified the conditions of uncertainty we are experiencing. I've developed this sense by highlighting the environmental crises, the increase in poverty and inequality, and institutional transitions. In addition to these crises and causes of uncertainty, at the start of Chapter 4 I set out a number of transitions taking place within political philosophy, sociology of religion and social policy, which all spoke to the need for a fresh understanding of the role of different world views in shaping faith-based organizations and the leadership that they can offer. From this, I have set out a paradigm shift in understanding for leadership within the Temple Tradition, using examples from different situated spaces found locally to the north-west of England and globally via virtual spaces. I have mapped the relationships between the different spaces in order to develop the transformational leadership for which I am arguing.

Within the three principles I've set out for informing transformational leadership thus far, comparisons can be found with the principles of William Temple. The fourth principle of affect marks a clear departure from Temple's work. This fourth principle speaks to the limitations that can be placed on our freedoms, and as a result calls for a more nuanced mapping of the affective flows of service we produce. I will set this out in terms of being attentive to scale, in terms of desire, and in terms of power.

Affect transcending scale

In the introduction to this book, I set out the definition of poly-crisis denoting the cumulative impact of multiple crises taking place at once. I have made reference to the Covid-19 pandemic in most detail, and referred to its impact as accelerating and intensifying the conditions of living with liminality that I set out in Chapter 3. The pandemic provides a powerful example of the principle of affect as transcending scale. The emergence of a virus on one side of the world entirely altered the day-to-day lives of others around the world, and almost overnight descended us into hybrid conditions where situated and virtual spaces became necessary and normal for everybody. The term 'affect' is the means of articulating the flows of difference through different spaces (Deleuze and Guattari, 2016, p. 7), and, as I discussed in Chapter 4, we must consider them as cutting across multiple levels from the micro or local level through to the macro or global level. This is not taken as a linear or sequential thing, but rather is a case of everything being potentially connected simultaneously.

Within the story of the scattered seeds this sense is exhibited most clearly through the imposition of NCSAN governance processes as one of the conditions set by the philanthropist, based on the national footprint and trustworthy reputation of NCSAN. Within the story of local trusted organizations, the community the story is taking place in receives extra significance and resources due to its status as, statistically speaking, one of the most depressed communities in the country. It is for this reason that there was such a strong local authority presence in the community, which served to draw attention to Beacon Community and the work Mark was doing. In the story of the uninvited and unexpected the connection between the bishop as a traditional intellectual and the prophetic influence of Eric, who would not be characterized even as an organic intellectual, opened up the legitimacy of transformational leadership in those spaces. In the account of the Dialogue Society, my reference has been consistently to the role of the Northern Director and their tactics as part of a conjunctural movement at the Iftar. I have noted that the movement overall is informed by the global flows of Hizmet (meaning service), which is in transition due to the July 2016 deterritorialization from Turkey, which is being felt most directly by refugees who, in spite of being part of the global Hizmet movement, are experiencing 'woundedness' because of the a-signifying rupture of being labelled terrorists and forced from their homes. These were recurring themes both in the Zoom room in 2022 and in a confounding sense at the Iftar in 2023. Multiple examples of affect transcending scale are present in the gatherings at Liverpool Hope University. The first example is the presence of a cardinal living and working in the Baltic Triangle in the city. Another example would be the connection established by the dialogues I ran between the periphery of the university and the Vice Chancellor as chair of the Mission and Values Committee. The legitimate connectivity between different forms of transformational leadership at these different scales surfaces both the opportunities for a culture of collegiality and the understanding of what Newman meant when he said, 'I do not ask to see the distant scene; one step enough for me.' If that one step is both at the periphery and in close proximity to activity that might previously have taken place on that distant scene, it could revolutionize the way the institution works, especially if it pertains to the working culture, practices, techniques and folklore of the university. The micro and macro scales within the Royal Society of Arts gatherings enabled the mapping of the affective flows of global gatherings of ideation with the Global Collaboration Institute, alongside the local gatherings in Liverpool addressing poverty in the city.

Affect, desire and power

Now I will highlight some important details about the distinction between service and servitude. The principle of affect helps us to understand not only how to map different expressions of transformational leadership, but the order in which to do it. I return here briefly to discussion of the postsecular in Chapter 4. There I highlighted the cultural struggle, where different world views were in dialogue with one another. These dialogues offer potential for forming new affinities, forms of connection, solidarity and leadership. I posed the question as to where the spaces in which this was taking place might be. I have detailed examples of those spaces in Chapter 3 in the 'By their fruits you will know them' section, stories in Chapter 4 (scattered seeds, local trusted organizations and uninvited and unexpected), and gatherings that made up the post-pandemic movement set out in Chapter 5. But it is here, in discussing these principles, that we begin to make 'good sense', as Gramsci would put it, of how to discern the role of different world views in guiding our transformational leadership in postsecular spaces. I argued in the last chapter, using Gramsci's political theory, that world views contribute to the formation of cultural hegemony, or the consent of the masses within civil society. His argument was essentially that power is informed by philosophy, folklore and common sense. So achieving power is the result of engaging with world views, not the other way around. Similarly, the case Habermas makes for the postsecular is that we bring pre-political motivations into the public sphere. To try and make this point clearer, I will refer back to the new materialist thinking of Gilles Deleuze. Deleuze does not find power flowing through every space, gathering or assemblage as if it is a foundational part. The scale of gathering space or assemblage means that the smaller they are, the less relevant power is. But instead, desire is central to the make-up of the spaces, gatherings or assemblages, or desire-assemblages as they are termed, as opposed to the force of power needed to realize our desires, which comes later. So, Deleuze does not dismiss the idea of power; he recognizes it as part of a hierarchy of affects, but puts desire first:

> If I speak with Felix [Guattari], of the desiring-assemblages, it's that I am not sure that the micro-systems can be described in terms of power. For me, the desiring-assemblage marks the fact that desire is never a 'natural' nor 'spontaneous' determination ... Systems of power would thus be a component of assemblages ... [However,] systems of power would never motivate, nor constitute, but rather desiring-assemblages

would swarm among the formations of power according to their dimensions. (Deleuze, 1997)

To clarify my meaning here I refer to Seigworth in his chapter 'From Affection to Soul' where he renders the relationship between power and desire within Deleuze's work as he sees it: 'Power is something like a coagulation or scabbing on the skin or surface of the social rather than the immanent breaks, flows and movements of desire' (Seigworth, 2011, p. 187). So the principle of affect draws our attention to the prepolitical motivations that we share, characterized as our desires, which are informed by the different world views that we hold, which drive movements for change, which may then express power. As these grow, the hegemony expressed as strategy, tactics and propaganda of conjunctural movements become more of a feature. Power is exerted by maintaining consensual cultural hegemony, as Gramsci would put it, as an expression of our world views, as opposed to acting or seeking power and domination by force.

So from the examples that we have throughout Chapters 3, 4 and 5, we can see the emergence of different values and world views, which are shaping and implicating the transformational leadership that I have discussed. In the story of scattered seeds, while the stated value of unity and a sense of only building one church was noted, this was at odds with the breaking down of relationships and the formation of a second Seed Project; the recognition of forgiveness, grace and reconciliation between the members of those different groups spoke to the prevailing influence of the Christian faith that was shared by those involved. Unearthing these different details addresses the contradictions within the stated values – unity in this case – and brings our attention to the foundations upon which those values were formed. I will come to the question of values within the Spaces of Hope movement in the next chapter. Likewise, in the story of local trusted organizations, Mark's leadership was tested. He expressed this in terms of the disagreements with colleagues over what it meant to share their lives, and to share the gospel, based on a verse from the Bible in a letter to the Thessalonians. He also noted within his decision-making process the prayer where he felt convicted of the risky path that he took. It was acknowledged elsewhere by the local authority officer that, while these details could not be communicated in public sector language, they were integral to the success of the leadership that was available, so finding ways to factor in these details mattered in terms of understanding the extent, richness and resilience of the work at Beacon Community. And then, of course, in the story of the uninvited and unexpected, we see the contrasting outcomes of power and desire, where, on the one hand, attempts were made to use violent force to control the homeless man within the House Church gatherings, suppressing the uninvited into the servitude of the host, which led to the breaking down of that relationship, and, on the other hand, we saw the ongoing maintenance of a relationship by volunteers, even under strained circumstances, that came to embody an attitude of service and a desire to help others.

These dynamics are observable once again in the Dialogue Society, Royal Society of Arts and Liverpool Hope gatherings. This time the hierarchy of desire and power can be seen within Sunni Muslim, ecumenical Christian and non-religious contexts. This was the case through gatherings with marginalized groups (asylum seekers and refugees), on the margins of institutions (through dialogues across Liverpool Hope University), and in response to marginalized experiences (poverty and inequality in the city of Liverpool). In all cases, people spoke of things they value and the desire they have for change – this was expressed as people's hopes for the future. This was then punctuated by dynamics of power, that is, in industrial disputes, populist political regimes, compound affects over generations, and so on. As the turn to power emerged, in each case we can see contrasting examples. Within the Royal Society of Arts gatherings there were calls for consensual power-sharing, characterized by cocreation in the case of LCVS, or the socio-psychological cure for fascism in the case of the Gramsci Society. In Liverpool Hope, consensual forms of power-sharing were exhibited through the willingness to hear and respond to recommendations for changes to working culture and practices from the periphery of the university and within spaces hosted by the most senior staff at the university. In contrast is the dynamic within the Dialogue Society, which they themselves recognize is the imposition of copy-and-paste tactics and modus operandi, insensitive to the woundedness of volunteers, as well as the capacity of outsiders to their group brokering an authentic welcome for them in new cities.

All this being said, during transitions through liminal spaces, it is possible for motives and the true nature of experiences to be masked or lost due to confusion and disorientation and fear. This can lead to confusion about what is motivating particular actions: desire driven by specific world views, or power. So, with this in mind, we need a final principle that can help us to authenticate the emancipatory potential that we share in relationships with one another. This can be experienced both as service and servitude, affected by both local and global considerations, by sources of desire and then expressions of power. As such, I will turn now to the fifth principle, authenticity.

Authenticity

This final principle is an outward question regarding the nature of transformational leadership. In this way, the idea of authenticity is understood not as a purely subjective and personal claim, as in my own assertion that I am being authentic to myself and professing what I determined to be my truth on my terms. Rather it is an understanding of authenticity as both inner authenticity, which equips us to form our own stories, and outer authenticity, which sets our sense of ourselves in relationship with trusted external sources of wisdom in the rest of the world. This dual sense of authenticity is both a caution against narcissism and other pathologies of power and a means of clarifying our sense of what is happening (Giddens, 2008, pp. 169–72). In Chapter 4, this sense of authenticity is coupled with a prophetic characteristic. This term is taken from the work of Walter Brueggemann, who similarly characterizes the prophetic as something that speaks truth not as part of a totalizing regime, autocracy, fascist dictatorship, or as in the DRC from my example in Chapter 3 a kleptocratic and failed state, but as a means of speaking truth in response to struggle and suffering. In this way, this principle of authenticity serves as a prophetic act, calling out beyond the scope and reach and influence of any one person, group, gathering, assemblage, network, institution, society or world view. It is a question of making sense of the truth claims we are making and relying on within the public sphere, and what they mean for both traditional and organic forms of transformational leadership.

One might query the legitimacy of speaking in such grand terms about the influence that the application of these principles might have on politics and on the state, in the way that I have just implied. But that connection is there to be seen in the arguments of William Temple, which I refer to in Chapter 2, and Antonio Gramsci in Chapter 6, as well as within the data itself, particularly in Chapter 5. I have used Gramsci to argue that it is the influence of each of us, and the potential that we have to be philosophers or intellectuals, in a way which shapes the folklore by which we live our lives. This is informed by the world views we hold and that are held by us as individuals, or by potential organic intellectuals, or by the traditional intellectuals who lead our institutions. Gramsci sought to inspire a revolutionary movement shaped almost in spite of the ecclesiastics and their control of the 'simple souls'. But I see a more hopeful scenario today. Over the last 15 years, I have encountered the kind of leadership that Gramsci points to, but I have also experienced traditional intellectuals, including but not limited to ecclesiastics, who want to facilitate a revolutionary movement of hope across our society. So, in this way, the principle of authenticity serves as a means of building the movement, not for our own ends but with respect to others. In terms of how this is done, we can authenticate our transformational leadership practice by drawing a distinction between cartography on the one hand and decalcomania on the other (Deleuze and Guattari, 2016, pp. 11–16). The distinction between the two made by Deleuze and Guattari calls out inconsistent motives, contradictions and empty rhetoric that might emerge. The principle of authenticity might be framed in much simpler language from the Sermon on the Mount: 'By their fruits, you will know them' (Matthew 7.16 and 20).

And so, in terms of this fruit, I will turn back to the stories that have shaped this book. In the story of scattered seeds, a question the philanthropist could have asked while imposing her conditions on the Seeds Project is, what story are we seeking to tell? Is it the seeds story, which has been present for a generation in this community, of how the gospel has been shared and lives changed? Or is it a new story, a different story, a story of unity, whatever that might mean? There's nothing to say that both aren't possible. But there is something to say about how it is done. In the story of the local trusted organizations, leadership exhibited by Mark was recognized by those who did not share his world view. They knew the people and they knew the context, they saw that something was working and they went to find out more. This was in stark contrast with the organization that was labelled as the 'trusted' organization. Their leadership was found to be untrustworthy. In the uninvited and unexpected story, the closure of House Church pointed to the fruit of its approach, and the changing of parish boundaries by the Old Town Church to include the most deprived community in the borough was a sign of recognition from above of the authenticity of its mission to marginalized communities. With the Dialogue Society, Liverpool Hope University and the Royal Society of Arts, the findings of the gatherings, as part of an emerging movement of hope, are authenticated by the folklore mapped out by books sponsored by each of those contexts: *Hizmet in Transitions*, *Serendipity of Hope*, *Arts and Minds*, *Rooted in the City* and the *Prison Notebooks*. The folklore in each indicates a recognition of the shortcomings of different periods of history, and opens up the desire for a more hopeful future.

In this chapter, I have set out principles for transformational leadership, which have been iteratively developed over the last nine years, through the initial proposition of principles as part of the social movement in South Manchester, the testing of those principles through ethnographic research, and the subsequent application of principles across gatherings within different institutions of different world views across local and global contexts that all contribute to civil society. The five principles of freedom, relationship, service, affect and authenticity provide a critical basis for guiding and developing transformational leadership. In Chapter 8 I will turn to the emerging values from Spaces of Hope, namely hope, unity and justice.

Notes

1 This stood out at a gathering in Stockport in 2018. One woman who had followed the movement for the last nine months joined a gathering one evening. When she sat down she noticed the principle 'honouring identity' written on a facilitation board, and quite abruptly got up and left. She was the first person in the room and there were no others present at that time, so I followed and inquired as to what the problem was. This is where it became apparent that this woman had an aversion to identity politics. She saw them as divisive and as something she had had enough of. I sought to explain that the rationale for the term was different from what she had become accustomed to. She heard this explanation and reassuring statement from me, and chose to return to the gathering for the full dialogue. This simple example from one of the earlier gatherings in the movement, which was then borne out by further research and reflection, serves as an important illustration of the value of the open and iterative cocreation of principles that has taken place over the last eight years. It also highlights the importance of lived experiences as part of the development of organizational paradigms.

8

Shared Values

In this penultimate chapter, I will turn to the values that have characterized curating Spaces of Hope as a social movement and can be used to guide the deployment of transformational leadership. Values of vulnerability, freedom and connection characterized the early dialogues from the movement and speak to the individual experience of opening up one's own personal story and sharing it with others, the liberating experience that can be, and the opportunity it offers to form connection with others. As I have suggested in previous chapters, there are also rhetorical values and lived values. Gramsci's analysis of the tactics and propaganda used within conjunctural movements point to the possible dangers of rhetorical values. With this in mind, I will analyse the value of unity as it has appeared in different contexts in previous chapters, the shortcomings of its application and the ways in which it might be redeemed. To finish the chapter, I will consider the value of justice and how it might be achieved. But first, I will turn to the value of hope.

Hope

Living hope

Here I refer to living hope as the diverse sources of hope that are present through our lived experience. The journey that I set out in Chapter 3 began with a sense of feeling hopeless. I was unemployed, suffering with poor mental health, and I felt as if my world had been turned on its head by things that were outside my control. I had been raised as a Christian in a Christian home. For that, I am grateful beyond measure. I was active in my local church and anyone who knew me would say I was a Christian. But I discovered that these foundations are not a guarantee of anything. This is not to forgo them, but to emphasize as we step into the world that we each have a responsibility to make sense of that and to give an account of ourselves and to find our way, however uncertain that experience might be. What I knew to be the case was that while I felt as if I was together, when it came to it I had no clue what to do and the promise of eschatological hope through the death and resurrection of Jesus Christ did little immediately to answer the question of how to live in the context I was in. I knew others had walked this road before me: they'd understood what it meant to be there for others; they had worked through contrasting experiences of hope and despair; they had heeded Jesus' call to be known by their fruits; and they had found their way in the wilderness.

In spite of the uncertainty, I knew there was living hope. I knew this because I'd heard the story of Jonah who was called to bring the gospel to people he was ideologically opposed to. I knew this because I had heard of the conversion of Saul to Paul from a murderous critic to an apostle of the church. I knew this because the apostle Peter said that struggles, when they do come, can prove faith to be of greater worth than gold when Christ is revealed. I knew this in 2014, when I heard of the work of Dietrich Bonhoeffer in the 1930s, who was calling for new ways to gather as church and to seek and serve God, even and especially when it's costly. I knew this in 2015, when I began to consider the work of William Temple, and his commitment to sharing Christ crucified with everybody; from the position of the Joneses trying to find out what there is to eat. I knew this when, quite serendipitously in 2016, spaces began to open up for questions of hope to be asked and answered. One after another, lived experiences were shared by different people, each from their own belief base and world view. Strangers were sharing stories of what hope meant to them, and how it might change things. This wasn't uncritical, it was with respect to the different concerns that were shaping individual lives, communities and our society at large. I knew this in 2017/18 and 2019, when these Spaces of Hope pointed to different conceptions of what hope means to people, the resources that might make further sense of where hope comes from and how we might share it as part of a vibrant civil society. I knew this in 2020 and each year thereafter, as hope became the means for developing responses to the intractable crises shaping our lives. However, I do not want you to think that, after all this, hope is simply rhetorical. My point here is that we can discern living hope from our lived experiences which can grow over time. In this sense, they offer seeds of hope.

Seeds of hope

There are different sources of living hope which are unearthed in every gathering that is curated, and in every space that opens up. Since the first gathering in South Manchester in 2016, it has been possible to see the seeds in all their richness and diversity. Early examples came in the form of a prophetic word from a woman from South Shields. She asked how the church might respond to the challenges of the day in a way that opens up Spaces of Hope for the future. From that seed much has grown! One might argue that seeds of hope are found by asking the right questions. Seeds of hope related to questions of personal well-being at Friendly Fridays, and seeds of hope were found with respect to disability and access to spaces. Seeds of hope were found in terms of broader questions around public service and the nurturing of health and hope for all through social prescription services. In this way, seeds of hope were as simple as offering a cup of tea or coffee and the opportunity to connect with somebody else from the community. And seeds of hope were also found around questions of identity, which did not descend into identity politics. Seeds of hope were also germinated within the context of the future of civil society. Seeds of hope were found by questioning what may or may not be shared in public spaces.

In these local contexts, attention was given to questions of love and value and what inspires people and communities and intermediate groups, as Temple put it, with seeds of hope for policymakers, on the one hand, for faith leaders themselves on the other. A seed of hope at the heart of the research process in this book has been the question, 'How might we live?' The Bishop of Chester pointed us to the Gospel of John referring to life in all its fullness (John 10.10). The Bishop of Stockport highlighted that from her perspective Spaces of Hope had endless potential, which is opened up by taking the right approach, for example carefully mapping the relationships between things; examining the cracks in the pavement, for example casting them in bronze and curating them as pieces of art. These are seeds of hope and can be seen as the multiplicity of different ways that the differences and creative potential that make up our lives might be made real, or incarnated. Seeds of hope are, as Canon Grace Thomas made clear at the Radical Hope gathering at Liverpool Hope University, already available to be found within each of our own contexts, however difficult or challenging these contexts might seem at the time. This is not simply Grace's perspective, as valuable as that is. The stories in Chapter 4 of scattered seeds, local trusted organizations, and the uninvited and unexpected made this point. Seeds of hope are everywhere in our communities – it is just a case of knowing how to look. It is not just a case of looking into the future. It is a case of considering our present position. Hope is both a present condition and a disposition to the future. One respondent in a 2017 gathering put it like this:

> Hope [is] not simply being an adjective but being a verb. That hope is something about being present... I'm sorry, my grammar isn't very good ... active continuous present? Is that a thing? ... but a verb that is done as well as something that is ... I think we talk about hope as if it's something that's going to happen. But I think [it is] part of leadership [that] is about being the action that forms now and is informed by now, about what will be next.

So this is a sense of being informed by what has happened before, such that our present sense of things can be hopeful. But it is also a future-facing consideration where whatever changes, however small, can be a seed of hope, too. In terms of the philosophical grammar used in Chapter 4, hope can be found there too, understood in terms of affect. Massumi argues in *Politics of Affect* that in fact hope is synonymous with affect:

> I use the concept of 'affect' as a way of talking about that margin of manoeuvrability, the 'where we might be able to go and what we might be able to do' in every present situation. I guess 'affect' is the word I use for 'hope'. One of the reasons it's such an important concept for me is because it explains why focusing on the next experimental step rather than the big utopian picture isn't really settling for less. It's not exactly going for more, either. It's more like being right where you are – more intensely. (Massumi, 2015, p. 3)

What he meant is that with each affect, each expression of our desires, either as a progressive movement forward or a regressive step back, potential seeds of hope emerge and are brought to life. And as we transition from gathering to gathering, and the concerns that are shaping our dialogue change – from feeling disconnected and alone, to deep worries caused by grinding poverty and inequality where we live, or indeed anxieties about the future of our climate and the world we live in – how we see these seeds of hope changes. However, to borrow a metaphor from the Gospel of Mark 4.3–8, some seeds will be scattered on the path, and some seeds on shallow ground, and others will take deep roots in fertile soil. This point is also emphasized later in the same chapter:

[Jesus] also said, 'This is what the kingdom of God is like. A man scatters seed on the ground. Night and day, whether he sleeps or gets up, the seed sprouts and grows, though he does not know how. All by itself the soil produces corn – first the stalk, then the ear, then the full grain in the ear. As soon as the corn is ripe, he puts the sickle to it, because the harvest has come.' (Mark 4.26–29).

A seed of hope that I hope stands out, but nonetheless bears repeating, is that the seeds have emerged from pre-political contexts, from before any sense of organized religion, from stories of everyday life. These stories are then spoken into the different gatherings and spaces and movements and networks and organizations and communities that we are part of. As such, seeds of hope are found each from our own positionality and perspective from within our lived experiences. In Chapter 5 I referred to the work of Professor Shakespeare to set out the need for us to be reoriented to the world around us and to turn to the hyper local for the small revolutions that can take place when we are attentive to the things that are growing around us in day-to-day life. In this way, we can equate seeds of hope to immanent sources of living hope that we might potentially draw upon. Gramsci's theory of the intellectuals encourages us to be critical in our thinking and to make good sense of these different sources. I suggest that naming seeds of hope from the broader and oftentimes unconscious sources of living hope around us is indicative of this Gramscian critical thinking. But even if we recognize and engage with them, how do we know which seeds of hope are good for us? Which seeds are producing good fruit, as Jesus would put it, or making good sense, as Gramsci would put it? This brings me to the question of authentic hope.

Authentic hope

The third way in which hope can be understood throughout the movement is as authentic hope. The idea of authenticity as a means of either articulating one's own truth or as checking against external sources of reference as to whether or not something has been done well has been present throughout the movement. The seeds of hope that we might see for ourselves are subjective and, while they may give us confidence or a personal sense of hope, I would suggest that these are akin to the first understanding of authenticity, that is, deciding for ourselves what is true without any external frame of reference. It is the second idea of authenticity I am interested in, where we test our hopes with respect to the world. In Chapter 3, as the Spaces of Hope social movement developed, the idea or phrase 'By their fruits you will know them' became a strap-line for the movement. This was indicative of the open process of curation and cocreation that was emerging, and it was also a sign that the outcomes were not predetermined. It was for others to decide if they were to attend our gatherings, or share a story, or contribute to a movement in a practical way, or host a gathering of their own through commissioning new work, for example. Each of these outcomes are indicative of authentic hope.

In Chapter 4, the sense of authentic hope is seen again in numerous ways. As part of the diversifying belief landscape in the UK, the question of authenticity pointed to a shared foundation in the public space. The sense is found in the work of Anthony Giddens (2008), which I noted in the previous chapter. As such, in a context where specific beliefs, values and world views are becoming more contested, authenticity offers a common denominator or means of determining what is working. In Chapter 7, the sense of authenticity was offered greater rigour and application when I set it in dialogue with the new materialist philosophy of Gilles Deleuze and Felix Guattari (2016) as a means of mapping affective hope. There was a distinction between cartography on the one hand, and decalcomania on the other. One carefully and authentically maps the affective flows of hope through different spaces, whereas the other calls out the inauthentic and ultimately hopeless. The story of scattered seeds gave an example of authentic hope in the form of Jane and her role as a linchpin in Mustard Seed for the five years she was there. Authentic hope was expressed through her personality and professionalism, from singing songs with volunteers to carefully managing the day-to-day running of the cafe. At Beacon Community, authentic hope was given by Pastor Mark through the contextual ways in which he cared for people. The poignant example of the man being brought to tears as he transitioned into the foodbank stands out, as it was met by reassuring words that helped the man come to terms with his experience. This kind of service was later recognized by the whole community. It was a beacon of authentic hope which the other organizations in the community sought to make sense of. This same sense was seen in Old Town Church where the volunteers went along with Eric the homeless man, even though his behaviour was not always comfortable. They and he were sources of authentic hope for Old Town Church as it found a way to overcome its existential crisis and change its parish boundaries to step further into care for marginalized people and communities. At Liverpool Hope University, the question, 'Are we hope by name and hope by nature?' was a question essentially of whether there is authentic hope within the institution. The willingness to commission new research in order to find the answers to the questions is a sign that there is some at least. Time will tell whether there is authentic hope for the Dialogue Society in Liverpool, which, like the Hizmet Movement at large, is in transition. The final example of authentic hope relates the Royal Society of Arts back to its roots in coffee houses and dialogues about how to respond to intractable social issues for the public good. This is where the RSA began 270 years ago through a movement of like-minded Fellows. This was the vision of former CEO Matthew Taylor, which appears still to be present. In each case this will look like transformational leaders from different positionalities, applying the principles of freedom, relationship, service and affect to realize authentic hope for the future.

Radical hope

The final way in which hope has been present in this movement, and this book is in terms of radical hope. The sense of being radical is a sense of reverting to one's roots:

> Of, belonging to, or from a root or roots; fundamental to or inherent in the natural processes of life, vital; spec. designating the humour or moisture once thought to be present in all living organisms as a necessary condition of their vitality; usually in radical heat, radical humidity, radical humour, radical moisture, radical sap. (Oxford English Dictionary, 2024)

Here I will look at the roots of Spaces of Hope set out in this book through the lens of what is referred to as radical theology, in order to see where hope is for the future of this movement. In Chapter 5 I referred to the Radical Hope gathering that took place at Liverpool Hope University. There, radical hope could be understood in terms of a democratic and social movement concerned with the environment, politics, poverty and inequalities, and education. In addition there is also a relationship with radical theology that has been below the surface throughout the book, but I will make explicit here. John Caputo situates radical theology as emerging from the unemployment line (2020, pp. 20–21). What he means is literal in one sense. He had seen colleagues who thought differently to the status quo go without work. However, he was also speaking of an experience of marginalization and how that shapes our world view. There is resonance here with my own experience of unemployment, which I set out at the beginning of Chapter 3. It is also worth noting that for Caputo radical theology is premised on the idea that 'God does not exist' (2023, p. 4). It might be off-putting for some at this late stage in this book. This might be heard as a move away from the source of living hope I have just talked about. It isn't. Stick with me. Caputo puts it like this:

> If I were now asked, 'who is God?', safely out of the reach of my priests and nuns, I would say that God – that one [the one he was taught about growing up], the guard a lot of us grew up with, not just Catholics or Christians; the one that is out there in general circulation; the star of stage and screen; the supreme being, who sees all, knows all, can do all, who is watching every move we make, and he's coming to get us if we do not behave ourselves, and to whom we turn when things takes a turn for the worse – does not exist. (Caputo, 2023, p. 4)

The point is that the God of the institutions that have shaped us and society, the institutions that are going through their own decline and transition, the God who has been distorted by the abuses cited by the Revd Crispin Pailing in Chapter 3, or the damaging experiences set out in the Scattered Seeds, Old Town Church and the Beacon Community stories in Chapter 4, or the lack of accountability flagged by Archbishop Rowan Williams in Chapter 5, is not who God actually is. Those failings do God a disservice and allow our conceptions of God to fall short of who God really is and the true glory of God. This is exactly the kind of issue that William Temple encountered in the early twentieth century and in response to which he led the Life and Liberty movement for reform of the church. There will, naturally, be push-back to this kind of claim. When Temple rallied the Life and Liberty movement he did so at odds with Archbishop Randall Davidson, who had been his mentor. However, he took on the hard task of speaking prophetically and honestly about the need for change, and change came about. As part of paradigm shifts such as the one set out in this book, we can use a new paradigm to look at content that has been present for some time, but see things entirely differently. In this way, paradigm shifts are transformational. Radical theology offers resources that can support this transformation. Grimshaw (2015) argues that 'central to radical theology is an engagement with the limits of authorities and their limits on the world.' Robbins and Crockett (2015)[1] develop their conception of radical theology along five lines, which one can also find, serendipitously (in the sense referred to by Lee (2023a) in Chapter 5), in earlier chapters of this book:

1 Radical theology is postsecular; we can find the question of the postsecular in Chapter 4 with reference to the work of Jürgen Habermas.
2 Radical theology is post-liberal; to develop this sense they refer to Dietrich Bonhoeffer, to whom I make reference in Chapter 3:

> Radical theology was born with Dietrich Bonhoeffer's prison cell writings wherein he issued the challenge to live in a world without the working hypothesis of God. This is the world come-of-age and represents a distinctly post-liberal sensibility in that like Barth before him, Bonhoeffer totally repudiated the cultural form of religion ... Bonhoeffer's call for a religion-less Christianity set the template for radical theology's self-distancing from religion. (Robbins and Crockett, 2015)

3 Radical theology is political theology; to some degree, Robbins and Crockett argue this is a case of self-identifying with the radical theology lineage beginning with John Caputo, and then considering the emancipation and transformation that can take place through engaging with questions of difference. I have done this throughout and explicitly in Chapters 4, 5, 6 and 7. I would argue that considering the political theory of Antonio Gramsci in the way that I have done opens up further the relationship and dialogue between radical and political, and, with reference to Temple, even public theology, with implications for each to be explored in future.
4 Radical theology is onto-theology; meaning, at its most basic, a new materialist ontology, or way of being that is oriented to change, transition and transformation, drawing on the work of Gilles Deleuze and Felix Guattari and their followers. (I refer you to Chapter 3 as the premise for this, Chapter 4 for the roots of my thinking within Spaces of Hope, and Chapter 5 onwards for the applications of it.)
5 Radical theology is eco-theology; this centres the relationship we are in with all of creation, and encourages consideration of the human and non-human and their affect on one another. This can be found explicitly in Chapters 3 to 7.

If the sense of what it means to be radical has been established as a foundation that can be built upon, how do we draw out understandings of radical *hope* that can drive the movement forward? For this I will turn back to the Temple Tradition. There are many comparisons to be found between the emerging Spaces of Hope and the Temple Tradition that has been present for the last 80 years. The attention to difference that Temple showed stands out, exhibited in his ecumenical work and his establishment of the Council of Christians and Jews. He advocated dialogue as a tool of action; not talking for the sake of talking, but dialogue as a tool for forming policy. Then there is the example of Temple's leadership, which bridged individual concerns, the role of intermediate groups in contributing to society, and the pursuit of justice through middle axioms or specific concerns or policy areas. While it is true to say that the Temple Tradition as was has come to an end, the synergies with the emerging movement speak to a rootedness that in all manner of ways gives hope for the future.

The Spaces of Hope movement and the transformational leadership approach I have set out speak to the opportunity for cocreating service together which can respond to the concerns shaping society: pandemics, the climate crisis, poverty and inequalities, wars and culture wars, and institutional change. The question of how this might happen was set out in the post-pandemic gatherings, culminating in the April 2024 'Radical Hope in an Election Year' gathering. In a context of leadership in the Temple Tradition, after Temple, this gathering pointed to the character of hope and also to the opportunities for democratic engagement by active citizens across civil society. Professor Peter McGrail noted, 'Hope is not a weak word', seeing it in the context of the cultural devastation that was experienced by Plenty Coups in the indigenous Crow tribe in north America, but equally finding that sense in the transitions or 'deterritorialization' I set out from the Spaces of Hope research – Mark's care and Nina's conversion, Eric's prophetic presence, Jane's musicality and personality, and the resilience of the members of the Seed Project after being deterritorialized from their own vision come to mind. Then there was the call by Professor Simon Lee to 'Deep Freeze Hope', which was a challenge to older generations to lay down their pursuit of a dream for today and to leave the space for new generations to step into that dream tomorrow. This points to a costly, powerful and intergenerational sense of hope. In Chapter 3 I reflected on the juxtaposition of hope and despair during a period of acute and devastating suffering in my own life. I found comfort in scripture from the apostle Paul in Romans 5 where he offered a rich process of emerging hope. However, it is Romans 4 where the richness of that hope finds its roots. Paul tells the story of Abraham who, in spite of what he quite understandably saw as impossible circumstances, had a family with his wife Sarah, which made Abraham father of many nations and father of the faith for Christianity, Judaism and Islam (see Genesis 12—17). Paul puts it like this:

> The promise comes by faith ... to those who have the faith of Abraham. He is the father of us all. As it is written: 'I have made you a father of many nations.' He is our father in the sight of God, in whom he believed – the God who gives life to the dead and calls into being things that were not.
>
> Against all hope, Abraham in hope believed and so became the father of many nations, just as it had been said to him, 'So shall your offspring be.' (Romans 4.16–18)

As offspring of Abraham in this book have attested too, there is hope in even the most existentially challenging of circumstances today. Caputo refers to this as the possibility of the impossible and 'something that shatters the horizon of expectation' (2020, p. 295). This is the kind of hope that should be invoked when we think of radical hope. It is deep and transformative and beyond anything you can possibly conceive of, and when it is realized it is embodied and visceral and explicates the essential nature of a God at work in our lives. Caputo reflects:

> We hope without why, hoping against hope in the coming of what we cannot see coming. The impossibility of hope ... is the very staging of hope. The impossibility of hope is the condition of its possibility ... If we have a good reason, it is not hope but a reasonable expectation. If it is utterly groundless, then it is not hope but an idle and arbitrary 'will-o-the-whisp'. [Between these is] the groundless ground of hope that does not rest on a ground but is nonetheless motivated. Hope does not have a sufficient reason ... but it does have a cause to fight for, a cause to hope in. (2020, p. 300)

Throughout the Spaces of Hope movement, a multiplicity of causes have emerged. In a postsecular public sphere with a diversifying belief landscape, and which is plagued by poly-crisis, I believe it is this fourth sense of hope, radical hope, that is needed to drive the way forward. Before turning to these ways forward, and the conclusion of the book, I will turn to the other values that have been prominent in the spaces of hope movement: unity and justice. If we do not have an adequate account of unity, then there is little chance of building a movement driven by radical hope.

Unity

At the root of the Temple Tradition there is a clear recognition of the importance of unity. First, unity is a oneness with Christ. The gospel tells us that this is already achieved through Christ's death on the cross and his resurrection. When the World Council of Churches was established, unity was based on the Nicene Creed. Beyond this sense of Christian unity there is also unity while living out our lives. I see that there is a distinction to be made here. Examples from Temple's life include the establishment of the Council of Christians and Jews, and his contributions to the public square, notably his contributions to the establishment of the welfare state, set out in *Christianity and Social Order*. There are contemporary examples of unity movements throughout the book. In Chapter 3, I referred to the work of Link Up. The leader of Link Up, the Revd Andy Glover, now Canon Ecumenical at Chester Cathedral, espoused a desire for unity rooted in the welfare of the city, which was nurtured through gathering for prayer, worship and developing shared and strategic agendas together. This unity movement was also characterized by the prophetic task of Ezekiel of 'standing in the gap', as they framed it, between community and the state and seeking to serve both through its work. The work of Link Up, as I saw it, spoke clearly to the kind of ecumenical leadership and unity Temple championed. There are examples in Chapter 4 of the strengths and indeed the weaknesses of unity movements. Unity cannot be forced. Christians are united as part of creation, united by the death and resurrection of Jesus Christ, and united in the kingdom of God. But that has nothing to do with *people*. That unity is afforded by God-given grace. Nothing has been done to achieve it, nothing has been done to merit it. So on the one hand, it is entirely true that we are united and therefore to claim unity in that sense is reasonable. But it does not give anyone licence to gazump the actions of others through expressions of strength, self-interest and power, in a way that does harm to others while using the rhetoric of unity. In Chapter 4, this kind of expression of unity was clearly present within the scattered seeds story. It was also present at Old Town Church, where that type of unity movement gave licence for physical aggression and force by senior leaders who hailed the presence of God, as the very people Christ came to save, and in the Sermon on the Mount called blessed, left the room. This is not unity. This is not transformational leadership. It is notable that the pastor of Beacon Community called out his concerns regarding this kind of unity, noting that it is based on a perfunctory level of agreement and that nothing changes. That pastor leaned into prayer and into the context of the community in a way that sought unity by submitting to the sacrifice of Christ on the cross, and giving away all power and authority that comes with leadership status, in a way that was ultimately recognized by secular authorities and as transformational for others.

Unity cannot be imposed. It requires the humility to acknowledge the role of grace in us having any hope at all. It requires the stories of those who are wounded to be heard – not as an aside or an afterthought, as was the case with the Dialogue Society gatherings, but as the seeds from which everything else might grow. And as with the seeds that we plant in the ground, which grow slowly and with respect to their environments and conditions, and are pruned back to encourage more resilient growth, unity should be hard won, if we achieve it at all. In each case, unity should involve a commitment to the differences that make up shared identities of those gathered, so that when fruit is produced it is fruit that lasts. This means that we need to be careful in our approach to seeking unity, and we need to be consistently attentive to changes in our relationships and the impact we have on one another. I would rather see unity as an unfulfilled aspiration accompanied by a process of integrity than something that is named over and over and claimed through our own hubris, but results in no change at all. Transformational leadership is a means of achieving this unity. But, if I have made the case I hope I have in previous chapters, we will understand together that this is by no means about us. Yes, we are to bring ourselves and our personalities to bear and to each take responsibility from our own positionality, but that means nothing if it is not authenticated through relationships and affective service, through the different spaces that make up civil society, as part of a radical and hopeful movement of justice for all. Temple was not naive in his outlook; where force was needed he advocated for it. But it was by no means a self-justification; instead, it was a case of sharing love with one another in the face of pure evil. Psalm 37 is an often quoted verse within contexts of unity movements, which speaks to this spirit,

> Do not fret because of those who are evil
> or be envious of those who wrong;
> for like the grass they will soon wither,
> like green plants they will soon die away.
> Trust in the LORD and do good;
> dwell in the land and enjoy safe pasture.
> Take delight in the LORD

and he will give you the desires of your heart.
Commit your way to the LORD;
trust him and he will do this:
He will make your righteous reward shine like the dawn,
your vindication like the noonday sun. (Psalm 37.1–6)

The value of unity within the scope of the Spaces of Hope movement has been highlighted when it emerges from a place of humility and repentance, or, as Temple put it, taking responsibility. Once we find something of this humility, the prospects of unity between those of different positionalities becomes more realistic and opportunities for justice in response to the different crises we face grow.

Justice

I began this book with different framing and examples of crises we are facing. Justin Welby referred to 'storms', Hans Ana and Ola Rosling referred to risks. The case at the heart of this book is that we are living in conditions characterized by liminal transitions catalysed not just by one crisis at a time but by multiple things all the time, a poly-crisis: 'a cluster of related global risks with compounding effects, such that the overall impact exceeds the sum of each part' (Torkington, 2023). In Chapter 3, the experiences of unemployment, poor mental health, low paid work and the influence of the global financial crash on opportunities for career progression could all be characterized as forms of injustice. The effects of colonialism and geopolitical manoeuvring in the DRC are profound examples of injustice, which was felt most keenly by those who were least able to respond, that is, street children. My own experience of abuse and discrimination, compounded by people's perceptions of a straight, white, middle-class Christian man as opposed to the content of my story set out in evidence, struck me as profoundly unjust. Within the Spaces of Hope social movement in South Manchester that followed, the different experiences of social division and poor mental health and unemployment, lack of access to services, and the precarious nature of the community voluntary sector and funding processes all spoke to injustices experienced by a wide variety of people in the sector, as they were trying to support people in their communities too. Likewise the stories of scattered seeds, local trusted organizations and the uninvited and unexpected offered more detailed and nuanced experiences of justice in local contexts. In Chapter 5, the context in Liverpool was set out, where different crises were impacting individuals and communities already experiencing grinding poverty that is intergenerational in nature. This injustice has been perpetuated for a century or more. It was not caused only by the global financial crash from 2008, nor by the Covid-19 pandemic from 2020 to 2022. Nor was it just the lack of access to jobs, or the crisis in leadership in the city that required government inspectors to be brought into the city council to ensure that acceptable standards of governance and leadership were being met. Nor was it the negative culture of competition reported in the third sector. Nor was it the history of sectarian division in the city. Nor was it the cognitive dissonance of claiming to be independent when this city is highly dependent on others, or claims of equality when the city is demonstrably unequal. And nor was it just the mercantile history of slavery in the city upon which everything else was built. It was all of these things, which have contributed through no fault of any one individual to experiences of injustice that have shaped a city for generations. But Liverpool does not need me to say this for people of the city to know it. The existence of the interdisciplinary Marmot Group speaks to this, taking inspiration from the eight policy areas set out by Michael Marmot, which, like Temple's middle axioms, speak to the lifelong pursuit of justice that is needed across provision for children and families, access to education, pathways into work, consideration of our environment, and our treatments of those who are different from us, calling for an end to racism and discrimination.

With these things in mind, there is living hope in the city. Seeds of hope are everywhere. Through the gatherings that I've been involved in alone, questions that seek to open up authentic hope are being asked, although answers might take some time. The Hillsborough disaster in 1989 finally received an adequate answer in the King's Speech in 2024, nearly 40 years on, when a Hillsborough Law was set out. King Charles said, 'My government will take steps to help rebuild trust and foster respect. Legislation will be brought forward to introduce a duty of candour for public servants.' It is not before time and is a powerful example of a return to the roots of public service, where public servants served the public. This sense of returning to the roots is emphasized through the dialogues that took place at Liverpool Hope University, where the question was asked, 'Are we Hope by name and hope by nature?' This institution was named from Hope Street, running through the centre of the city, between the two cathedrals, and spoke to a period of partnership between the Anglican and Roman Catholic Churches, personified by Bishop David Sheppard and Archbishop Derek Worlock, which sought justice in the city during a period of protracted division in city and nation. In a similar way, I am sure a return to the roots of the Dialogue Society as a movement of service across society would be welcomed. However, after the catastrophic events of July 2016 (detailed in Chapter 5), the movement no longer had roots in the nation it emerged from and is in transition. The injustices of this period will not be overcome quickly, nor will the woundedness of volunteers forced to seek asylum in other countries and cities, including Liverpool.

In all these cases for justice to be realized something radical has to happen. This is why at the start of the book I made reference to the meta-crisis. Rowson (2021) breaks this down in terms of understanding who 'we' are, how we 'know' things, how we 'learn' things, and our capacity to 'imagine' and 'believe' things. We need to attend to the details of who we are, what and how we know things, how we learn and how we might reimagine things, and indeed what it is that we believe as part of our pursuit of justice. This book has set out the case for transformational leadership that can build resilience to both poly-crisis and meta-crisis, such that we might unite as transformational leaders with radical hope, in this pursuit of justice for all.

Notes

1 Robbins and Crockett are characterized by Grimshaw (2015) as the Deleuze and Guattari of radical theology. This indicates the prominence of their work within the field, and also highlights the distinctive nature of it, in the same way that Deleuze and Guattari's poststructuralist and emerging new materialist philosophy is distinct from other schools of thought.

9

Conclusions: Ways Forward

I finished writing this book in the summer of 2024. I found myself, quite unexpectedly, at Virginia Theological Seminary, just outside Washington DC in the USA.[1] During my time there, I watched as a new Labour government was elected in the United Kingdom. This followed 14 years of leadership by the Conservative government since their election in 2010, which is also when my journey in Chapter 3 began. In his first speech as Prime Minister, Kier Starmer gestured to the 'sunshine of hope' shining once more. Within a month of the new government being established, three primary school-aged girls were murdered while attending a Taylor Swift-themed dance event in Southport, a coastal town near Liverpool. In the fortnight that followed, riots took place in towns and cities across the UK, characterized by violence against police and minority groups, including asylum seekers and refugees, and attacks on mosques and Muslim communities. This violence did not originate in the attacks in Southport, but appeared to be the result of organizing tactics by political groups on the far right. Some violence, such as that which took place in Walton in Liverpool, surfaced the disaffection of an already impoverished community as a community hub that received seven-figure investment in 2023 was burned to the ground. This lamentable act of self-harm by community members gave a visceral reminder of the compacted and grinding nature of the challenges being faced. The riots elsewhere in the country appeared organized and sustained, and were stoked by misinformation online including from the owner of X (Twitter), Elon Musk, who said of the events, 'Civil war is inevitable.' These events highlighted how important the call for genuinely radical forms of democratic engagement are and how important transformational leadership is to bring about the change that is needed.

In the USA, a number of historic events took place too: first, there was the presidential debate between Donald Trump and Joe Biden. The debate was much earlier in the election year than usual and was seen as a test, by his own party, of President Biden's capacity to communicate and lead the Democratic Party into the future. This is a test Biden ultimately failed and in the weeks that followed he announced that he would not accept his party's nomination to be re-elected as president. Instead he backed his Vice President, Kamala Harris, in a move that has no precedent in history and tested the limits of the US constitution, with some calling it a political coup. Days after the Trump–Biden debate came the judgement from the Supreme Court which gave the president immunity from criminal prosecution if the person being tried was deemed to be undertaking official business as president. At the time of this judgement, Trump was facing multiple criminal prosecutions, including one related to what some called an attempted coup on 6 January 2020 as protesters stormed the Capitol building in response to what they saw as an illegitimate election result. Weeks later came the attempted assassination of Donald Trump at a campaign rally. He survived, which should be a relief to everybody. However, the use of potentially lethal violence and the image of a presidential candidate dripping blood and chanting 'fight, fight' in defiance of what had taken place was shocking. In the aftermath of these events and as part of the election campaigns, both sides claimed that they would unite a nation. Based on the events that unfolded, it is tough to see how that will happen in the near future. In light of the arguments in this book, one can't help but see connections between what happens in the USA and in the UK, and indeed in other places around the world. In all of this, living hope will continue and seeds of hope will continue to be planted. The question is, will we also see this grow through the proliferation of spaces of authentic and radical hope, cocreated and curated by transformational leadership across the public square in a way that will make the seemingly impossible possible again? I will conclude by drawing attention to some areas in this book that might present ways forward, to equip us for the transitions that are ahead.

Transformational leadership and the Temple Tradition after Temple

In 2022, time was called on the Temple Tradition and Temple's most significant contributions, represented by *Christianity and Social Order*. I set this out in Chapter 2. As I conclude the book and look to the future, I want to draw attention to three points from Temple's work – one from the start of his ministry, one from the end, and one that points to his methodology – and indicate their relevance to transformational leadership today: (1) Temple's contribution through the Life and Liberty movement; (2) Temple's contribution to the welfare state; (3) the use of dialogue to form action in public life.

1. Life and Liberty was a reform movement that set Temple at odds with the leaders of the church of the day, including his mentor Archbishop Randall Davidson. Temple called for the reform of the Church of England to enable it to move on from the abuses of the past, such that there might be hope for the future both within the governance of the institution and through the gospel it preached. This book has not sought to address directly any of the ongoing issues within the Church of England; however they are noted by former Archbishop Rowan Williams in Chapter 5. The tension exists between the freedom of the church to determine its future and how it works, while also being held to account in the public sphere for how it operates and for historic abuses that were not dealt with as they should have been. Williams' point highlights that where change can happen, then the church can be positioned to respond to the vulnerabilities of people in communities and offer prophetic and practical responses that can nurture authentic hope in public life. This kind of lived experience is at the root of the Spaces of Hope movement and could be brought into being through transformational leadership applied to a radical new monasticism rooted in the prison cell writings of Dietrich Bonhoeffer.
2. The second point relates to the welfare state, which Temple situated as a means of supporting all in society, contrasted with the power state, of which we have plenty of examples to draw on today. At the 2022 roundtable at Balliol College, Professor Anthony Reddie questioned whether it might be possible for three black women on a park bench in Handsworth, Birmingham, to have the same influence over the policies that affect their lives as the Balliol three, Temple, Beveridge and Tawney, did on the formation of the welfare state. What I have set out in this book is an approach to transformational leadership that is cognizant of the Temple Tradition, and also offers answers to the question raised by Reddie. In Chapter 3, a shared conceptual basis is established of living with liminality. In Chapter 4, the capacity to map these liminal spaces was opened up and the basis for transformational leadership from them was offered using examples from some of the most marginalized communities in the country. This approach will only benefit from further applications. In Chapter 5, the case was made that these spaces can be curated and cocreated as part of a social movement, which can address myriad

concerns that are shaping the public square. The case I have made is one of hope for the future. The task is by no means complete, not by any stretch of the imagination. It is only just beginning. However, in Chapter 6, I have opened up the case for transformational leadership from different positionalities across the public square. The case is then developed in Chapter 7 for principles to guide the deployment of transformational leadership, each of us from our own positionality. And in Chapter 8 I have drawn out the relationship between transformational leadership practice and the pursuit of radical hope, unity and justice. I suggest that the tools for the job are available for the case that Reddie wishes to be made.

3 A third point, following Reddie's question, can be found in the synergy between the Spaces of Hope gatherings and the Malvern Conference that Temple hosted in 1941, through the reference to 'micro-Malverns'. From this, the possibility of spaces of dialogue that form policy, as Temple advocated, looks deeply plausible. To add strength to this case from this book, there is the influence of Antonio Gramsci and his concept of the modern prince as a means of political engagement and party-building, which can be explored further too. So with this in mind, what connections might be made between Spaces of Hope and concepts of micro-publics or citizens' assemblies as a means of cocreating policy insights, recommendations and leadership from the ground up? This was hinted at in Chapter 3 with reference to the movements advocated by the likes of Jon Alexander and Camilla Vegara, and in Chapters 5 and 6 through reference to the work of Antonio Gramsci. This is an opportunity that should be taken up, and the Spaces of Hope movement offers a foundation for how this might be developed.

Hope for higher education

The careers advice I got when graduating into the global financial crash in 2008 was to get a temp job. As tough as the circumstances were, this is an indictment of higher education institutions and their ability to serve their students through a vision such as Newman's which called our sector to mother, or more accurately 'nurture', those who are within our space for their journey through life. This was a vivid calling set out by Simon Lee in *Serendipity of Hope*, which he noted was at the root of the vision for Liverpool Hope University. Temple and his contemporaries at Balliol received nurture of this kind within the school of T. H. Green, delivered under the guidance of Master Edward Caird. Their legacy is clear from earlier chapters. The question raised during the Spaces of Hope dialogues, however, is about how might we recover such a legacy for students today and for Higher Education Institutions. This question is set within numerous additional contexts: situated and virtual learning environments; declining engagement with humanities and a hostile environment for the subjects in recent years; declining collegiality across institutions, highlighted by protracted strike action throughout the sector; the contested role of faith in the sector and within faith-based higher education institutes themselves; the perceived lack of safety for students in higher education because students might hear ideas that they deem to be offensive; and students having no sense of what their futures might look like when they graduate (this point was highlighted by the chaplain at Hope, the Revd Julia Pratt). There is a case to be made for the hope that higher education can offer young people seeking a way in the world through a renewed sense of nurture and culture of collegiality between staff. There is also a case to be made for hope in higher education itself in terms of the way that different ideas are engaged with, and the public impact and contributions that can be made. More must be done to develop these agendas, not just at Liverpool Hope University but through all universities, and particularly through the transformational leadership of faith foundation universities and colleges.

Authentic communications

A theme that was present throughout the book, which would benefit from explicit attention in the future is the relationship between situated and virtual spaces and the nature of communication between the two as part of, in Gramscian terms, a conjunctural movement.

Virtual spaces were cited by faith leaders and local authority workers in the pandemic as facilitating a shift to a more open and democratic modus operandi. Within higher education, virtual spaces also served as a means of connecting students with one another during the pandemic, while access to situated spaces was limited. Virtual spaces acted as sources of hope for students in Ukraine when the war with Russia began. Access to virtual spaces ensured that students and teachers could stay in touch when they had to flee for their lives. Within the post-pandemic movement of hope, respondents from the RSA Coffee House gathering noted the anxiety of transitioning from virtual spaces back to physical spaces, and curating spaces using a curtain to separate themselves so as to replicate the conditions of being present but having your screen off in a Zoom room. The volunteers from the Dialogue Society also cited virtual spaces and remote communications tools as a source of hope while they transitioned between countries and into a new city. During the movement, developments in artificial intelligence became prominent, opening up the relationship between the human and non-human through questions of what is authentically human communication and what is AI, and indeed how we receive it. The presence of these contrasting experiences merits further attention. The presence of AI and its impact as a non-human actor within shared Spaces of Hope should also be subject to further research.

However, beyond these examples is the basic question of what is authentic communication across physical and virtual spaces. There are different ways of communicating in each space, for example within virtual spaces the creation of avatars can mask identities, the circulation of fake news is prevalent in these spaces too. Trolls and bots can stir up counter-narratives and propaganda, which can be used for political ends. Donald Trump has become synonymous with fake news, social media tirades, and the establishment of his own social media platform, Truth Social. How do people with different world views relate to one another in these spaces? Are there differences based on the world views you hold? How do these spaces mediate global networks and movements of hope beyond establishing the space to meet? Who or what governs access to and flows of information through these spaces, and to what extent are theses spaces still considered public? How do we discern the folklore that fuels the counter-hegemonic movements within civil society and inform the consent that is needed for lasting change? How do we know what is truth and what is not? What does this mean for networked institutions such as the William Temple Foundation, the Royal Society of Arts, Dialogue Society, higher education institutes such as Liverpool Hope University and Virginia Theological Seminary, CVS infrastructure networks such as Liverpool Charity and Voluntary Services, dioceses such as Manchester and Salford, city-wide policy and partnership networks such as the Marmot Group in Liverpool, and international networks such as the Global Collaboration Institute and the Gramsci Society? More must be done through exploring authentic communications further.

Sustainable transitions

The context for this book was set out using terms of poly-crisis and meta-crisis. The crises that were most prominent in the early chapters of the book were the Covid-19 pandemic and the climate crisis. While the pandemic is over, the climate crisis is a substantially bigger challenge with much more significant consequences for the lives of millions of people around the world over a much longer period. It has implications for poverty, inequalities and experiences of welfare in the city. These sit alongside wars being fought around the world and the impact they're having on situated and virtual spaces in terms of lives lost and the perpetuation of propaganda and culture wars in a post-truth era. As such, responses need to be offered to aid transitions through these crises such that a more hopeful future might be found. This is not in the sense of *Kimbilio* (refuge; see Chapter 3), but in terms of life in all its fullness. In addition to these challenges there is the crisis of identity, in terms of who we are, how we learn, lost imagination, and how to make sense of what we believe. These outer and inner challenges point to transitions that transformational leadership is equipped to respond to. In Chapter 3 I highlighted the idea of common but differentiated responsibilities, which is an underpinning principle for sustainable development. In the final section of the chapter, I also highlighted local and regional strategies for responding to the policy of net zero carbon, which is informed by the Intergovernmental Panel on Climate Change (IPCC). The IPCC convene annual gatherings or Conference of the Parties, known as COP climate change summits. COPs should be attuned to the contributions that faith-based organizations can make and to the need to integrate all our resources to ensure sustainable transitions for all. Could there be Spaces of Hope at COP gatherings in years to come which support the cocreation of sustainable transitions including climate-change policy and mitigation? Likewise, spaces that seek to respond to inner development goals and the meta-crisis should draw on theological resources and processes that open up authentic and radical hope.

Another process that is squarely within the Temple Tradition, and indeed finds its roots in the tradition, is Faith in the City. A follow-up to Faith in the City could include a sustainable transitions agenda that would develop transformational leadership from faith communities, in the spirit of the work led by David Sheppard and Derek Worlock in Liverpool in the 1980s (Sheppard was involved in the original Faith in the City process). These different spaces are part of what Pope Francis refers to as an integral ecology, which are both rooted locally and connected globally. Sustainable transitions that pick up on these factors and hold space for both human and non-human contributions can promote transformational leadership in urban contexts and deepen resilience for the future. There is work to be done to explore this agenda further and Spaces of Hope can offer tools for that job.

Hope, unity and justice for future generations

In Chapter 8 I referred to the tradition of radical theology emerging from the unemployment line. Caputo (2020) calls this out as the cost of expressing something different from colleagues within the academy. I can speak from experience in saying that unemployment is costly, materially, spiritually and in terms of mental health. Unemployment is often the cost counted by those least able to adapt. Often that is new generations. Canon Grace Thomas cited her own experiences of being impoverished while raising her child. The Revd Julia Pratt noted that students she encountered at Hope could not see what their future might hold after completing their degrees. This is undoubtedly a tough experience, but these tests and transitions build resilience and offer hope for the future. I grew up as the public square was becoming increasingly secular. The first UK election that I was aware of was the 1997 election of the New Labour government, after which Alistair Campbell famously said, 'We don't do God' (Brown, 2003). Out of a secular context where God was not done, we have experienced a new visibility of religion in public life, which has shown me the deeply transformational power that Christ crucified has today. Post-pandemic, the Bloom review (2022) asked afresh the extent to which we do God in the public sphere. And we now have a public narrative from the government of the day that once again refers to service and hope, reminiscent of that which came in 1945, which received posthumous influence from Temple. In a post-secular public sphere, where faith-based organizations are both an asset to be harnessed and a problem to be solved (Baker and Dinham, 2018; Levin, 2020, 2021, 2022), it is right that an account is given of the authentic hope that is on offer. This will inevitably involve a paradigm shift in how we organize and lead, which I have argued for in this book. With paradigm shifts come new generations of leaders who can take up the hope that has been put into deep freeze by those who have gone before us. The task ahead will be transformation both for you and for those you bring hope to, but there is time enough for hope to emerge for generations to come. The groundless grounds are set. If institutions want to continue into the future, they will welcome you and the service you can offer in a way that nurtures you to step into leadership and into the rest of your lives. For them it is an opportunity to return to their roots and unite across differences through a movement of radical hope across the public sphere. This is a task that is recognizable to the 1500-plus people that contributed to the Spaces of Hope movement from 2016 to the present. It is also recognizable to numerous institutions, including, but not limited to, those featured in this book. If a movement of hope is to grow, it will do so through transformational leadership from diverse positionalities, within our institutions and across civil society. It starts with you.

Notes

1 There is a sense of serendipity about this connection with Virginia Theological Seminary (VTS). VTS has governance responsibilities for another seminary; the General Theological Seminary (GTS) which is in New York. In 1914–15, William Temple gave the William Paddock Lectures at GTS. It is reputed that the time Temple spent in America, including through his time at GTS and through his connection with Reinhold Niebuhr, was a time where Temple's idealism was replaced by realism. Maybe my time as a Dean's Scholar at VTS might have a similarly formative quality to it.

References

Acemoglu, D. and Robinson, J., 2012, *The Origins of Power, Prosperity, and Poverty, Why Nations Fail*, Crown Publishers, New York.
Alexander, J., 2020, *Citizens: Why the key to fixing everything is all of us*, London: Canbury.
Alinsky, S., 1971, *Rules for Radicals: A Pragmatic Primer for Realistic Radicals*, Random House, New York.
APPG, 2020, 'Keeping the Faith: Partnerships between Faith Groups and Local Authorities during and beyond the Pandemic', All Party Parliamentary Group for Faith and Society, Westminster, https://www.faithandsociety.org/keeping-the-faith/, accessed 30.10.2023.
APPG, 2022, 'Keeping the Faith II: Embedding a new normal for partnership working for post-pandemic Britain', All Party Parliamentary Group for Faith and Society, Westminster, available at https://www.faithandsociety.org/keeping-the-faith/, accessed 30.10.2023.
Archbishop of Canterbury's Commission on Urban Priority Areas, 1985, *Faith in the City: A Call for Action by Church and Nation*, London: Church House Publishing.
Archbishops' Council, 2016, Section E1.4, *Canon Law*, London: Church House Publishing.
Arendt, Hannah, 1998 (1958), *The Human Condition*, Chicago, IL: Chicago University Press.
Arnold, J., 2024, 'Radical Hope in an Election Year' in Barber-Rowell, R. (ed.), *Radical Hope in an Election Year? Reflections from a Roundtable at Liverpool Hope University*, Liverpool: Temple Books, https://williamtemplefoundation.org.uk/temple-books.
Ashworth, P., 2024, 'Liverpool rector to quit a Church that validates "homophobic and misogynistic views"', *Church Times*, 25 March, https://www.churchtimes.co.uk/articles/2024/28-march/news/uk/liverpool-rector-to-quit-a-church-that-validates-homophobic-and-misogynistic-views.
Atherton, J., 2018, 'By their fruits you will know them: The economics of material wellbeing and a Christianity fit for purpose', in C. Baker and E. Graham, *Theology for Changing Times: John Atherton and the Future of Public Theology*, London: SCM Press, pp. 20–36.
Atherton, J., Baker, C. and Reader, J., 2011, 'Faith and the new social and welfare policy: How do we understand the Big Society?' in J. Atherton, C. Baker, J. Reader, *Christianity and the New Social Order: A Manifesto for a Fairer Future*, London: SPCK, pp. 75–107.
Attride-Stirling, J., 2001, 'Thematic Networks: An analytic tool for qualitative research', *Qualitative Research*, 1 (3), pp. 385–405.

REFERENCES

Aupers, S. and Houtman, D., 2003, 'Oriental Religion in the Secular West: Globalization, new age and the re-enchantment of the world', *Journal of National Development*, 6 (1/2), pp. 67–86.

Baerveldt, C., 1996, 'New-Age Religiositeit als individueel constructieproces [New Age-religiosity as a process of individual construction]', in J. V. Arkel (ed.), *De kool en de geit in de nieuwe tijd: Wetenschappelijke reflecties op new age [The fence, the hare, and the hounds in the new age: Scientific reflections on new age]*, Utrecht, pp. 19–31.

Baker, C., 2015, 'Where Politics, Theology and Philosophy Meet', *William Temple Foundation*, 3 September, https://williamtemplefoundation.org.uk/book-review-christ-in-all-things-spencer-william-temple/.

Baker, C., 2016, 'Faith in the Public Sphere – in search of a fair and compassionate society for the twenty-first century', *Journal of Beliefs and Values*, 37 (3), pp. 259–72.

Baker, C., 2017, 'Mission and Authenticity', *Anvil: Journal of Theology and Mission*, 3 (33), pp. 30–7.

Baker, C., 2020 see APPG, 2020.

Baker, C., 2022 see APPG, 2022.

Baker, C., Crisp, B. and Dinham, A., 2018, *Re-imagining Religion and Belief: 21st Century Policy and Practice*, Bristol: Policy Press.

Baker, C. and Dinham, A., 2017, 'New interdisciplinary Spaces of Religions and Beliefs in Contemporary Thought and Practice: An Analysis', *Religions*, 8 (16), pp. 1–12.

Baker, C. and Dinham, A., 2018, 'Renegotiating Religion and Belief in the Public Square: Definitions, Debates, Controversies' in C. Baker, B. Crisp, A. Dinham, 2018, *Re-imagining Religion and Belief: 21st Century Policy and Practice*, Bristol: Policy Press, pp. 15–32.

Baker, C. and Graham, E., 2018, *Theology in Changing Times: John Atherton and the future of public theology*, London: SCM Press.

Baker, C., James, T. and Reader, J., 2015, *A Philosophy of Christian Materialism: Entangled Fidelities and the Public Good*, Farnham: Ashgate.

Baker, C. and Haecker, R. (eds), 2023, *Re-envisioning the British State in a Time of Crisis: A Critical Revisiting of the Balliol Connection of Temple, Tawney and Beveridge for the 21st Century*, Rochdale: Temple Books.

Barbato, M., 2012, 'Postsecular Revolution: Religion after the End of History', *Review of International Studies*, 38 (5), pp. 1079–97.

Barber, M., 2017, 'Curating Spaces of Hope: A New Definition and Model of Faith Based Organisations', *Temple Tract Series*, William Temple Foundation, available at https://williamtemplefoundation.org.uk/wp-content/uploads/2017/12/Matthew-Barber-Spaces-of-Hope.pdf, accessed 1.04.2019.

Barber, M., 2020, 'What is unseen is eternal', *Magnet Magazine*, 121, available at https://ourmagnet.hymnsam.co.uk/articles/121/bible-studies/bible-study-what-is-unseen-is-eternal/, accessed 24.03.2020.

Barber, M., 2020, 'Lockdown, liminality and leadership', *William Temple Foundation Blog*, https://williamtemplefoundation.org.uk/blog-lockdown-liminality-and-local-leadership/, accessed 26.07.2024.

Barber-Rowell, M., 2021, *Curating Spaces of Hope: Towards a Liminal, Rhizomatic and Productive Paradigm of Faith Based Organisations (FBOs)*, London: Goldsmiths, University of London.

Barber-Rowell, M., 2022a, 'Curating Spaces of Hope: Intra-Communities Dialogue and Local Leadership in Post-pandemic Society', *William Temple Foundation Blog*, https://williamtemplefoundation.org.uk/curating-spaces-of-hope/, accessed 31.07.2022.
Barber-Rowell, M., 2022b, 'Curating Spaces of Hope: Intra-Communities Dialogue and Post-Pandemic Society', London: William Temple Foundation, https://williamtemplefoundation.org.uk/curating-spaces-of-hope-2/, accessed 14.03.2023.
Barber-Rowell, M., 2022c, 'Curating Spaces of Hope: Local Leadership for Post-pandemic Society', *William Temple Foundation Blog*, https://williamtemplefoundation.org.uk/curatspaces-of-hope-3/, accessed 31.07.2022.
Barber-Rowell, M., 2023a, 'Curating Spaces of Hope: exploring the potential for Faith Based Organisations in uncertain times', *Social Policy Review* 35, https://doi.org/10.51952/9781447369219.ch007.
Barber-Rowell, M., 2023b, 'Curating Spaces of Hope: Coproducing Shared Values in Uncertain Times', *Sociology Study*, https://doi.org/10.17265/2159-5526/2023.02.004.
Barber-Rowell, M., 2023c, 'Curating Spaces of Hope: a new paradigm of post-secular partnership for uncertain times', *Journal of Church and State*, 65, pp. 418–27.
Barber-Rowell, M., 2024a, 'Radical Hope: Reflections from a Roundtable at Liverpool Hope University', *William Temple Foundation Blog*, 3 May, https://williamtemplefoundation.org.uk/radical-hope-reflections-on-a-roundtable-at-liverpool-hope-university/, accessed 26.07.2024.
Barber-Rowell, M. (ed.), 2024b, *Finding Radical Hope in an Election Year? Reflections from a Roundtable at Liverpool Hope University*, Liverpool: Temple Books.
Beaumont, J., 2004, 'Workfare, associationism and the "underclass" in the United States: contrasting faith-based action on urban poverty in a liberal welfare regime' in *European Churches Confronting Poverty: Social Action against exclusion*, Bochum: SWI Verlag, pp. 249–78.
Beaumont, J., 2008a, 'Dossier: "Faith-based organisations and human geography"', *Tijdschrift voor Economishe en Sociale Geografie*, 99(4), pp. 377–81.
Beaumont, J., 2008b, 'Faith Action in urban social issues', *Urban Studies*, 45(10), pp. 2019–34.
Beaumont, J. and Baker, C., 2011, *Postsecular Cities*, London: Continuum.
Beaumont, J. and Cloke, P., 2012, 'Introduction' in *Faith based Organisations and Exclusion in European Cities*, Bristol: Policy Press, pp. 1–36.
Beaumont, J. and Dias, C., 2008, 'Faith Based Organisations and Urban Social Justice in the Netherlands', *Tijdschrift voor Economishe en Sociale Geografie*, 99, pp. 382–92.
Beck, U., 1992, *Risk Society: Towards a new modernity*, London: Sage.
Beck, U., 1998, *World Risk Society*, London: Wiley Press.
Beck, U., 2009, *World at Risk*, London: Polity Press.
Beckford, J. A., 2012, 'SSSR presidential address: Public religions and the post-secular: Critical reflections', *Journal for the Scientific Study of Religion*, 51 (1), pp. 1–19.
Berger, P., 1999, 'The desecularization of the world: A global view' in P. Berger (ed.), *The Desecularization of the World: Resurgent Religion and World Politics*, Grand Rapids, MI: William B Eerdmans, pp. 1–18.

REFERENCES

Bloom, C., 2022, *The Bloom Review: Does the Government do God?*, https://assets.publishing.service.gov.uk/government/uploads/system/uploads/attachment_data/file/1152684/The_Bloom_Review.pdf, accessed 1.12.23.

Bolz-Weber, N., 2014, *Accidental Saints: Finding God in all the wrong people*, Norwich: Canterbury Press.

Bonhoeffer, D., 1935, 'Letter to Karl-Friedrich Bonhoeffer, 14 January 1935' in Keith Clements (ed.), Isabel Best (trans.), *Dietrich Bonhoeffer, London, 1933–1935*, Dietrich Bonhoeffer Works, volume 13, Minneapolis, MN: Fortress Press, p. 285.

Bonta, M. and Protevi, J., 2006, *Deleuze and Geophilosophy: A Guide and Geophilosophy*, 2nd ed., Edinburgh: Edinburgh University Press.

Brandsen, T. and Honingh, M., 2018, 'Definitions of Co-Production and Co-Creation' in Brandsen, T., Steen, T., Verschuere, B. (eds), *Coproduction and Cocreation: Engaging Citizens in Public Services*, London: Routledge, online, https://library.oapen.org/bitstream/id/186359f7-aac1-42e2-8aeb-7c28671869d5/9781138700116_text.pdf, accessed 29.11.2023.

Brandsen, T., Steen, T., Verschuere, B., 2018, 'Co-Creation and Co-Production in Public Services: Urgent Issues in Practice and Research' in Brandsen, T., Steen, T., Verschuere, B. (eds), *Coproduction and Cocreation: Engaging Citizens in Public Services*, London: Routledge, online, https://library.oapen.org/bitstream/id/186359f7-aac1-42e2-8aeb-7c28671869d5/9781138700116_text.pdf, accessed 29.11.2023.

Brown, C., 2003, 'Campbell interrupted Blair as he spoke of his faith: "We don't do God"', *Telegraph*, 4 May, https://www.telegraph.co.uk/news/uknews/1429109/Campbell-interrupted-Blair-as-he-spoke-of-his-faith-We-dont-do-God.html, accessed 24.07.2024.

Brown, M., 2014a, 'The Case for Anglican Social Theology Today' in *Anglican Social Theology*, London: Church House Publishing, pp. 1–27.

Brown, M., 2014b, 'Anglican Social Theology Tomorrow' in *Anglican Social Theology*, London: Church House Publishing, pp. 175–89.

Brown, M., 2016, 'Reflections on Bishop David Jenkins', *William Temple Foundation Blog*, https://williamtemplefoundation.org.uk/reflections-on-bishop-david-jenkins/, accessed 24.07.2024.

Bruce, S., 2002, *God is Dead: Secularisation in the West*, 1st ed., Oxford: Blackwell.

Brueggemann, W., 2018 (1978), 'In Retrospect: Prophetic Imagination at Forty' in W. Brueggemann, *The Prophetic Imagination: 40th Anniversary Edition*, Minneapolis, MN: Fortress Press.

Bullivant, S., 2017, *The 'no religion' population of Britain*, London: St Mary's University Twickenham.

Calhoun, C., 1993, '"New Social Movements" of the early nineteenth century', *Social Science History*, 17 3 (Fall 1993), pp. 385–427.

Calhoun, C., 2014, 'Religion, Government and the Public Good', William Temple Foundation 70th Anniversary Conference Public Lecture, online, https://williamtemplefoundation.org.uk/celebrating-a-successful-conference-temple70/, accessed 13.03.2020.

Calhoun, C., Juergensmeyer, M. and Van Antwerpen, J., 2011, *Rethinking Secularism*, Oxford: Oxford University Press.

Caputo, J. D., 2020, *In Search of Radical Theology: Expositions, Explorations, Exhortations*, New York: Fordham University Press.
Caputo, J. D., 2023, *What to Believe? Twelve Brief Lessons in Radical Theology*, New York: Columbia University Press.
Carson, R., 1962, *Silent Spring*, New York: Penguin.
Chesters, A., 2001, 'Foreword' in S. Spencer, *William Temple, A Calling to Prophecy*, London: SPCK.
Chesters, G. and Welsh, I., 2011, *Social Movements: The Key Concepts*, Oxford: Routledge.
Civil Society Futures, 2018, *Inquiry into the Future of Civil Society in England*, online, https://civilsocietyfutures.org/wp-content/uploads/sites/6/2018/11/Civil-Society-Futures_Civil-Society-in-England_small-1.pdf, accessed 24.03.2020.
Clark, C. and Woodhead, L., 2018, *Westminster Faith Debates, A New Settlement Revised: Religion and Belief in Schools*, http://faithdebates.org.uk/wp-content/uploads/2018/07/Clarke-Woodhead-A-New-Settlement-Revised.pdf, accessed 30.03.2020.
Cloke, P., 2010, 'Theo-ethics and radical faith-based praxis in the postsecular city' in Molendijk, A., Beaumont, J. and Jedan, C. (eds), *Exploring the Postsecular, The Religious, the Political and the Urban*, Vol. 13, Leiden: Brill, pp. 223–41.
Cloke, P., 2016, 'Understanding the Economic Realm', in P. Cloke, M. Pears, *Mission in marginal places: The Praxis*, Milton Keynes: Paternoster, pp. 517–1023.
Cloke, P., Baker, C., Sutherland, C., Williams, A., 2019, *Geographies of Postsecularity: Re-envisioning Politics, Subjectivity and Ethics*, London: Routledge.
Cloke, P., Sutherland, C. and Williams, A., 2016, 'Postsecularity, Political Resistance, and the protest in the Occupy Movement', *Antipode*, 48 (3), pp. 497–523.
Cloke, P., Thomas, S., Williams, A., 2013, 'Faith in Action: Faith based Organisations, Welfare and Politics in the Contemporary City' in P. Cloke, J. Beaumont, A. Williams (eds), *Working Faith: Faith Based Organisations and urban social justice*, Milton Keynes: Paternoster, pp. 1–24.
Cloke, P., Williams, A., Thomas, S., 2013, 'Faith based Action Against Poverty: Christians Against Poverty and Church Action on Poverty' in P. Cloke, J. Beaumont, A. Williams (eds), *Working Faith: Faith Based Organisations and Urban Social Justice*, Milton Keynes: Paternoster, pp. 34–42.
Cnaan, R. A., Wineburg, R. J., Boddie, S. C., 1999, *A Newer Deal: Social Work and religion in partnership*, New York: Columbia University Press.
Coleman, J., 2024, 'Liverpool City Council handed back decision making powers', *BBC News*, 8 May, https://www.bbc.co.uk/news/articles/cz5dx73j3m1o, accessed 26.07.2024.
Conde-Frazier E., 2006, 'Participatory Action Research: Practical Theology for Social Justice', *Religious Education*, 101 (3), pp. 321–9.
Congo Children's Trust, 2020, *Congo Children's Trust – Centre Kimbilio*, https://congochildrentrust.org, accessed 24.03.2020.
Council of Christians and Jews (CCJ), 2020, *Council of Christians and Jews*, http://www.ccj.org.uk, accessed 31.03.2020.
Curtice, J., Clery, E., Perry, J., Phillips M. and Rahim, N. (eds), 2019, *British Social Attitudes Survey 36*, London: National Centre for Social Research, https://natcen.ac.uk/sites/default/files/2023-08/BSA_36.pdf, accessed 26.11.2024.

REFERENCES

Dando, C., 2014, 'New Look William Temple Foundation, same enduring values', *William Temple Foundation blog*, 27 March, https://williamtemplefoundation.org.uk/new-look-william-temple-foundation-same-enduring-values/, accessed 25.07.2024.

DeLanda, M., 2016, *Assemblage Theory*, Edinburgh: Edinburgh University Press.

Deleuze, G., 1992, 'Postscript on the Societies of Control', *October*, 59 (Winter 1992), pp. 3–7, https://cidadeinseguranca.files.wordpress.com/2012/02/deleuze_control.pdf, accessed 29.11.2023.

Deleuze. G., 1997, *Desire and Pleasure*, McMahon, M. (trans.), unpublished.

Deleuze, G., 2014 (1968), *Difference and Repetition*, London: Bloomsbury.

Deleuze, G. and Guattari, F., 2016 (1988), *A Thousand Plateaus*, London: Bloomsbury.

Deleuze, G. and Parnet, C., 2007 (1977), *Dialogues II*, New York: Columbia University Press.

Dinham, A., 2008, 'Commentary: From Faith in the City to Faithful Cities: The "Third Way", the Church of England and Urban Regeneration', *Urban Studies*, 45 (10), pp. 2163–74.

Dinham, A., 2015, 'Religious Literacy and Welfare', in Dinham, A., Francis, M., *Religious Literacy in Policy and Practice*, London: Policy Press, pp. 101–12.

Dinham, A., 2016, 'Grace Davie and Religious Literacy: Undoing a Lamentable Quality of Conversation', in A. Day, M. Lövheim (eds), *Modernities, Memory and Mutations: Grace Davie and the Study of Religion*, London: Routledge.

Diocese of Manchester, 2023, 'Eco Stepping Stones Promo Video', *Diocese of Manchester*, https://www.manchester.anglican.org/faithlife/ecodiocese/eco-stepping-stones/, accessed 26.07.2024.

Dorling, D., 2010, 'New Labour and Inequality: Thatcherism Continued?', *Local Economy*, 25 (5/6), pp. 397–413.

Easthope, L., 2023, *When the Dust Settles: Searching for Hope After Disaster*, London: Hodder.

Enlow, J., 2008, *The Seven Mountain Prophecy: Unveiling the Coming Elijah Revolution*, Creation House Publishing.

Esping-Andersen, G., 1990, *The Three Worlds of Welfare Capitalism*, Cambridge: Polity Press.

Giddens, A., 1998, *Third Way: The Renewal of Social Democracy*, Cambridge: Polity.

Giddens, A., 2008, *Modernity and Self-Identity: Self and society in the Later Modern Age*, Cambridge: Polity Press.

Goldman, L., 2023, 'The British State and its Limits, 1870–1945. Tawney, Temple and Beveridge Compared' in C. Baker and R. Haecker (eds), *Re-envisioning the British State in a Time of Crisis: A Critical Revisiting of the Balliol Connection of Temple, Tawney and Beveridge for the 21st Century*, Liverpool: Temple Books.

Goodwin, J. and James, J. M. (eds), 2015, *The Social Movements Reader: Cases and Concepts*, 3rd ed., Chichester: Wiley Blackwell.

Gorski, P., Kim, D., Torpey, J. and Van Antwerpen, J., 2012, *The Postsecular in Question*, New York: New York University Press.

Graham, E., 2013, *Between a Rock and a Hard Place: Public Theology in a Post-Secular Age*, 1st ed., London: SCM Press.

Gramsci, A., 1920, 'Controllo di classe', *L'Ordine Nuovo*, 3 January, https://www.centrogramsci.it/riviste/nuovo/ordine%20nuovo%20p3.pdf.

Gramsci, A., 1920, 'Per un rinnovamento del partito socialista', 8 May 1920: *L'Ordine Nuovo*, p. 117. In Joll (1977), *Gramsci*. Fontana Modern Masters.

Gramsci, A., 1921, *Introduction to Socialismo e Fascismo: L'Ordine Nuovo*. In Joll (1977), *Gramsci*. Fontana Modern Masters.

Gramsci, A., 1957, *The Modern Prince and Other Writings*, Louis Marks (trans.), New York: International Publishers.

Gramsci, A., 1965, *Lettere Dal Carcere a cura di Sergio Caprioglio e Elsa Fubini*, Torino: Einaudi.

Gramsci, A., 1971, *Selections from the Prison Notebooks*, Smith, Q., Hoare, N. (ed. and trans.), London: Lawrence & Wishart Limited.

Greeley, A., 1966, 'After Secularity: The Neo-Gemeinschaft Society – A Post-Christian Postscript', *Sociological Analysis*, 27 (3), pp. 119–27.

Greenbelt, 2024, 'Our Story', *Greenbelt*, https://www.greenbelt.org.uk/greenbelt-festival/#our-story, accessed 22.08.2024.

Grimley, M., 2023, 'Christianity and Social Order in Context' in C. Baker and R. Haecker (eds), *Re-envisioning the British State in a Time of Crisis: A Critical Revisiting of the Balliol Connection of Temple, Tawney and Beveridge for the 21st Century*, Liverpool: Temple Books.

Grimshaw, M., 'Radical theologies', *Palgrave Commun* 1 (2015), 15032, https://doi.org/10.1057/palcomms.2015.32.

Habermas, J., 1976, *Knowledge and Human Interests*, London: Heinemann.

Habermas, J., 1987, *Theory of Communicative Action*, Vol. 2, The Critique of Functionalist Reason, Cambridge: Polity Press.

Habermas, J., 2005, 'Equal Treatment of Cultures and the limits of Post-modern Liberalism', *Journal of Political Philosophy*, 13 (1), pp. 1–28.

Habermas, J., 2008a, 'Notes on Post-Secular Society', *New Perspectives Quarterly*, 25 (4), pp. 17–29.

Habermas, J., 2008b, 'Religion in the Public Sphere: Cognitive Presuppositions for the "Public Use of Reason" by Religious and Secular Citizens' in *Between Naturalism and Religion: Philosophical Essays*, London: Routledge, pp. 114–47.

Habermas, J., 2010, *An Awareness of what is missing: Faith and Reason in a postsecular age*, 1st ed., Cambridge: Polity.

Habermas, J. and Ratzinger, J., 2004, *The Dialectics of Secularisation: On Reason and Religion*, 1st ed., San Francisco, CA: Ignatius Press.

Hamilton, M., 2000, 'An analysis of the festival for Mind-Body-Spirit' in S. Sutcliffe, M. Bowman (eds), *Beyond New Age: Exploring alternative spirituality*, Edinburgh: Edinburgh University Press, pp. 188–200.

Hankins, D., 2018 (1978), 'Foreword' in W. Brueggemann, *The Prophetic Imagination: 40th Anniversary Edition*, Minneapolis, MN: Fortress Press.

Hardin, G., 1968, 'Tragedy of the Common', *Science*, new series, 162, pp. 1243–48.

Harvey, D., 2000, *Spaces of Hope*, Edinburgh: Edinburgh University Press.

Harvieu-Leger, D., 2000, *Religion as a Chain of Memory*, New Brunswick, NJ: Rutgers University of Press.

Hastings, Adrian, 1995, *The Dictionary of National Biography*, Oxford: Oxford University Press.

REFERENCES

Heelas, P. and Woodhead, L., 2005, *The Spiritual Revolution: Why Religion is giving way to spirituality*, 1st ed., Oxford: Blackwell.

Held Evans, R., 2015, *Searching for Sunday: Loving Leaving and Finding the Church*, London: Harper Collins.

Herman, A., Beaumont, J., Cloke, P. and Walliser, A., 2012, 'Spaces of post-secular engagement in cities' in *Faith Based Organisations and Exclusion in European Cities*, Bristol: Policy Press, University of Bristol, pp. 59–80.

HM Government, 2023, *National Risk Register*, London: HMSO, https://assets.publishing.service.gov.uk/government/uploads/system/uploads/attachment_data/file/1175834/2023_NATIONAL_RISK_REGISTER_NRR.pdf, accessed 24.07.2024.

Hoare, G. and Sperber, N., 2016, *An Introduction to Antonion Gramsci: His Life, Thought and Legacy*, London: Bloomsbury.

Hobsbawm, E., 2012, *How to Change the World: Tales of Marx and Marxism*, London: Abacus.

Houtman, D. and Aupers, S., 2007, 'The Spiritual Turn and the Decline of Tradition: The spread of post-Christian spirituality in 14 Western Countries, 1981–2000', *Journal of Scientific Study of Religion*, 46 (3), pp. 305–20.

Howes, A., 2020, *Arts and Minds: How the Royal Society of Arts Changed a Nation*, Princeton, NJ: Princeton University Press.

Howson, C., 2011, *A Just Church: 21st Century Liberation Theory in Action*, London: Continuum.

Hughes, J., 2014, 'After Temple: The Recent Renewal of Anglican Social Thought' in M. Brown (ed.), *Anglican Social Theology*, London: Church House Publishing, pp. 74–101.

Interfaith Network, The, 1999, *The Local Interfaith Guide – Faith Community in Action,* London: Interfaith Network and the Office of the Deputy Prime Minister.

Iremonger, F. A., 1948, *William Temple: Archbishop of Canterbury*, Oxford: Oxford University Press.

Johnsen, S., 2014, 'Where is the "F" in FBO? The evolution and Practice of Faith Based Homelessness Services in the UK', *Journal of Social Policy*, 43 (2), pp. 413–30.

Joll, J., 1977, *Gramsci*, London: Fontana Modern Masters.

Kaufmann, E., 'Shall the Religious Inherit the Earth?', *Studies: An Irish Quarterly Review*, Winter 2010, pp. 387–94.

Klandermans, B., 1991, 'New social movements and resource mobilization: The European and the American approach revisited', *Politics & the Individual*, 1 (2), pp. 89–111.

Kong, L., 2010, 'Global shifts, theoretical shifts: Changing geographies of religion', *Progress in Human Geography*, 34 (6), pp. 755–76.

Kuhn, T., 2012 (1962), *The Structure of Scientific Revolutions: 50th Anniversary Edition*, Chicago, IL: University of Chicago Press.

Laclau, E. and Mouffe, C., 2001 (1985), *Hegemony and Socialist Strategy: Towards a Radical Democratic Politics*, London: Verso.

Lansley, J., 2010, 'Charities and Philanthropy in Liverpool' in R. Morris and H. Russell (eds), *Roots in the City, Recollections and Assessments of 100 years of voluntary action in the city*, Liverpool: Liverpool Charity and Voluntary Services Press.

Latour, B., 2007, *Reassembling the Social: An Introduction to Actor Network Theory*, Oxford: Oxford University Press.

Lear, J., 2008, *Radical Hope: Ethics in the Face of Cultural Devastation*, Cambridge, MA: Harvard University Press.

Lee, L., 2016, 'The nonreligious are Britain's hidden majority', *London School of Economics and Political Science*, 4 January, http://blogs.lse.ac.uk/politicsandpolicy/the-nonreligious-are-britains-hidden-majority/, accessed 3.11.2017.

Lee, S., 2023a, 'Balliol Influences: How One College Lost an Empire and Found a Common Wealth of Ideas' in C. Baker and R. Haecker (eds), *Re-envisioning the British State in a Time of Crisis: A Critical Revisiting of the Balliol Connection of Temple, Tawney and Beveridge for the 21st Century*, Rochdale: Temple Books.

Lee, S. 2023b, 'The Serendipity of Hope in the Peripheral Vision of a University' in S. Lee and I. Markham (eds), *The Serendipity of Hope*, Eugene, OR: Pickwick Publications, pp. 1–38.

Lee, S., 2024, 'Afterword' in Barber-Rowell, R. (ed.), *Radical Hope in an Election Year? Reflections from a Roundtable at Liverpool Hope University*, Liverpool: Temple Books, https://williamtemplefoundation.org.uk/temple-books.

Levin, J., 2020, 'The faith community and the SARS-CoV-2 outbreak: part of the problem or part of the solution?', *Journal of Religious Health*, 59, pp. 2215–28.

Levin, J., 2022, 'Human flourishing in the era of COVID-19: how spirituality and the faith sector help and hinder our collective response', *Challenges*, 13 (1), p. 12, https://doi.org/10.3390/challe13010012.

Levin, J., Idler, E. and VanderWeele, T., 2022, 'Faith-Based Organizations and SARS-CoV-2 vaccination: challenges and recommendations', *Public Health Reports*, 137 (1), pp. 11–16, https://journals.sagepub.com/doi/full/10.1177/00333549211054079.

Ley, D., 2011, 'Preface: Towards a Postsecular City?' in J. Beaumont, C. Baker (eds), *Postsecular cities: Space, Theory and Practice*, London: Continuum, pp. xii–xiv.

Link Up, 2015, 'About Us', *Link Up*, https://www.linkup.uk.net/Groups/109040/Link_Up/About_Us/About_Us.aspx, accessed 24.03.2020.

Liverpool City Council, 2021, 'Religion – Census 2021, Key Stats and Data', *Liverpool City Council*, https://liverpool.gov.uk/council/key-statistics-and-data/census-2021/religion/, accessed 29.11.2023.

Liverpool Post, 2024, 'Joe Anderson doesn't have many defenders, but he has two in the house of Lords', *The Post*, 22 April, https://www.livpost.co.uk/p/joe-anderson-doesnt-have-many-defenders?utm_source=post-email-title&publication_id=107018&post_id=143850676&utm_campaign=email-post-title&isFreemail=true&r=2lplap&triedRedirect=true&utm_medium=email, accessed 26.07.2024.

Local Trust, 2019, 'Locally trusted organisations', *Local Trust*, https://localtrust.org.uk/big-local/programme-guidance/locally-trusted-organisations/, accessed 24.07.2024.

Lövheim, M., 2013, *Media, Religion and Gender: Key issues and Challenges*, London: Routledge.

Lucas, S., 2018, *The 'Glorious Liberty of the Children of God': Reimagining Freedom Beyond Liberalism between William Temple and Hannah Arendt*, Temple Tracts, 2 (4), William Temple Foundation.

REFERENCES

Lukianoff, G. and Haidt, J., 2018, *The Coddling of the American Mind: How Good Intentions and Bad Ideas Are Setting Up a Generation for Failure*, London: Penguin.

Lyon, D., 2000, *Jesus in Disneyland: Religion in Post-Modern times*, 1st ed., Oxford: Polity Press.

Makin, Keith, 2024, *Independent Learning Lessons Review: John Smyth QC* (The Makin Review), https://www.churchofengland.org/sites/default/files/2024-11/independent-learning-lessons-review-john-smyth-qc-november-2024.pdf.

Manchester Guardian, 1920, 'The New Bishop of Manchester. Canon William Temple. An Appreciation', *Manchester Guardian*, 1 December.

Markham, I., 2024, 'Hope and higher education' in Barber-Rowell, R. (ed.), *Radical Hope in an Election Year? Reflections from a Roundtable at Liverpool Hope University*, Liverpool: Temple Books, https://williamtemplefoundation.org.uk/temple-books.

Marmot, M., et al., 2010, 'Fair Society, Healthy Lives (Marmot Review)', *Institute of Health Equity*, https://www.instituteofhealthequity.org/resources-reports/fair-society-healthy-lives-the-marmot-review, accessed 30.10.2023.

Marmot, M., 2020, 'Health Equity in England: The Marmot Review 10 years on', *The Health Foundation*, https://www.health.org.uk/publications/reports/the-marmot-review-10-years-on, accessed 30.10.2023.

Marmot Group, 2023, *Wider Determinants of Health Group*, https://phar.liverpool.gov.uk/wider-determinants-of-health/, accessed 1.12.2023.

Massumi, B., 2015, *Politics of Affect*, Cambridge: Polity Press.

Massumi, B., 2016 (1988), 'Preface: Translator's Foreword, Pleasures of Philosophy' in G. Deleuze and F. Guattari, *A Thousand Plateaus*, London: Bloomsbury, pp. i–xviii.

Mavelli, L., 2012, 'Postsecular Resistance, the body, and the 2011 Egyptian Revolution', *Review of International Studies*, 38 (5), pp. 1057–78.

May, J. and Cloke, P., 'Modes of Attentiveness: Reading for Difference in Geographies of Homelessness', *Antipode*, 46 (2014), pp. 894–920.

May, T., 2005, *Gilles Deleuze: An Introduction*, Cambridge: Cambridge University Press.

McAuley, P., 2024, '"Sombre and dark period" leaves Christians "invigorated and fuller" in their faith', *Echo*, 14 February, https://www.liverpoolecho.co.uk/news/liverpool-news/sombre-dark-period-leaves-christians-28624122, accessed 25.07.2024.

McFarlane, C., 2011, 'Assemblage and Critical Urban Praxis: Part One', *City*, 15 (2), pp. 204–24.

McGrail, P., 2024, 'Afterword' in Barber-Rowell, R. (ed.), *Radical Hope in an Election Year? Reflections from a Roundtable at Liverpool Hope University*, Liverpool: Temple Books, https://williamtemplefoundation.org.uk/temple-books.

Melucci, A., 1980, 'The New Social Movements: A Theoretical Approach', *Social Science Information*, 19 (2), pp. 199–226.

Melucci, A., 1985, 'The symbolic challenge of contemporary movements', *Social Research*, 52 (4), pp. 789–816.

Melucci, A., 1989, *Nomads of the Present*, London: Radius Hutchinson.

Milbank, J., 2011, 'The Church is the site of true society', *Church Times*, 14 December, https://www.churchtimes.co.uk/articles/2011/16-december/comment/the-church-is-the-site-of-the-true-society, accessed 24.07.2024.

Mill, J. S., 1859, *On Liberty*, London: John W. Parker and Son.
Molendijk, A., Beaumont, J., Jaden, C., 2010, *Exploring the Postsecular: The Religious, the Political and the Urban*, Leiden: Brill.
Morris, R., Russell, H., 2010, *Rooted in the City: Recollection and assessments of 100 years of voluntary action in Liverpool*, Liverpool: Liverpool Charity and Voluntary Services Press.
Mountford, R., 2013, *The Mantle of Chad*, Stoke on Trent: Tentmaker Press.
Nest, M. et al, 2006, *The Democratic Republic of Congo; Economic Dimensions of War and Peace*, Boulder, CO: Lynne Rienner Publishers.
Niebuhr, R., 1944, 'Dr William Temple and His Britain', *The Nation*, 12 November.
North, P., 2016, 'How the Hills of the North are supposed to Rejoice', *Church Times*, 29 April, https://www.churchtimes.co.uk/articles/2016/29-april/books-arts/book-reviews/how-the-hills-of-the-north-are-to-rejoice, accessed 25.07.2024.
Nynas, P., Lassander, M., Ultriainen, T., 2015, *Postsecular Society*, New Brunswick NJ: Transaction.
Offe, C., 1985, 'New Social Movements: Challenging the Boundaries of Institutional Politics', *Social Research*, 52 4 (Winter), p. 817.
Office for National Statistics, 2022, *Religion, England and Wales: Census 2021*, https://www.ons.gov.uk/peoplepopulationandcommunity/culturalidentity/religion/bulletins/religionenglandandwales/census2021#how-religious-affiliation-varies-across-england-and-wales, accessed 4.11.2024.
Olson, E., Hopkins, P., Pain, R., Vincent, G., 'Retheorizing the postsecular present: Embodiment, Spatial Transcendence, and Challenges to Authenticity Among Young Christians in Glasgow', *Annal of the Association of American Geographers*, 103 (2013), pp. 1421–36.
Ostrom, E., 1999, 'Coping with the Tragedy of the Commons', *Annual Review of Political Science*, pp. 493–535.
Ostrom, E., 'Beyond markets and states: Polycentric Governance of complex economic systems', *American Economic Review*, 100 (2010), pp. 1–33.
Ostrom, E. and Whitaker, G., 1973, 'Does Local Community Control of Police make a Difference? Some Preliminary Findings', *American Journal of Political Science*, 17 (1).
Oxford English Dictionary, 2024, 'radical adj. & n.', *Oxford English Dictionary*, September, https://www.oed.com/dictionary/radical_adj?tl=true, accessed 24.07.2024.
Parmaksiz, U., 2018, 'Making Sense of the Postsecular', *European Journal of Social Theory*, 21 (1), pp. 98–116.
Partridge, C., 2006, 'The Spiritual and the Revolutionary: Alternative Spirituality, British Free Festivals, and the Emergence of Rave Culture', *Culture and Religion: An Interdisciplinary Journal*, 7 (1), pp. 41–60.
Percy, M., 2021, 'Preface' in *Crossing Thresholds: A Practical Theology of Liminality*, T. Carson, R. Fairhurst, N. Rooms and L. Withrow (eds), London: The Lutterworth Press.
Phillips, R. (ed.), 2009, *Muslim Spaces of Hope: Geographies of Possibility in Britain and the West*, London and New York: Zed Books.
Pidd, H., 2019, 'Is this the most depressed place in England?', *The Guardian*, 6 May, https://www.theguardian.com/uk-news/2019/may/06/is-brinnington-stockport-the-most-depressed-place-in-england.

REFERENCES

Pope Francis, 2023, *Laudate Deum*, Vatican Press, https://www.vatican.va/content/francesco/en/apost_exhortations/documents/20231004-laudate-deum.pdf, accessed 19.04.2024.

Pope Francis and Ahmad Al-Tayyeb, 2019, *A Document on Human Fraternity For World Peace and Living Together*, Vatican Press, https://www.vatican.va/content/francesco/en/travels/2019/outside/documents/papa-francesco_20190204_documento-fratellanza-umana.html, accessed 24.07.2024.

Possamai, A., 2003, 'Alternative spiritualities and the cultural logic of late capitalism', *Culture in Religion*, 4 (1), pp. 31–45.

Pratt, J., 2024, 'Hope in Higher Education' in Barber-Rowell, R. (ed.), *Radical Hope in an Election Year? Reflections from a Roundtable at Liverpool Hope University*, Liverpool: Temple Books, https://williamtemplefoundation.org.uk/temple-books.

Putnam, R., 1993, *Making Democracy Work. Civic traditions in modern Italy*, Princeton, NJ: Princeton University Press.

Putnam, R., 2000, *Bowling Alone*, 1st ed., New York: Simon and Schuster.

Putnam, R., Campbell, D., 2010, *American Grace: How Religion Divides Us and Unites Us*, 1st ed., New York: Simon and Schuster.

Raleigh, V., 2022, 'Deaths from Covid-19 (coronavirus)', *The King's Fund*, 23 August, https://www.kingsfund.org.uk/insight-and-analysis/long-reads/deaths-covid-19, accessed 26.07.2024.

Reader, J., 2014, 'Paradigm Change in Theology', *William Temple Foundation Blog*, https://williamtemplefoundation.org.uk/paradigm-change-in-theology/, accessed 24.07.2024.

Reddie, A., 2023, 'The Balliol Legacy Remembered', in C. Baker and R. Haecker (eds), *Re-envisioning the British State in a Time of Crisis: A Critical Revisiting of the Balliol Connection of Temple, Tawney and Beveridge for the 21st Century*, Liverpool: Temple Books.

Reeve, G., 2023, *Navigating 2020 as a Social Researcher*, William Temple Foundation Blog. Available at https://williamtemplefoundation.org.uk/blog-navigating-2020, accessed 17.02.2025.

Richards, A. and the Mission Theology Advisory Group, 2017, *The Five Marks of Mission*, https://www.churchofengland.org/sites/default/files/2017-11/mtag-the-5-marks-of-mission.pdf, accessed 22.08.2024.

Robbins, J., Crockett, C., 2015, 'A radical theology for the future: five theses', *Palgrave Commun* 1, 15028, https://doi.org/10.1057/palcomms.2015.28.

Romanillos, J., Beaumont, J., Sen, M., 2012, 'State–Religion Relations and Welfare Regimes in Europe', in Beaumont, J. and Cloke, P. (eds), *Faith-based Organisations and Exclusion in European Cities*, Bristol: Policy Press, pp. 37–58.

Rosling, H., Rosling, A., Rosling, O., 2018, *Factfulness: Ten reasons we are wrong about the world – and why things are better than you think*, London: Sceptre.

Rowson, J., 2021, 'Tasting the Pickle: Ten flavours of meta-crisis and the appetite for a new civilisation', *Perspectiva*, 9 February, https://systems-souls-society.com/tasting-the-pickle-ten-flavours-of-meta-crisis-and-the-appetite-for-a-new-civilisation/, accessed 24.07.2024.

Royal Society of Arts, 2018, 'Health as a Social Movement', *RSA*, https://www.thersa.org/action-and-research/rsa-projects/public-services-and-communities-folder/health-as-a-social-movement, accessed 1.04.2019.

Royal Society of Arts Journal, '50 Famous Fellows', *Royal Society of Arts Journal*, 1 (2024), pp. 32–7.
Schmitt, C., 1922, *Political Theology: Four chapters on the concept of Sovereignty*, Chicago, IL: University of Chicago Press.
Schmitt, C., 1970, *Political Theology II: The myth of the closure of any political theology*, Cambridge: Polity Press.
Sedgwick, P., 2018, 'The Manchester School', in C. Baker, E. Graham, *Theology in Changing Times: John Atherton and the future of public theology*, London: SCM Press, pp. 50–64.
Seigworth, G., 2011, 'From Affection to Soul' in C. Stilvale, *Gilles Deleuze, Key Concepts*, London: Routledge.
Shakespeare, S., 2024, 'Ecological Hope' in Barber-Rowell, R. (ed.), *Radical Hope in an Election Year? Reflections from a Roundtable at Liverpool Hope University*, Liverpool: Temple Books, https://williamtemplefoundation.org.uk/temple-books.
Shaw, D., '"William Temple" Fellowship and Service in Blackburn, Lancashire and Manchester', *Journal of Church and State*, 65 4 (Winter 2023), pp. 385–95, https://doi.org/10.1093/jcs/csad064.
Silvoso, E., 2017, *Ekklesia: Rediscovering God's Instrument for Global Transformation*, Minneapolis, MN: Chosen Books.
Skinner, Simon, 2023, 'The Greenian Movement' in C. Baker and R. Haecker (eds), *Re-envisioning the British State in a Time of Crisis: A Critical Revisiting of the Balliol Connection of Temple, Tawney and Beveridge for the 21st Century*, Liverpool: Temple Books.
Smith, G., 2002, *Faith in the Voluntary Sector: A common or distinctive experience of religious organisations*, London: Centre for Institutional Studies, University of East London.
Spencer, S., 2001, *William Temple, A Calling to Prophecy*, London: SPCK.
Spencer, S., 2015, *Christ in all things: William Temple and his Writing*, Norwich: Canterbury Press.
Spencer, S., 2017, 'William Temple and the "Temple Tradition"' in S. Spencer (ed.), *Theology Reforming Society: Revisiting Anglican Social Theology*, London, SCM Press, loc. 1598–1959.
Spencer, S., 2022, *William Temple: A Study in Servant Leadership*, London: SCM Press.
Sridhar, D., 2022, *Preventable: How the Pandemic Changed the World and How to stop the next one*, London: Penguin Random House.
Staggenborg, Suzanne, 2011, *Social Movements*, New York: Oxford University Press.
Suggate, A., 2014, 'The Temple Tradition', in *Anglican Social Theology*, London: Church House Publishing, pp. 28–73.
Taylor, C., 2004, *Modern Social Imaginaries*, London: Duke University Press.
Taylor, C., 2007, *A Secular Age*, Cambridge, MA: Harvard University Press.
Temple, W., 1919, *Mens Creatrix*, London: Macmillan Publishers.
Temple, W., 1924, *Christus Veritas*, London: Macmillan Publishers.
Temple, W., 1925, *Christ's Revelation of God*, London: SCM Press.
Temple, W., 1928, *Christianity and the State*, London: Macmillan Publishers.
Temple, W., 1936, Speech to the Pilgrims of the United States at the Waldorf Astoria, New York, 13th January 1936, The Pilgrims, New York.

REFERENCES

Temple, W., 1941, *Citizen and Churchman*, London: Eyre and Spottiswoode.

Temple, W., 1976 (1942), *Christianity and Social Order*, London: Penguin.

Thomas, G., 2024, 'Radical Hope; Poverty in the City' in Barber-Rowell, R. (ed.), *Radical Hope in an Election Year? Reflections from a Roundtable at Liverpool Hope University*, Liverpool: Temple Books, https://williamtemplefoundation.org.uk/temple-books.

Tilly, C. and Wood, L. J., 2013, *Social Movements 1768–2012*, 3rd ed., London: Routledge.

Torkington, S., 2023, 'We're on the brink of a poly-crisis – how worried should we be?', *World Economic Forum*, 13 January, https://www.weforum.org/agenda/2023/01/polycrisis-global-risks-report-cost-of-living/#:~:text='Polycrisis', accessed 24.07.2024.

Touraine, A., 1977, *The Self-productivity of Society*, Chicago, IL: University of Chicago Press.

Touraine, A., 1981, *The Voice and the Eye*, Cambridge: Cambridge University Press.

Touraine, A., 1983, *Anti-Nuclear Protest: The Opposition to Nuclear Energy in France*, Cambridge: Cambridge University Press.

Turner, V., 1967, 'Betwixt and Between; The Liminal Period in Rites of Passage' in L. C. Mahdi, S. Foster and M. Little (eds), *Betwixt and Between: Patterns of Masculine and Feminine Initiation*, La Salle, IL: Open Court, https://books.google.co.uk/books?id=YohoOEe19pcC&lpg=PA3&dq=victor%20turner%20liminality&lr&pg=PA18#v=onepage&q&f=false, accessed 24.03.2020.

Turner, V., 1969, *Liminality and Communitas, in the Ritual Process: Structure and Anti-Structure*, Chicago, IL: Aldine Publishing.

Van Gennep, A., 1960 (1929), *Les Rites Du Passage*, London: Routledge and Keegan Paul.

Vasquez, M., 2011, *More than Belief; A materialist theory of religion*, Oxford: Oxford University Press.

Vegara, C., 2020, *Systemic Corruption: Constitutional Ideas for an Oligarchic Republic*, Princeton, NJ: Princeton University Press.

Voorberg, W., Bekkers, V. and Tummers, L., 2015, 'A Systematic Review of Co-Creation and Co-Production: Embarking on the Social Innovation Journey', *Public Management Review*, 17 (9), pp. 1333–57.

Wallnau, L., 2016, *God's Chaos Candidate: Donald J. Trump and the American Unravelling*, Keller, TX: Killer Sheep Media Inc.

Watson, T., 2012, 'How might Bonhoeffer's new Monasticism shape today's church?' MA in Theology and Ministry Dissertation, University of Chester, unpublished.

Watson, T., 2014a, *Old Lost and Broken Dreams: Poems Liturgies Prayers and Blessings*, Proost.

Watson, T., 2014b, *Restore: A Service of Compline and Examen*, self-published.

Welby, J., 2024, 'Keynote address: "Embracing Courage" at the Royal Society of Arts', *The Archbishop of Canterbury*, 31 January, https://www.archbishopofcanterbury.org/speaking-writing/speeches/keynote-address-embracing-courage-royal-society-arts, accessed 24.07.2024.

Weller, P., 2022, *Hizmet in Transitions: European Developments of a Turkish Muslim-Inspired movement*, London: Palgrave Macmillan.

Wilford, J., 2010, 'Sacred Archipelagos: Geographies of Secularisation', *Progress in Human Geography*, 34, pp. 328–48.
William Temple Foundation, 2014, 'Celebrating a Successful Conference #Temple70', *William Temple Foundation*, https://williamtemplefoundation.org.uk/celebrating-a-successful-conference-temple70/, accessed 24.03.2020.
William Temple Foundation, 2019, 'Annual Lecture 2019 – Archbishop Justin Welby "Reimagining Britain: Faith and the Common Good"', *YouTube*, 19 May, https://www.youtube.com/watch?v=n1bAhuQszdY, accessed 24.07.2024.
William Temple Foundation, 2024, *Religious Capital in Regenerating Communities*, Manchester: William Temple Foundation, https://williamtemplefoundation.org.uk/wp-content/uploads/2014/03/Religious-Capital-in-Regenerating-Communities-.pdf, accessed 22.08.2024.
Williams, A., Cloke, P. and Thomas, S., 2012, 'Co-constituting neoliberalism: faith-based organisations, co-option and resistance in the UK', *Environment and Planning*, 44.
Williams, R., 2023, 'Response', *Journal of Church and State*, 65 4 (Winter 2023), pp. 457–60, https://doi.org/10.1093/jcs/csad073.
Winter, T., 2023, 'Response', *Journal of Church and State*, 65 4 (Winter 2023), pp. 457–60.
Woodhead, L., 2016, 'The rise of "no religion" in Britain: The emergence of a new cultural majority', *Journal of the British Academy*, 4, pp. 245–61.
Woodhead, L., 2017, 'The Rise of "No Religion": Towards an Explanation', *Sociology of Religion: A Quarterly Review*, 78 (3), p. 247–62.
Woods, D., Walker, J. and Watson, T., 2015, *Lighting Beacons: A Liturgy for Life*. Self-published under Creative Commons License.
World Commission on Environment and Development, 1987, *Our Common Future* (Brundtland Report), United Nations, https://www.are.admin.ch/are/en/home/media/publications/sustainable-development/brundtland-report.html, accessed 25.07.2024.
Wrong, M., 2000, *Footsteps of Mr Kurtz*, London: Forth Estate.

Index of Names and Subjects

abuse 9, 15, 45, 46, 67n13, 168, 196, 202, 211
affect 2, 11, 25, 62, 70, 80–6, 91, 92, 93, 97, 102–3n14, 103n15, 117, 139, 142, 165–6, 167, 170, 172, 174, 179, 180–5, 188, 192, 194, 195, 197, 201, 205, 207
agency 41, 51, 52, 63, 74, 80, 81, 125, 138
archbishop 3, 6, 8, 13, 14, 15, 16, 19, 34, 58, 72, 111, 117, 118, 166, 196, 203, 207
assemblage 5, 10, 77, 79, 80–2, 85, 88, 93, 92, 94, 100, 102n8, 102n9, 102n10, 102n11, 102n12, 103, 162, 164, 174, 183, 186
authenticity 4, 11, 51, 52, 63, 75, 103, 172, 186–8, 193

belief 2, 9, 32, 49, 54, 56, 70, 74, 76, 77, 78, 102n5, 107, 149, 153, 158, 163, 190, 194, 199
beacon 44, 83–91, 173, 176, 178, 182, 184, 194, 196, 200
Bonhoeffer, Dietrich 44, 47, 65, 66n11, 190, 197

Chester 42–3, 47, 49, 55, 66n11, 68n22, 191
  Cathedral 49, 50, 72, 200

University of 30, 32, 43
Christ 18, 21, 27, 28, 39, 40, 44, 45, 85, 111, 190, 200, 201, 212
Christian 2, 5, 10, 15, 16, 18, 21, 27, 32, 39, 75, 76, 83, 88, 89, 93, 94, 95, 96, 101n4, 108, 112, 114, 115, 116, 117, 118, 142, 157, 158, 166, 170, 171, 174, 176, 184, 185, 189, 196, 200, 202
Christianity 3, 8, 10, 14, 19, 20, 21, 22, 23, 25, 26, 28, 31, 32, 33, 34, 43, 50, 54, 63, 70, 99, 171, 197, 198, 199, 200
Christendom 74, 75
church 10, 13, 15, 16, 17, 18, 19, 20, 21, 25, 28, 29, 32, 40, 41, 42, 43, 44, 45, 46, 47, 48, 49, 53, 55, 56, 57, 58, 59, 60, 61, 62, 66n7, 66n11, 67n19, 71, 83, 84, 85, 87, 88, 89, 90, 92, 93, 94, 95, 96, 97, 98, 99, 100, 101, 103n23, 103n24, 111, 112, 113, 117, 118, 127, 128, 129, 138, 145, 146n3, 152, 156, 157, 158, 162, 165, 169n3, 174, 176, 178, 184, 185, 187, 189, 190, 191, 194, 196, 200, 203, 207
citizen 9, 16, 17, 19, 21, 23, 24, 25, 26, 27, 64, 69, 105, 106,

229

107, 108, 110, 117, 123, 145, 162, 172, 180, 198, 208
colonial 40, 176, 202
community 9, 18, 21, 26, 32, 37, 41, 46, 47, 48, 49, 50, 51, 53, 54, 55, 56, 61, 62, 63, 64, 66n11, 71, 83, 84, 85, 86, 87, 88, 89, 90, 91, 92, 93, 94, 100, 105, 106, 107, 110, 111, 112, 113, 115, 118, 120, 121, 122, 123, 127, 128, 129, 131, 132, 138, 157, 162, 173, 176, 178, 180, 182, 184, 187, 191, 194, 196, 200, 201, 202, 205
consent 56, 90, 118, 153, 157, 159, 171, 175, 183, 210
control 23, 35, 39, 42, 45, 79, 97, 105, 109, 135, 138, 147n7, 149, 157, 158, 185, 187, 189
Covid-19 7, 10, 33, 57, 63, 65, 101, 101n2, 104, 105, 107, 110, 114, 129, 162, 164, 177, 181, 203, 211
crisis 3, 4, 8, 35, 40, 56, 70, 86, 101, 105, 159, 164, 180, 179, 203
  climate 7, 33, 60, 62, 82, 129, 140, 162, 198, 211
  ecological 62
  environmental 145
  existential 97, 174, 194
  financial 9, 33, 65, 129
  mental health 7, 9, 39, 55, 83, 89, 104, 127, 134, 162, 189, 202, 212
  meta 7, 204, 211
  poly 7, 164, 181, 199, 202, 204, 211
curate 3, 10, 11, 33, 53, 70, 85, 119, 127, 128, 161, 163, 167, 169, 191, 206, 207

curating 2, 7, 11, 55, 65, 77, 102n12, 107, 110, 117, 134, 166, 189, 191, 209
curation 3, 51, 52, 117, 161, 162, 169, 194

Deleuze, Gilles 69, 77, 78, 79, 144, 167, 183–4, 204n1 *see also* rhizome
  and Guattari, Felix 69, 77, 79, 81, 82, 85, 93, 103n22, 174, 179, 187, 194, 197, 204n1
dialogue 3, 4, 5, 10, 47, 48, 49, 50, 51, 53, 55, 59, 64, 66n10, 72, 73, 76, 77, 84, 89, 101, 102n12, 103n15, 105, 110, 112, 113, 114, 115, 117, 122, 136, 137, 138, 139, 141, 145, 146, 147n6, 148, 162, 163, 165, 166, 174, 177, 179, 182, 183, 185, 188n1, 189, 192, 194, 195, 197, 198, 203, 207, 208, 209, 210
The Dialogue Society 119, 120, 121, 122, 123, 124, 125, 135, 167, 174, 177, 182, 185, 187, 195, 201, 204 *see also* the Hizmet movement
difference 3, 10, 14, 18, 25, 47, 69–71, 72–3, 77–85, 87, 93, 94, 102n7, 102n9, 118, 124–5, 138, 146n3, 160, 161, 162, 172, 174, 177, 181, 191, 198, 201, 210, 213

ecumenical 8, 5, 17, 21, 25, 42, 55, 83, 111–12, 113, 118, 185, 198, 200
emerge 8, 11, 13, 20, 48, 49, 51, 52, 64, 67n15, 68n22, 69, 73, 74, 76, 78, 83, 109, 110, 105,

124, 136, 146, 148, 150, 162, 163, 172, 179, 185, 187, 192, 193, 199, 202, 204, 212
emergent 5, 75, 84, 123, 165
emergence 8, 10, 20, 30, 40, 42, 48, 49, 70, 73, 74, 79, 91, 97, 102n11, 103n15, 110, 119, 134, 140, 143, 158, 159, 160, 164, 167, 181, 184
experience, lived 3, 35, 55, 56, 69, 82, 84, 85, 87, 92, 101, 111, 114, 125, 142, 160, 163, 164, 172, 174, 176, 177, 188n1, 189, 190, 193, 207

faith 1, 7, 17, 21, 23, 24, 25, 26, 27, 30, 31, 32, 35, 38, 39, 40, 42, 45, 48, 49, 50, 54, 55, 56, 57, 61, 62, 70, 71, 73, 83, 92, 95, 98, 104, 105, 106, 110, 115, 117, 120, 122, 123, 127, 128, 133, 136, 138, 145, 146n2, 157, 178, 184, 190, 191, 199, 209, 211, 212
faith-based 5, 7, 9, 10, 32, 41, 42, 43, 53, 54, 69, 70, 71, 73, 76, 77, 82, 83, 85, 86, 101n1, 101n3, 103n16, 104, 105, 106, 107, 112, 118, 145, 176, 181, 209, 211
faithfully 1, 45, 67n19, 174
inter 50, 120, 162
and Order 17, 19
in the City 29, 211
Faith-based Organization (FBO) 70–1, 83, 101n2
Link Up 42, 43, 66n9, 66n10, 200
freedom 11, 17, 21, 22–5, 52, 55, 104, 106, 117, 134, 135, 136, 138, 149, 170, 172–5,
176–7, 179, 181, 188, 189, 195

gathering 1, 2, 10, 15, 29, 42, 47–55, 64–5, 66n11, 68n22, 81, 83, 85, 92, 97–101, 102n7, 103n23, 107–8, 110, 112–15, 117, 119, 121–4, 126–7, 129, 132–4, 136–8, 139, 140, 144–6, 147n5, 148, 162, 164–8, 172, 174, 177, 179, 180, 182, 183, 185–8, 188n1, 191–5, 198, 200–1, 203, 208, 209, 211
General Synod 57, 61
governance 57–8, 86, 91–4, 98, 162, 181, 203, 207, 213n1
Gramsci, Antonio 10–11, 108, 109, 126, 132, 136–7, 138, 146, 147n8, 148, 169n1, 169n2, 169n3, 170, 171, 175, 177, 180, 183, 184, 185, 186, 187, 189, 193, 197, 208, 209, 210
cell 150–2
intellectuals 153–6, 160–9
and the church 156–8
and philosophy 158–9
hegemony 148, 152–3, 155, 157–9, 179, 183–4
Society 126, 136, 146, 148, 167, 168, 180, 185, 210
Greeley, Andrew 71

Habermas, Jürgen 9, 31, 71, 72, 77, 78, 146n2, 183, 197
Hizmet movement 119–24, 167, 179, 182, 195
hope 1–4, 7, 9, 10, 11, 19, 23, 27, 28, 38, 41, 42–9, 57, 61, 62, 64, 68n21, 68n22, 85,

103n14, 104, 108, 111–12, 113, 115–19, 123–5, 127, 129, 132, 133, 134, 137, 138, 140, 144, 145, 146, 146n2, 146n4, 148, 164, 165–7, 172, 177, 188, 189, 190, 198, 207, 209, 211, 212, 213
  authentic 193–5, 203, 206, 207
  living 189–90, 196, 203, 206
  radical 33, 65, 138, 140, 195–9, 204, 206, 211, 213
  seeds 191–3, 203, 206

Incarnation 20, 21, 28, 84–5, 91, 95, 123, 164, 168, 169, 174, 179
Imago Dei 23
Islam 4, 10, 54, 123, 119–20, 124, 141, 147n5, 162, 166, 199

justice 4, 7, 11, 18, 19, 21, 22, 25, 26, 30, 31, 47, 55, 130, 133, 140, 145, 170, 188, 189, 198, 199, 201–4, 208, 212

Latour, Bruno 80–1, 161, 174
leadership 2, 3, 9, 10, 14, 16, 19, 21, 22, 25, 27, 29, 31, 32, 34, 42, 49, 50, 56, 58–62, 64–5, 66n7, 66n10, 69, 81, 84–5, 88, 92, 97, 100, 103n14, 117–18, 131, 133–6, 140, 142, 145, 146, 146n2, 147n8, 148, 153, 160, 163–5, 170–88, 192, 203, 206
  transformational 3, 10, 11, 38, 70, 67n15, 80, 82, 84–6, 89, 91, 95–6, 99, 101, 108, 110, 146, 148, 152, 160–1, 164–5, 167, 169, 170–89, 198, 200–1, 204–6, 207–9, 211–13

liminality 5, 9, 10, 34, 35–68, 69, 76–7, 79, 82–3, 85, 101, 104, 107, 110, 146, 148, 172–4, 180–1, 185, 202, 207
Liverpool 4, 17, 41, 56–7, 59, 60, 64, 66n5, 110–13, 116, 117, 121, 122, 124, 126–33, 135, 137, 143, 144, 147n4, 147n5, 147n6, 162, 165–8, 172, 177, 179, 180, 182, 185, 195, 202–5
  Hope University 62, 111, 113, 116–17, 124, 1392, 165, 171, 174, 177, 179, 182, 185, 187, 191, 194, 195, 203, 208–11
  Liverpool Charity and Voluntary Services (LCVS) 126, 127–9, 134, 147n6, 177, 185, 210

Malvern Conference 19–20, 21, 208
Micro-Malverns 145, 208
Manchester 13, 15, 16, 17, 19, 29, 30, 41, 46, 49, 53, 55, 61, 62, 98, 105, 121, 125, 131, 135, 139, 148, 188, 191, 202, 210
Marmot, Michael 128, 147n7, 203
Marmot Group 128, 129, 203, 210
  Reviews 128
metanoia 63
movement 1, 2, 4, 8–11, 15–17, 19, 21, 25, 31, 34, 40, 42, 46, 48–55, 64, 65, 67n15, 67n17, 68n22, 69, 72–4, 77, 80, 83–4, 103n15, 104–49, 152, 157–8, 161, 163, 164, 166–70, 172, 179, 180, 182, 183, 184, 186, 187, 188n1, 189, 192, 193,

194–9, 200, 202, 204, 207–10, 213
Muslim 4, 34n4, 72, 76, 112, 117, 119, 121, 122, 143, 167, 171, 174, 185, 205

net zero 57, 58, 61, 211
non-religious 10, 54, 56, 83, 102n5, 110, 171, 185
  nones 74–6, 102n4, 102n5

postsecular 5, 9, 32, 49, 70–6, 119, 145, 146n2, 171, 183, 197, 199 *see also* Greeley, Andrew
poverty 6, 7, 15, 40, 83, 101n3, 111, 120, 127–32, 134, 137, 138, 140, 142, 148, 162, 168, 180, 182, 185, 192, 195, 198, 203, 211
power 15–19, 33, 34n2, 37, 40, 44, 45, 60, 63, 66n4, 92, 93, 98, 105, 111, 113, 114, 116–18, 131, 132, 133, 135, 138, 139, 144, 146n2, 149, 150, 153, 159, 172, 176, 179, 181, 183–6, 198, 200, 201, 203, 207, 212
public square 3, 10, 33, 34, 72, 76, 110, 117, 118, 125, 140, 159, 171, 175, 200, 206, 208, 212

reform 9, 16, 19, 20, 21, 34, 60, 142, 160
  Life and Liberty movement 8, 15, 21, 196, 206–7
rhizome 79, 81, 82, 84, 91, 102n8, 103n18, 110 *see also* Deleuze, Gilles
  connectivity 43, 51, 52, 103n8, 178, 182

heterogeneity 71, 76, 79, 80, 102n5, 102n9, 103n18, 128
multiplicity 7, 78–9, 102n9, 103n18, 110, 161, 191, 199
assignifying rupture 92, 94, 96, 102n9, 103n22, 168, 182
cartography 91, 93, 102n9, 167, 187, 194
decalcomania 81, 91, 102n9, 167, 187, 194

seeds 138, 201
  of hope 138, 191–3, 203, 206
  Margery 'Seeds' Bennett 91–2, 173
  Seeds Project (The Mustard Seed and The Seed Café) 83, 91–4, 184, 187, 194, 196, 198
  scattering, scattered 170, 173, 176, 178, 181, 184, 187, 200, 202
  vision 94–6
service 2, 11, 24, 25, 34n3, 41–4, 46, 48, 49, 52, 58, 67n15, 70, 75, 84, 90, 92, 99, 100, 104, 106, 107, 119, 121, 126, 127, 134, 135, 136, 147n6, 148, 170, 172, 177–83, 185, 188, 191, 193, 194, 196, 198, 201–4, 210, 212, 213
Spaces of Hope 2–5, 7, 9, 10, 11, 32, 35, 46–55, 64, 65, 67n15, 69–103, 107, 110, 112, 114, 117, 126, 127, 128, 134, 136, 137, 140, 144, 146, 146n4, 147n5, 147n6, 148, 161–2, 163, 168, 169, 172, 180, 184, 185, 187, 198, 202, 207, 211, 213
stories 9, 10, 11, 38, 48, 51, 55, 67n18, 69, 82–5, 91, 127, 129,

141–4, 159, 165, 167, 172, 186, 190, 191, 193, 201

Temple, William 1, 3, 6, 8, 9, 12n2, 13–34, 34n2, 34n3, 43, 48, 51, 52, 56, 62, 69, 70, 73, 77, 82, 84, 85, 108, 117, 118, 140, 139, 144, 145, 147n5, 147n7, 148, 160, 161, 170–3, 175, 176, 178, 179, 181, 186, 190, 191, 196–8, 200–3, 206–8, 210–12, 213n1
territories 79, 80, 164
  deterritorialization 79, 87, 103n22, 165, 182
  reterritorialization 79, 86
theology 1, 3, 8, 14, 29, 30, 31, 33, 34n4, 72, 110–11, 116, 118, 139, 146n2, 195, 196, 197, 204n1, 212
Turner, Victor 34, 35–7, 76, 79, 82, 173

unity 8, 11, 17–19, 42, 58, 81, 93, 94, 96, 97, 99, 120, 125, 132, 149, 157, 167, 176, 184, 187, 189, 199, 200–2, 208, 212
USA 31, 40, 66n3, 108, 113, 138, 168, 172, 205, 206

welfare state 3, 8, 14, 17–19, 24, 27–8, 29, 34n2, 200, 207
wilderness 9, 38, 56, 59, 61–3, 65, 68n21, 190
William Temple Foundation 6, 14, 29, 30, 31, 33, 43, 56, 62, 117, 139, 145, 147n5, 171, 210
world view 2, 3, 4, 9, 10, 11, 34, 39, 49, 55, 71–4, 76–8, 84, 106, 112, 115–17, 119, 121, 123–5, 143, 146, 147n8, 159, 162, 163, 171, 174–5, 177, 181, 183–8, 190, 194–5, 210

www.ingramcontent.com/pod-product-compliance
Lightning Source LLC
Chambersburg PA
CBHW022051290426
44109CB00014B/1058